MORE AND LESS THAN A FRIEND

More and Less than a Friend

The Songwriting Partnership

of Tamás Cseh and Géza Bereményi

in Hungary

Diana Senechal

Paperback ISBN: 9781972482193

Cover art: Juan Gris, *Still Life with a Guitar* (1913), Wikimedia Commons

Cover concept by Diana Senechal

Cover design by Jacob Arms

Editor-In Chief William K. Lawrence
Serving House Books
Lawrence Landing Company
Raleigh, North Carolina 27609, USA

www.servinghousebooks.com

Serving House Books is a proud member of:

Independent Book Publishers Association
 and
Community of Literary Magazines and Presses

CONTENTS

Acknowledgments

I am grateful to the following individuals and entities for making the book possible:

To William K. Lawrence, publisher of Serving House Books, for supporting my work and seeing this book into print; and to Serving House Books itself.

To the staff of the MNMKK-PIM-Cseh Tamás Archívum (the Tamás Cseh Archive) in Budapest for allowing me to spend hours there perusing documents, recordings, and photos; for their ample research assistance; for the conversations and recommendations along the way; and for the November 2025 conference on Cseh's life and work, hosted by the University of Pécs – Department of Humanities and Social Sciences, and the MNMKK Petőfi Irodalmi Múzeum – Cseh Tamás Archívum.

To those who have inspired and informed me with their renditions of Cseh and Bereményi's work: in particular, SICC Production, with their reimagination and performance of *Frontátvonulás*; Miklós H. Vecsei, Balázs Szabó, and Huba Ratkóczi, with their song-play *Füst a szemében* ("Smoke in His Eyes"); Sándor Sárkány Jr.; Mihály Víg and his band Balaton; and the students and teachers of the Alternatív Közgazdasági Gimnázium in Budapest. Many thanks, also, to those who have brought me Cseh and Bereményi's work indirectly, through its influence on their own art.

To Gyula Jenei, who first mentioned Cseh and Bereményi to me, sent me links to their songs, and told me about László Bérczes, whose *Cseh Tamás: Bérczes László beszélgetőkönyve* ("Tamás Cseh: László Bérczes's Conversation Book") has been a great source for this book. To Bérczes I give thanks for continuing Cseh's legacy and helping us understand who he was.

To András Cseh, Tamás Cseh's son. One of my fondest memories is of singing Cseh and Bereményi's songs at *közös éneklés* ("common singing") events hosted by András and others. I hope for many more of these and thank them for what they brought to the book.

To the journals that published my essays on aspects of Cseh and Bereményi's work: *Literary Matters, Asymptote, Hungarian Cultural Studies*, and *Hungarian Literature Online*.

To Géza Bereményi, who not only gave me permission to quote and translate song lyrics for this book, but answered my questions along the way and heartily supported the project.

To the music itself, its authors, and its audiences.

Playlist

The main songs considered in this book are presented in the accompanying Spotify playlist, accessible through the full link, short link, and QR code below. Here the songs are listed in order of appearance, by chapter. The full citations for the albums can be found in the bibliography. (One song, "Keresztben jégeső," the focus of the ninth chapter, is not available on Spotify; a link to a YouTube video is provided below.) Lyrics can be found on the website of the Cseh Tamás Archívum (https://csehtamasarchivum.hu/).

Link:
https://open.spotify.com/playlist/51bUCf9iNIPUCYxw2NVZWZ?si=dRaspp6FQFK6WrnOFrd7lQ

Short link: https://bit.ly/4lxpf9u

Chapter 1

- "Antoine, Désiré és a szél" ("Antoine, Désiré, and the Wind"), *Antoine és Désiré* ("Antoine and Désiré") (1978.
- "Az ócska cipő" ("Shabby Shoes"), *Antoine és Désiré* (1978.
- "I Love You So," *Fehér babák takarodója* ("White Dolls' Curfew") (1979).
- "Désiré megnémul" ("Désiré Falls Silent"), *Antoine és Désiré* (1978).

- "Az égboltsapkájú" ("The One in the Sky Cap"), *Jóslat.*

Chapter 7

- "Lee van Cleef," *Műcsarnok.*

Chapter 8

- "Váróterem" ("Waiting Room"), *Utóirat* ("Postscript").

- "Életem utolsó gesztusa" ("The Last Gesture of My Life"), *Utóirat.*

- "A 100. éjszaka" ("The Hundredth Night"), or, "Amikor Désiré megérkezett Budapestre," *Antoine és Désiré.*

Chapter 9

- "Keresztben jégeső" ("Sideways Hail"), *Az igazi levél nővéremnek* ("The True Letter to My Sister"), https://www.youtube.com/watch?v=0sy-my9-ukA. This song is not on Spotify and thus not in the playlist; the URL points to a YouTube video—a documentary excerpt—of Cseh and Másik performing the song at Cseh's last concert on August 26, 2006.

Chapter 11

- "Csönded vagyok" ("I Am Your Silence"), *Új dalok* ("New Songs").

- Csaknekedkislány (band), "Cseh Tamás," *Na ná ba bám.*

Chapter 12

- "Désiré megnémul." (This is the fourth item in the playlist, since the song comes up in Chapter 1 as well.)

PREFACE

With this essay collection I hope to give readers—particularly those who do not speak Hungarian—an entrance into the songs and albums of Tamás Cseh (1943–2009) and Géza Bereményi (1946–), legendary Hungarian songwriters of the 1970s and beyond. While interconnected and sequentially arranged, the chapters can be read independently. Some readers may speak Hungarian, others not; this book is intended for anyone curious enough to listen to the songs. Treasured by a range of listeners, including several generations of musicians, actors, writers, and other artists, their music gives a glimpse into a Hungary that tourists and reporters rarely see.

While their work reflects on life in Hungary in the Kádár era and beyond, it breaks through barriers of time and place. At the same time, it treats time and place seriously and is often interpreted in this light. Cseh and Bereményi described their songs as *helyzetjelentések* ("situation reports"), a word that can be understood in many ways. To report on a situation, a song must capture its essence: that is, transform it imaginatively. It is this imaginative transformation that has amazed and moved listeners across the decades.

Cseh and Bereményi met one midnight at a pub, among friends, in December 1970. They were both in their twenties. Cseh, at the time an art teacher, had already gained informal renown for his informal performances; Bereményi's first story collection had just been published. They began talking; Bereményi wanted to know why Cseh didn't write his songs in Hungarian. Cseh said (more or less) that he feared he could not live up to the standard of his forebears. Bereményi replied (more or less), "Tell you what. I'll write lyrics in Hungarian for you." They made an appointment to meet at Cseh's apartment the next day at four in the afternoon. Not only did Bereményi show up, but they wrote their first two songs together that day and continued with hundreds more over the years.

Beloved and admired in Hungary, Cseh and Bereményi are little known internationally; I hope the book will help change this. My aim is not to insist on a particular interpretation but to enable readers to encounter the music on their own. At the same time, I present it in a personal and somewhat idiosyncratic way.

The topic may appeal to those interested in Hungarian language, arts, history, and culture; to songwriters and song-listeners; and to anyone else willing to step in and give it a try. My dream is for someone to stumble upon the book, begin reading it and listening to the songs, and continue listening independently. Perhaps on a visit to Hungary you will find a Cseh- and Bereményi-related event to attend. Perhaps certain songs, texts, albums will become your favorites. If a friend has ever recommended music to you with true enthusiasm and knowledge, if you have listened to this music together, if your friend has pointed out favorite moments in it (a phrase, a solo, a tempo change, a tone), this book might remind you at times of those sessions.

Over the decades of their collaboration, Cseh and Bereményi released twenty albums, produced hundreds of concerts and shows, and took part in theatre and film (Bereményi is a film director as well as a writer; Cseh appeared in numerous films and plays).[*] They received some of Hungary's most prestigious prizes, are honored today at numerous events, and have profoundly influenced Hungarian song and literature. Their external achievements aside, their songs have a way of taking up residence in the mind. The versatile, playful melodies and rhythms, the lyrics with their wordplay, stories, characters, and objects—all of this makes for discoveries and returns. Thus their fame is somewhat private and internal; whoever takes to their songs will likely spend many hours with them and come to understand them in happily lonely ways.

Bereményi called Cseh "both more and less than a friend"—more, because the relationship was more intimate than most friendships, and less, because they had set strict limits on it from the start. They established, first, that they would continue working together until one of them called it quits— and should this happen, the other would not ask why—and second, that there would be no performance of the songs unless both gave their consent.[1] This phrase is the source of the present book's title. It can apply to the listener too, although differently: we may be drawn intimately into the songs yet removed culturally and historically. Beyond that, an encounter with their music is bound to be somewhat solitary, since the music itself is filled with certain kinds of solitude. Cseh and Bereményi kept separate

---

[*] In this book I use the "theatre" spelling except when mentioning an institution that uses "theater."

domains when writing the songs: Bereményi wrote the lyrics, Cseh the music, and Cseh performed them.[2]

Cseh and Bereményi's relationship had no sexual component or even anything romantic in an ordinary sense. Yet the intimacy, intensity, and boundaries of their working relationship led them to liken themselves at times to a married couple. Their songs are filled with friendships of a similar kind: for instance, between the characters Antoine and Désiré, or Vizi and Ecsédi. It would be misleading to equate these characters with their creators, but some resemblances poke through. These fictive pairs also represent aspects of the human soul: they exist within us, in different ways and to different degrees. I am both Vizi and Ecsédi, both Antoine and Désiré; that accounts for a small part of my attraction to the songs.

What draws Hungarians and others to the music of Cseh and Bereményi? What is this music about, what makes it unusual, how and to what extent does it cross generations, eras, countries? What light does it shed on Hungarian culture? How can someone come to appreciate it without a knowledge of Hungarian? These and other questions shape the book. I have combined formal research with personal observations; having lived in Hungary since 2017 and immersed myself in its musical and literary life, I have a special opportunity to report and reflect on what I have seen. For research, I have access to a trove of primary and secondary sources through the Tamás Cseh Archive (MNMKK-PIM-Cseh Tamás Archívum), where I spent many hours; also, I know many people who have been affected by Cseh and Bereményi's work. Yet this is not a scholarly book; for secondary sources it relies more on interviews and newspaper articles than on academic literature. This is because I want to keep the language relatively simple within the complexities.

The first two chapters will introduce the reader to Cseh and Bereményi and their historical, political, and cultural surroundings. The following four will look at three albums and the various characters running through their opus. The next three will focus on specific songs, and the final three will consider Cseh and Bereményi's influence from different perspectives, including my own reflection at the end.

I came to Hungary in 2017 to teach and to follow a hunch and a longing. I had left my previous teaching position to write a book; this almost complete, I found my way to Szolnok. I plunged into my new work, the language, literature, music. At some point in 2019 or so, my colleague Gyula

Jenei, whose poetry collection *Mindig más* (*Always Different*) I translated, recommended the songs of Cseh and Bereményi to me, thinking that I would like them. He told me about the writer and director László Bérczes, who had taught at our school, come to know Cseh well, and written a book of conversations with him. I listened to the songs and was struck by their understated beauty and wit, their contradictions and mysteries.

Over time, I heard more and more musicians refer to Cseh and Bereményi as influences. I started listening to more of their music. Many songs took me by surprise. Funny, moving, hummable, they held some kind of secret, something I could possibly uncover one day. I sensed their layers, their way of making people laugh and then shocking them with sadness. Simple on the surface, the music itself was unlike anything I had heard before, playful in its rhythms and tempos, evocative of styles ranging from klezmer to Gregorian chants to country laments. You could compare it to the work of Leonard Cohen, Simon and Garfunkel, Bob Dylan, or Jacques Brel, but it would always escape the comparisons and go its own way.

That is the miracle of Cseh and Bereményi's music. In a particular song you might detect wry references to the details of life in the communist-socialist era,[*] but then one day, listening to the same song, you might be struck by the internal rhymes, particular words and phrases, or the way Cseh sings and plays it. While the songs speak, to a great degree, of the experience of a particular generation in Hungary (the generation that came of age in the 1960s), they are not limited to that context in the least.

Many in Hungary seemed surprised by my interest in this music. "What can it say to you?" they would ask—hinting that because I had not lived through the experiences that these songs allude to, I could not understand them. Many who attended the concerts in the 1970s and 80s felt such a strong connection to the work—and to the concert atmosphere—that they viewed even the younger audience members with some suspicion.

But Cseh and Bereményi's work has great meaning for younger generations. Part of this has to do with the tension in their work between saying something and keeping it secret. Young artists in Hungary may

---

[*] The Kádár era has been called both "communist" and "socialist." From here on I use the term "socialist" in reference to this era--but the Soviet Union's political and economic control over Hungary justifies the term "communist" as well. Kádár's economic policies are often dubbed "goulash communism" because of of their mixture of elements.

perceive the songs as outspoken, guarded, or cryptic, but in either case they sense the double pull.

Cseh and Bereményi's art is political to the extent that it has to do with the *polis*, the city, and the forms of movement within it. If you cannot move, if trains are not departing from the station—as in their stage show and album *Frontátvonulás* ("Frontal Passage")—even the teller of the story takes a risk. By portraying reality (through their particular imagination), they risked running afoul of the censors, yet their songs do not make overt political statements or call for specific changes. This kind of political abstinence accounted in part for their "tolerated" status during the Kádár era in Hungary. Yet the songs abound with allusions that can be understood politically; many analyses focus on these possible political references and meanings. Without ignoring such elements, this book tilts away from a political focus, simply because there is so much more to be found in the songs.

Each album's graphics, credits, and lyrics can be found on the Cseh Tamás Archívum website (https://csehtamasarchivum.hu/); the recordings can be found on Spotify and elsewhere. A playlist of the main songs discussed in this book can be found at the start of the book. I encourage the reader to listen to the main songs of each chapter before reading the chapter itself—and then, after reading, to listen to them again and to the full albums. Each reader will find a different approach; some may listen to the songs in the midst of reading, others only after finishing the book. Some may end up so absorbed by the songs that they listen to more and more.

This book is an essay collection, not a comprehensive treatise; it has significant omissions. For example, only in passing does it bring up Cseh's collaboration with Dénes Csengey—with whom he created the show and album *Mélyrepülés* ("Flying Low" or "Deep Dive"). In addition, it focuses mainly on Cseh and Bereményi's earlier work (between 1970 and 1987) and on their songs in particular, barely touching on their work in theatre and film. The book is bound to have additional limitations and imperfections; they are necessary for the larger endeavor.

Throughout the book, I translate selected song lyrics, as well as quotes from Hungarian texts. These translations contain the book's soul, since they came out of many hours of listening. Song translation has a particular challenge and joy: one must consider not only the text on the page, but the texture, melodies, and rhythms of the music. Sometimes a literal translation will do, if the purpose is just to convey some of the meaning—but to reach deeper layers, one must take liberties and risks, rearranging phrases here and there and sometimes altering their sense. Along the way, I explain some of the challenges involved in translating these songs. For ease of reading, I present the lyrics in English translation only (except when commenting on particular phrases or words); in the notes and bibliography I provide links to the original texts and albums.

By examining the songs from different angles, I hope to give a glimpse of what they have meant to people across several generations, and how much more might be discovered in them. If this book brings readers to the music and starts to open it up for them—or, for those familiar with it, reveals something new in it—then it will have accomplished, or started to accomplish, what it set out to do.

CHAPTER 1

Introduction to Tamás Cseh and Géza Bereményi

In January 2024, in a neighborhood pub in Szolnok, a small city on the Great Hungarian Plain, the inner room has been set up for an informal concert. In the darker rear, some men in their sixties and seventies relax by the bar. The pub is hosting a *Cseh-est*, an event devoted to the work of Tamás Cseh and his songwriting partners, particularly Géza Bereményi.[*] A young man sits down behind the keyboard: Sándor Sárkány, a composer and musician born in 2001. Listeners young and old wander in with their drinks. The grey-haired barflies lean back into the darkness. A short hush, then the concert begins.

> *Antoine-t s Desirét*
> *fújja a szél,*
> *előredőlve közelednek.*
>
> *Mindkettő énekel,*
> *s velük a dal*
> *szintén megbillen egy kissé.*
>
> *Tűrüpp, türűrüpp, türűrümm,*
> *tűrüpp, türűrüpp, türűrümm.*

Even without knowing Hungarian, one can tell that this song—by Cseh and Bereményi—tells of a certain Antoine and Désiré and has a *tűrüpp, türűrüpp, türűrümm* refrain. An approximate translation, with some

---

[*] Cseh's name is pronounced *approximately* "Tamash Cheh"; Bereményi's is pronounced approximately the way it looks in English, but with subtle differences that would be too difficult to describe in a footnote. In IPA phonetic notation, they are /ˈtɑmaːʃ ˈtʃɛh/ and /ˈɡeːzɑ bɛrɛmeːɲi/. In Hungarian, the family name precedes the given name; hence they are known as Cseh Tamás and Bereményi Géza.

liberties, reads, "Antoine and Désiré / are blown by the wind; / slightly tipped forward, they scuttle. // Both of them sing, / and with them the song / likewise tips forward a little."[*] The song proceeds to talk of this wind and tipping, in which the narrator and the song take part. This comical tipping seems to hold some secret significance—there seems to be a risk in it (political? social? existential? physical?)—but remains as elusive as the wind itself. Still, a meaning teases the air. The song reaches a slow point, quiets down… and then someone in the somnolent rear of the room cries out, *istenem!* ("my God!"), the next word of the song. ("my God, just now, now let us not topple forward.") A few more cries of *istenem* from around the room; then Sárkány responds with his own *istenem*, finishes the line, and brings the song to a close with an exuberant final refrain.[1]

Most of the crowd has come for the music, it turns out, even those reclining in the dark. They range in age from twenties to seventies, drinking a little, a lot, or not at all, but listening, singing along, knowing the songs. Over time, a newcomer might learn about this crowd and what brings them here. At events like this, some participants knew Cseh personally and have many stories to tell. Perhaps they worked with him on a project or talked with him through the night; perhaps he slept on their couch more than once. Others know the music inside out, along with its recordings and variations. Conversations unfold and then continue after the music is over. But it isn't over yet; there will still be a few more songs, more conversation, and finally, when the pub closes, a parting of ways into the night.

During Cseh's lifetime, a Cseh concert was not just a concert. First of all, he usually performed solo. (Bereményi stayed offstage but was often present.) Cseh inhabited the different characters of the songs, narrating and singing. The immediacy of these performances brought the audience close. After the official concert was over and many had left, those who lingered would get treated to the after-hours concert (the "real concert," as some called it) that sometimes lasted through the night. Cseh was far from rich; instead of staying in hotels, he would accept offers of couches.[2] His audiences were both devoted and talented; they not only collected cassettes, albums, bootlegs, posters, photos, autographs, anything they could get their hands on, but they collaborated with him, arranged concerts for him, interviewed him, and argued about the meanings of the songs.[3]

---

[*] A full translation of the song appears in the fourth chapter.

For some, Cseh and Bereményi's work offered a way of resisting the system without succumbing to slogans or dogma. The sociologist Anna Szemere locates their work in a "semi-underground": neither officially prohibited nor officially promoted. In terms of the infamous "three Ts" (*támogatott, tűrt, tiltott*, "supported, tolerated, prohibited") of the Kádár regime's official arts policy, they belonged to the *tűrt* ("tolerated") category and were keenly aware of its dangers, particularly unconscious self-censorship.[4] They had more freedom from censorship in songwriting than in performances (although files were kept on them), and more in performances than in record releases (all songs had to be scrutinized by the *sanzonbizottság*, or "song committee," before they could be published); thus the risks were both external and internal, ranging from the banning of a song to the stifling of a thought.[5]

For the listeners, it was particularly at performances that Cseh and Bereményi's work came to life; the albums mainly served to preserve what had been made. Cseh gave the songs slightly different nuances with each performance; sometimes he brought out songs that the devoted audience had never heard. Some of his performances could even be perceived as an expression of protest; in 2009, *Titkos dalok* ("Secret Songs"), a DVD of a 1984 concert video recording (in a dimly lit winery) gives a glimpse of some of the hidden layers of Cseh and Bereményi's work. The concept of the *titok* (secret) pervaded their early songs, which were filled with allusions and could be understood in numerous ways.[6] Yet Cseh and Bereményi eschewed political statements and political interpretations of the songs; they wanted their creations to have their own life. Moreover, the lyrics were Bereményi's, and the music Cseh's; in some cases, Cseh did not understand the meanings of the songs until much later.[7]

The story of how Cseh and Bereményi met could be considered a microcosm of their career. Various versions of the tale have been told many times—including in three of my articles—so I will convey the bare gist.

One night in December 1970, close to midnight, near the Keleti train station in Budapest, Tamás Cseh, an art teacher in his twenties, was trying to figure out how to get home to his illegal sublet on Iskola Street, on the Buda side of the Danube. He decided to take a cab as far as he could afford and then take it from there.

While watching the meter in the cab, he glimpsed a group of young people heading toward the Astoria intersection, a hub of nightlife. He recognized one of them, called out to him, and ended up joining them; they wound up at a pub. Then came the fateful moment: one of them leaned toward him and said he had heard about his songs.

Cseh had been playing guitar since high school and writing songs in English and French (languages he did not know). His music had already attracted some attention; the director Péter Bacsó had included it in his 1965 film *Szerelmes biciklisták* ("Bicyclists in Love") and his 1967 film *Nyár a hegyen* ("Summer on the Mountain").

The young man wanted to know why Tamás didn't write songs in Hungarian. He offered his help; they made an appointment. Cseh assumed nothing would come of it. The next day, his doorbell rang at four in the afternoon. It was the same young man, Géza Bereményi, a writer whose first story collection had just been published.

They wrote their first two songs together that day; the next day, Bereményi moved into the sublet (and remained Cseh's roommate for a year and a half). They established strict rules for their working relationship: there would be no public performances of the songs without the consent of both parties, and if one of the two should ever wish to call it quits, he would say so, and the other would not ask for explanations.[8] Yet their relationship was filled with humor; they left each other amusing notes day by day and developed a special language of their own. Today, if you stop by the building (35 Iskola Street, near the Batthyány tér metro station), you will see a commemorative nameplate listing fifteen of their song characters as residents of the apartments.

Their first song spoke a language they must have grasped at once, without being able to explain it. In a 1980 interview, Cseh and Bereményi said that they didn't know what this song was about when they wrote it, that it took on its own life.[9] The uncommon intuition, this communication without formalities, must have set the tone for what was to come.

This song, "Az ócska cipő" ("Shabby Shoes"), has several qualities that would later characterize their work: the classic onomatopoeic refrain, *tárá-ráálá-rálárám*, an imitation of singing itself; the characters Antoine and Désiré (Hungarian, but with French monikers), who came into being in the song; and the musical flexibility.[10] The sound is bare, with voice and a single guitar. Listening carefully, I hear the initial hesitation and freedom, the changing tempo, the variable syllable counts. It is the *tárá-ráálá-rálárám* that grounds the song, yet even this *tárá-ráálá-rálárám* changes subtly and ends irresolutely. The lyrics can be translated as follows:

The shabby shoes one evening were
so thickly covered up in mud
that at last Désiré
could only stop and stare.

Désiré whispered aloud:
"My God, my God!
What surroundings!
What shabby surroundings!
And my shoes, how shabby they are now!"

Tárá-ráálá-rálárám,
táráá-rárám,
táá-ráláá-rárám,
táráá-rárám.

Táá-ráláá-rárám, etc.

Right in front of a pub,
Désiré had a thought:
What was it that Antoine said?
Maybe a year ago.
"Don't stare like a fool
if it rains, if it rains."
Very well then, thought Désiré,
I'll keep on going, then.

Tárá-ráálá-rálárám, etc.

The sparseness rotates, revealing unpinpointable, uncatchable moods, something like disappointment, dejection, resignation, thoughtfulness, remembrance, courage, and even then, a patch of comedy, because nothing happens here except that Désiré stops, whispers, thinks, and keeps on going. Nothing like an ode to persistence, it captures a moment of perception in the life of a nonexistent, hapless Désiré, the *tárárá* refrain capturing what cannot be said. Hidden in the slight silliness is genuine misery: not only the shabbiness, but its shock: being so stunned by your own tattered shoes and surroundings that you can only gawk.

Cseh performed it with a quiet liveliness and rubato, starting out slow, then finding his way into the tempo, then pausing, starting up, pausing. Even in this little song, there is much to discover in the words; this is where Bereményi's art comes in. An irregular placement of rhymes, an unusual grouping of syllables, an intuitive imagination (who are Antoine and Désiré? We have no idea yet, but they exist within the song), an expressiveness without sentimentality, a simplicity without clichés.

The songs of Cseh and Bereményi differed markedly from pop music with its *I-love-you-so* mannerisms; in fact, their song "I Love You So" (from their 1979 album *Fehér babák takarodója*, or "White Dolls' Curfew") does something surprising with the title. The song bewails how people in Hungary sing along to English songs without understanding them, believing that they must mean something that Hungarians haven't put into song yet. It ends with a bitter lament, "Perhaps we were wrong there, / Oh that rotten singer, / too bad he sang in English! / Oh, the singer, / why didn't / he sing / to us, somehow, / anyhow, / any which way, / in Hungarian?" Thus the song topples not only its own apparent cliché, but an industry built on clichés of this kind. Yet like the others, the song eschews statements; it stands out for its play, its unique take on a title of this sort.[11]

A few general principles can help newcomers approach Cseh and Bereményi's work: the primacy of the songs and shows; the recurring characters; the different eras of their work; the interaction of their work with literature, theatre, and film; and their relation to musical traditions and musicians around the world.

While many bands and songwriters think in terms of albums, Cseh and Bereményi worked first with songs, then with shows. The albums came as an afterthought or afterword, partly because of the censorship practices of the era; their shows usually underwent less scrutiny than their releases. Also, the shows allowed them to develp their special genre, which was difficult to translate onto albums.

From their songs and accompanying text, they began to create stories with recurring characters (to be discussed in the fourth chapter). Some of these story-texts are included in the albums—for instance, in their 1983 album *Frontátvonulás* ("Frontal Crossing")—while others are absent from the albums entirely but present in the stage performances. These romping yet subtle narratives summoned, justified, and unified the songs.

Their work spans both the socialist era of the 1970s–80s and the post-socialist era from 1989 onward. These two halves of their repertoire are also divided by Bereményi's seven-year hiatus from songwriting (1982–1989). During this period, the *Jóslat* ("Prophecy") stage performance, the *Frontátvonulás* album, the *Jóslat* album, and the 1987 *Utóirat* ("Postscript") album came into being; the songs for these had been written earlier. Cseh also created the 1988 album *Mélyrepülés* ("Flying Low" or "Deep Dive") with Dénes Csengey.

The first era of their work was marked by allusiveness, secret references, clever evasions of censorship, and their intimate yet bounded collaboration—in which they worked closely together, day by day, while maintaining their delineated roles (Cseh as composer and performer, Bereményi as lyricist). In the second era, that of Bereményi's hiatus, they released songs they had already written; in the case of *Jóslat* ("Prophecy), Bereményi added the spoken text. In the third era, marked by regime change in Hungary, they not only released new material, but reworked several of their albums into updated versions. Thus their first album, *Levél nővéremnek* ("Letter to My Sister") was later followed by a sequel, *Levél nővéremnek 2* (1994), and a concert recording, *Az igazi levél nővéremnek* (2004).[12] They also released compilations and more concert recordings.

In both eras, many musicians played on the albums (with some exceptions), but only a few of these collaborated with Cseh and Bereményi outside the studio. By the time of *Antoine és Désiré* (the live show was titled *Désiré és Antoine*), Cseh generally performed alone; this remained the case until much later. Yet the contributions of János Másik, János Novák, and others are central to some of the albums and songs. These composers and musicians recognized something exceptional in Cseh and Bereményi's work and helped to bring it out.

Their work participated in a variety of literary as well as musical traditions while also departing from them. The songs not only refer to literary works and authors, but create ambiences evocative of a Paris-like

Budapest, or, in contrast, a Hungarian Wild West. While they were devoted to writing in Hungarian—that was, after all, Bereményi's patent reason for offering to help Cseh with his songs in 1970—their imagination was captured by books, films, songs, and lore from around the Western world. Songs about Arthur Rimbaud, William Shakespeare, and Fyodor Dostoevsky combine with "Lee van Cleef" and other allusive airs.

Cseh and Bereményi's theatrical and film activity influenced and sometimes combined with their music. Cseh sang their songs in a number of films; in addition, he was a member of the 25th Theatre company, then the Katona József Theatre and later the Bárka Theatre. Bereményi, for his part, wrote and directed films and plays—his famous films include Ferenc András's *A nagy generáció* ("The Great Generation"), for which Bereményi wrote the screenplay, and *Eldorádó,* which he both wrote and directed. He taught for years at the Academy of Theatre and Film Arts in Budapest.

Their attraction to American Western lore had roots in Cseh's "Indian" lifestyle, a practice that began in Germany in the late nineteenth century and in Hungary and Eastern Europe from the 1920s onward. In Cseh's time, many Hungarians and others looked up to Native Americans as exemplars of integrity, strength, spirituality, connection to nature, and independence from the prevailing social and political currents. They formed secret tribes, held meetings, and taught themselves to survive in the wild with their handmade "Indian" clothes, weapons, tools, and teepees. Cseh and Bereményi's songs have many hints of this labor of love; for instance, part of their song "Antoine és Désiré történelemkönyve" ("Antoine and Désiré's History Book") from the 1978 album *Antoine és Désiré* has a section in Lakota, or what Cseh and Bereményi were able to glean of the language. The "Indian" movement in Hungary has had an array of political connotations; in any case it was a form of resistance, spiritual practice, and discipline.[13]

Cseh and Bereményi respected some of their literary and musical colleagues around the world and made contact with them in various ways. At one point there was talk of a joint concert with Leonard Cohen, but when Cseh and Bereményi contacted Cohen's secretary to work out the details, she told them that he was at a year-long Zen Buddhist retreat and thus not available. Cseh once met Vladimir Vysotsky; as Cseh spoke no Russian and Vysotsky no Hungarian, they sat down in a room together and conversed through songs, taking turns playing for each other. For Cseh, this opened up a new way of thinking of songs; he realized that a song could roar if that was what it was meant to do. That is, one could follow the impulse of the songs as they came out.[14]

Alongside these many influences, collaborations, and meetings or near-meetings, both Cseh and Bereményi had a solitary streak. This can be sensed in the songs themselves and in the way they left each other alone, even while working directly together. The lyrics were Bereményi's domain; the music, Cseh's. They left the songs themselves alone; they did not even discuss their meanings. Moreover, their relationship—as Bereményi described it, both more and less than a friendship—allowed either one of them to make a break. Perhaps it is a sense of solitude, in part, that draws people together to hear and sing the songs: not loneliness, but rather the knowledge that even when talking with our best friends, we cannot explain what a song means or how we hear it. We can call a song this or that: melancholic, funny, playful, brooding, but these words do not convey how the song reaches us. The world is filled with "false measures" (a phrase from the song "Pridem").[15] We find refuge in those places where we do not have to explain ourselves or the things that matter.

The following overview of Cseh and Bereményi's shows and albums is meant to give the reader a basic map of their work, particularly in the early period. The second chapter will explore Cseh and Bereményi's social and political context, with attention to their particular generation; the third through ninth chapters will take up individual albums, songs, and concepts; and the final three chapters will consider audience responses, both during their time and later.

In this chapter, instead of plodding through the discography, I will move through it somewhat whimsically (though sequentially), as if pulling records out of a collection. I will consider their work in terms of three main eras: the initial era (1970–1981), Bereményi's hiatus (1982–1989), and Cseh and Bereményi's reunification—which more or less coincided with the regime change in Hungary—and further collaboration (1989–2007).

The initial era of their collaboration began with intensive songwriting. Cseh and Bereményi had already composed hundreds of songs—and had considered emigrating—before accepting an invitation from the writer and director László Gyurkó (which they initially declined) for Cseh to perform at the 25th Theatre in Budapest. It was on March 1, 1973, that Cseh gave his first public performance, the debut of the first show created by Cseh and Bereményi, *A Dal nélkül* ("Without Song"). The band Ad libitum (János Novák, István Márta, Gábor Kecskeméti, and László Jakobi) accompanied him. For this occasion, Levente Szörényi (already famed for his musicianship in Illés and earlier bands) lent him his own guitar, as Cseh did not have a good instrument. Cseh later recalled standing in front of the stage, almost with his back to the audience. Before he went out to the audience, Bereményi gave him advice that would help him for the rest of his life: "Tamás, it isn't you who are important here, it's the songs." From this, he understood, "It's not about me here, I should just be alert to the songs, sink into each one separately, in its own way, hide in their skin, pull them into myself." He went out onto and down from the stage, and as he recalls, this concert became almost a sacred rite.[16]

This concert likely differed from anything the audience had seen or heard before. First, it was ingenious on Gyurkó's part to invite Cseh to perform in the theatre rather than in a music club, thus signaling that this was no ordinary pop music performance. Second, the accompanying musicians were exceptional, not only in their technical prowess and versatility, but in their ability to grasp the art in these seemingly simple songs. Third, Bereményi did much more than provide lyrics; along with Cseh and the others, he envisioned and planned the show and encouraged Cseh. More performances of *A Dal nélkül* were to follow.

In September 1973, this debut performance received its first review (Cseh's first critical review overall), written by András Szeredás and published in *Színház* ("Theatre"). Szeredás praised the performance, drawing attention to "the playful dialectic of seriousness and frivolity" and observing that "it is actually not the genre itself, but its function that the songs of Tamás Cseh and Bereményi shed a spotlight on. The special feature of their show is that it offers an opportunity for a dramatic comparison, a comparison between singing as a continuous human expression, a social function, and the song as reality."[17]

Their next show, *Levél Nővéremnek* ("Letter to My Sister") created in collaboration with János Másik and János Novák, premiered in 1976, again at the 25th Theatre, and was released as an album in 1977. (I will take up this show and album in Chapter 3.) Framed as a letter broken into episodes, alternating between chanted narration and song, it is wistful, bittersweet, and humor-trodden. On the album, Cseh and Másik sing together; in the chanted narrated parts, they stagger their voices, Cseh first, then Másik, creating the effect of an echo or a double person. Bereményi commented in an interview: "Two people, as one, write a letter to their sister. We know that the sister as a woman is different from other women in a man's life. She embodies a man's feminine side. The better side. An ideal woman. ... The female half of our soul. So the two people, who are one person, personally address the better half of their soul."[18]

The album begins, "This is a letter. / Its envelope is blue. / I bought the stamp for a forint. / The place and date: / Dated: Budapest. / All right, all right. / Let this be the scene... / The place and date... / Let there be scenery. / This is a letter. / This is a letter. / The place and date. / The place and date. / 1976 is the year. / 1976 is the year. / This is that year. / Let it be, let it be... / This much is known. / This is a letter. / I write to my sister. / Her name is Irén. / This much is known. / Right now it's winter. / A regular season. / All right, all right. / This is a letter. / Let there be a letter. / The place and date. / Let there be scene. / Let there be scenery."[19]

From that very introduction, we can glean that time and place both matter and do not; we know the year at this point, and the season, but not much more. The letter, in fact, seems to come into being with the words "Let there be scene. / Let there be scenery," which suggests the quietly theatrical aspect of the album. The songs have to do with questions over whether to leave (the country?) or stay at home in Budapest; a train ride to Kraków; an infernal night in a *eszpresszó* (in this case a euphemism for a bar); the speaker's father's hat; memories of youthful summers on Lake Balaton, before they had a sailboat; contemplation of a possible meeting with former love who emigrated and has returned to Hungary; a dream about meeting with a married woman; a ceremony; a memory of a class field trip; a story of almost moving but ending up staying; a state of drunken reverie after a concert, with Mozart and alcohol on the breath, memories of holding hands, a doorbell being rung, an imaginary name next to it. In the final song of the album, "Kézbesítés" ("Delivery"), the letter-writer wonders, at the end, "An important ceremony, who knows where it comes to a halt? / Irén doesn't answer, because she has to take care of the kids. / Sealed in an envelope, who knows where it tosses about? Tell me, Irén, where does this all come to a halt?"

Their 1978 show *Désiré és Ántoine* and album *Antoine és Désiré* ("Désiré and Antoine," "Antoine and Désiré"), to be examined further in the fourth chapter, signaled the beginnings of their story-song genre. While the album consists only of songs, it hints at a surrounding fiction; in the show, Cseh told stories between the songs. An insert in the record contains the biographies of the two fictional protagonists, both of whom are known by these monikers but "actually" (still fictionally) have Hungarian names. The songs mark episodes in these characters' lives and friendship. Antoine apparently is the more dominant and successful of the two, Désiré the more hapless; Antoine has practical knowhow, Désiré soul (yet that is too simple). Désiré is really the hero of their joined story, the focus of nine of the album's seventeen songs, and possibly more, depending on one's interpretation.

Partly inspired by the persona of János Gémes ("Dixi"), an iconic figure in the Hungarian underground scene, Désiré could be anyone whose sensitivities put him in continual danger. There is something fascinating though silly about Désiré; his biography in the record insert reminds us that if Antoine had not propped him up under the arm, he would have sunk still deeper. The songs on this album are Cseh and Bereményi classics, often covered at concerts or sung at gatherings. The mood ranges from the exuberance of the aforementioned "Antoine és Désiré történelemkönyve" ("Antone and Désiré's History Book") to the comic-elusive "Demonstráció" ("Demonstration") to the reflective "Désiré megnémul" ("Desiré Falls Silent"), a song to pause on here.

In this song, which brings the album to a close, Désiré reflects on the roads he has taken, the confusion, mistakes, perhaps lies, but then comes upon a sentence that he cannot finish, "*és volt egy kevés*" ("and there was a little"). He searches for what to call it, and then finally decides it could be "perhaps one or two evenings / that have not been named / and by now, probably will stay / empty of name." The song then breaks into a *táráráráram*, reflecting the end of words. In the second verse, Désiré goes on to consider what will happen if he doesn't name them, and no one else does either: he will go silent ("dumb"), and this little something or other will probably disappear. "this little, I don't know / what to call that, maybe just this: there were one or two evenings," and then the *táráráráram* comes back and takes us to the end of the album. This tender, hesitant song touches on death and the loss of memory and words, as well as the things that cannot be said because expression itself is forbidden. Decades later, in 2006, the song took on another level of meaning when Cseh, by now ill with lung cancer, opened his final concert with it on Bakáts Square in Budapest.

The next two albums, *Fehér babák takarodója* ("White Dolls' Curfew") and *Műcsarnok* ("Art Gallery"), released in 1979 and 1981 respectively, are likewise based on live shows, but with differences between them. *Fehér babák takarodója* is an album about women and relationships with women; some songs take up particular liaisons, while others reflect on relationships more generally. In the stage shows, these songs were part of a dialogue between Antoine and Désiré.[20] In *Műcsarnok*, which did not have a stage show of its own, almost all of the songs refer to literature, film, and visual art. There are homages to Rimbaud, Shakespeare, and Dostoevsky as well as the Hungarian poets Sándor Petőfi and Endre Ady; the iconic song "Lee van Cleef" (to be discussed in the seventh chapter; and surreal but pointedly satirical phenomena such as "Valóság nagybátyám" ("Uncle Reality"). Many of these songs appeared in earlier shows, including Cseh's 1973 debut.

It is with the fifth show and album, *Frontátvonulás* ("Frontal Passage")—the focus of the fifth chapter—that Cseh and Bereményi arrive at the apex of their form. Here, both in the stage performance, which premiered in 1979, and on the 1983 album, narration alternates with songs, which themselves tell stories within the larger story. Cseh performed it solo, but the album has musical accompaniment and sound effects (both of them likely synthesized, as no additional musicians are credited).

The gist of the story is as follows: After a drunken evening with his friend Ecsédi, which ends with Ecsédi shouting women's names and street addresses, Vizi decides to leave and start a new life.[*] A magic trick he performs with a glass in the kitchen—where the glass floats in the air—tells him that he is capable of everything; he takes off. Ecsédi, finding him gone, rushes around desperately in search of him. Over the course of various encounters and songs—featuring a certain Comrade Eagle, a ticket clerk, a suicidal man, an aged man, a restroom attendant, a *diseuse* (nightclub singer), a group of graduating seniors, and other characters stuck in various forms of stagnation or despair— they both end up at Keleti Station, where Vizi learns to his astonishment and dismay that no trains are departing. When Ecsédi finds his friend at last, he urges him to do a trick he has performed many times before (the same one he performs in the kitchen at

---

[*] The Hungarian surnames 'Vizi' and 'Ecsédi' derive from words meaning 'water' and 'younger brother,' respectively.

the start of the story): to hold up a glass and release it. Vizi does so; just as before, the glass floats in the air instead of falling. Buoyed by this miracle, the following morning they drive a locomotive through the glass façade of the station and take it on a victory tour around the city. After much confetti and cheering, they watch the event later that night on television, back at Vizi's place. Vizi watches it to the end—Ecsédi has fallen asleep in the other room, slumped over his arms—and turns off the television. Then he goes up to Ecsédi, pulls him by the hair, and roars in his face: "If you yell women's names at me here one more time, and street addresses, it's over, get it?" The album ends with Cseh addressing the audience: "It's over. Get it?"

Frontátvonulás has been interpreted in myriad ways: as a story of a generation, as a political allegory, as a piece of brilliant absurdity, as art for art's sake. The possibilities continue to multiply. In 2024, graduating students of the University of Film Arts in Budapest (who have since formed their own company, SICC Production) reimagined it in space and time while remaining scrupulously faithful to the text. Their production featured new arrangements—six actors playing multiple instruments and creating vocal sound effects—and a challenging stage set (a two-tiered metal structure that they clamber up, down, and around). The paradox inherent in this structure—the majestic, spacious Keleti Station imagined as a structure that makes you bend, twist, and duck—brings out the deeper paradoxes of the work itself, its mixture of ingenuity and despair, its transcendence.

Between the time of the *Frontátvonulás* premiere and the album's release, Bereményi had declared a hiatus from songwriting, without giving reasons (and Cseh, in keeping with their initial agreement, did not ask for any). Without reading biographical innuendo into *Frontátvonulás*, one can nonetheless find in it a serious question that might have been on their minds. At what point does creation itself become routine, like a magic trick performed night after night? At what point does a person have to break with the routine and do something new, wherever it might lead?

During Bereményi's hiatus, Cseh and Bereményi released three new albums and premiered a new stage performance; in addition, Cseh collaborated with Dénes Csengey on the album *Mélyrepülés* ("Flying Low" or "Deep Dive"). The Cseh-Bereményi albums, *Frontátvonulás* (1983), *Jóslat* ("Prophecy," 1984), to be discussed in the sixth chapter, and the double album *Utóirat* ("Postscript," 1987), to be discussed in the eighth, all consisted of previously unreleased songs written before the hiatus. To someone familiar with Cseh's performances but unaware of the situation, this interim period might have seemed stagnant. But not only did it allow them to revisit their vast repertoire of songs and choose what to release and how, but it provided, over time, a new perspective.

When Bereményi resumed songwriting with Cseh in 1989, the regime in Hungary was changing, their was hope in the air, and censorship relaxed— yet the initial exuberance was soon followed by disillusionment, reflected in the somber, angry tone of some of the songs. Cseh and Bereményi's newfound collaboration took several forms. First, they released albums of entirely new material, beginning with *Új dalok* ("New Songs," 1990). Second, they reworked some of their previous material by creating sequels and updated versions. For example, as mentioned before, their first album, *Levél nővéremnek* ("Letter to My Sister," 1977), was followed by *Levél nővéremnek 2.* (1994) and the concert album *Az igazi levél nővéremnek* ("The Real Letter to My Sister," 2004)—both of these in collaboration with János Másik, who likewise had resumed his work with Cseh. Third, they released a number of concert recordings and compilations of previously recorded songs. Between 1989 and 2006, Cseh continued to perform prolifically. A documentary film about him, directed by Gergely Fonyó, was released in 2001; in the same year, he and Bereményi received the Kossuth Prize. Thus this era of their collaboration involved formal recognition as well as intense activity on several fronts.

On August 26, 2006, Cseh gave his last concert for a large crowd on Bakáts Square in Budapest. He was accompanied by János Másik; a documentary film shows them playing "Keresztben jégeső" ("Hail in the Face") with all the exuberance they can muster. Cseh later commented to László Bérczes that he had not wanted the audience to be weepy on this occasion: "laughing, I looked at the audience," he said, "taking damn good care that God save us from some kind of mournful mood." Yet it is impossible to ignore the pain as he sings, "*Most jókedvem lesz, jó kedvem lesz, akkor is jókedvem lesz. / Valaki elpusztul, talán az én leszek, de jó kedvem lesz!*" ("I will be cheerful now, I will be cheerful, I will be cheerful then too. / Someone's about to perish, maybe that's me, but cheerful I will be!").[21]

We who never attended these performances will never know exactly what it was like to be in a room where Cseh was playing, no matter how much we can glean from audio recordings, videos, interviews, descriptions, or evenings dedicated to Cseh and Bereményi's work. Yet a leap of imagination can land us in the room anyhow—because their work, and Cseh's stage presence, had to do with such a leap to begin with. What does that mean here, a "leap of imagination"?

For listeners today, it means to dare to enter these works even if we do not qualify for admission: that is, if we are not old or experienced enough, did not live through their eras, do not recognize all of the allusions. It means to believe, while the song or performance lasts, that Ecsédi is actually running around looking for Vizi, that Antoine and Désiré are prophesying on the subway, that Ádám Balogh is passing by in his velvet hat, and that Cseh is conveying his personal secrets. People often forgot that the lyrics were Bereményi's, but this was part of the conjuration. Bereményi, who disliked adulatory fans, stayed in the background at Cseh's shows and avoided attention from the audience; that was Cseh's role, to draw attention.[22]

These leaps are remarkably easy: first, because the songs make their own leaps, and second, because any event devoted to the songs of Cseh and Bereményi may evoke the atmosphere of the original concerts. It sometimes seems that Cseh is right there in the room, about to call out, *Istenem!* if a barfly in the shadows does not beat him to it.

The following chapter will consider the generational experience of Cseh and Bereményi and the extent to which it figures in their music.

Chapter 2

The Question of the "Great Generation"

Hungarians of Cseh and Bereményi's generation, born during or shortly after World War II, emerged from the end of the war and the Soviet takeover; endured the Rákosi dictatorship in their childhood; felt the jolts of the 1956 revolution; perhaps took part in the "Beat" era with its rock rhythms, free poetry, and rebellious lifestyle; and—unless they died young or emigrated—lived through the Kádár era (1956–1989), followed by the fall of the Iron Curtain and a succession of new regimes. Given the differences between segments of the population and among individuals, generic descriptions of this generation falter; nonetheless, the idea of generational identity took hold, influencing many interpretations of Cseh and Bereményi's work. Later dubbed the "Great Generation," this cohort was known for both its impulse toward freedom and its thwarted (possibly self-sabotaged) potential.

In his 1983 treatise … *és mi most itt vagyunk* ("And We Are Here Now"), Dénes Csengey (1953–1991 described this generation and analyzed the role of Cseh and Bereményi's work within it.[1] While he did not call it the *nagy generáció* ("great generation")—he usually referred to it as a *nemzedék*, a weightier word for "generation," which he put in quotes—he defined its parameters and analyzed its characteristics. Subsequent critics have challenged his arguments, but because of their daring and depth, they have attained canonical status and continue to assist our understanding.

This essay examines a few key events in the lives of Cseh and Bereményi in the aftermath of World War II, the 1956 Revolution, and the Kádár era, mentioning a few of their contemporaries along the way (János Baksa-Soós, János Gémes, Zsuzsa Koncz, and Pál Szécsi); then it considers and responds to Csengey's arguments.. Throughout it, I refer to the Kádár era as "socialist," but "communist" or "socialist-communist" could be used as well. In a sense it was both communist and socialist: communist in ideology and socialist in its economic policies. (Many refer to the Kádár government's economic policies as "goulash communism" because of their mixture of elements.) When speaking of the "system," I refer to a specific (but changing and sometimes contradictory) set of institutions and policies of the era; for a detailed analysis of the arts policy of this period, see Gábor Bolvári-Takács's 2024 article "Arts Policy in Kádár Era in Hungary, 1957–1989."[2] For convenience, I refer to this as the "Kádár era" (as do many historians), but Kádár was not its sole architect. In fact, the entire "Great Generation" contributed to it, at least passively. It is difficult in such a short space to convey the essence of the Kádár era: its relative lenience combined with its censorship and surveillance. However, the book would be incomplete without an attempt.

From the outset, I acknowledge the complexity of generational questions. On the one hand, generations themselves are difficult to define, as the cutoff years are somewhat arbitrary; on the other, even within a defined cohort, differences may outweigh common traits. Nonetheless, when a country goes through upheavals of war, revolution, cultural influx, and foreign occupation, the common experiences become pronounced, especially in a small nation where it can seem at times that *mindenki rokon* ("everyone is a relative," an ironic phrase in the final song of *Frontátvonulás*).

Hungary both suffered and inflicted trauma in World War II; historians disagree on the proportion of the two. Allied with the Axis powers since 1940 (with hopes of regaining the territory it had lost through the Trianon agreement), it participated in the invasions of Yugoslavia and the Soviet Union. It subsequently began restoring relations with the U.S. and U.K.; in response, Germany invaded it in 1944. This marked the beginning of the deportation—by German and Hungarian officials—of Hungarian Jews and Roma to concentration camps; before this, these groups had already suffered severe discrimination under the racial laws. Altogether, some 900,000 Hungarians, including Jews and Roma, died in World War II; the cities were bombed, in some places to ruins.

For a long time afterward, instead of grappling with what had happened, many Hungarians (Jews and others) fell silent. In a 2018 interview with Gábor Mórocz, the historian Gábor Hanák—the founding director of the Tamás Cseh Archive—spoke of the silences of this era: "Families guarded the traumas of 1944–49 and 1956–63 as their innermost secrets. Thus it could happen that a generation grew up whose members did not know, for example, that they were Jews. Or that their grandfather was a decorated soldier and a hero of the World War. ... If the child told anyone what the parents thought, this posed an existential danger. That is why the parents did not tell them... and they did not tell them en masse."[3]

Tamás Cseh was born on January 22, 1943, on Bakáts Square in Budapest; after his birth, his family returned to their residence in Tordas, Fejér County, where Cseh's father, Ferenc Cseh, was the local representative of the business cooperative Hangya ("Ant") National Consumer and Sales Cooperative, founded in 1898. In 1944, the family fled westward to the edge of the village to escape the German front. Cseh's father served in the Hungarian army from 1942 to 1944, when he was one of a group of sixteen who stayed in the rearguard while others blew up the Danube bridge at Dunaföldvár to halt the advance of the German troops. The bombing succeeded, but he and others were taken as war prisoners; it would be another three years or so before he could return to his family. "He hated the war, hated weapons," Cseh recollected. When, as a boy, he attempted to ask his father about the war, he replied, "My Tamáska, I didn't fire a single shot."[4]

The 1944–1945 Soviet offensive in Hungary, which accelerated the end of the Second World War, was followed immediately by the establishment of the Second Hungarian Republic (communist in ideology), succeeded in 1949 by the Soviet-controlled Hungarian People's Republic. It was into the Second Hungarian Republic that Géza Bereményi was born, on January 25, 1946, in Budapest. His biological father, Géza Vetró, had fled from Transylvania to Hungary to escape Romanian military conscription; barely after the baby's birth he fled onward, to escape further drafting. Neither he nor Bereményi's teenage mother, Éva, opted to take care of him; thus it was Bereményi's grandparents, the merchants Róza and Sándor Bereményi, who raised him until his sixth year, when Éva and her second husband, István Rózner, took custody of him. (He met his biological father when he was thirteen and remained on good terms with him until the end of the latter's life.) Bereményi's surname was initially Vetró, then Rózner; when, at the age of twenty, he was about to publish his first story collection, he was told that he needed a Hungarian name, so he chose his grandfather's surname, Bereményi.[5]

At age ten, Bereményi witnessed the immediate aftermath of the 1956 Revolution. In his autobiographical novel *Magyar Copperfield* ("Hungarian Copperfield") he tells of how, on October 22, 1956, his classmate Gabi Rácz called him and told him not to come to school, as the city was on curfew. Just barely over a flu, he lay down and sank into Hemingway's *For Whom the Bell Tolls*. The next day, on October 23, upon hearing that the curfew was over, his parents announced that they were going shopping and that he had to stay home. They took the key and left him alone. Géza climbed out the window and down to the ground. He and Gabi met near the Nyugati train station; together they headed toward the Parliament, where a large crowd had assembled and more were arriving. The newer arrivals asked those present what was happening, and were told "nothing," that this had been going on for a long time. A few moments later, shots rang out, and Géza and Gabi rushed to the Rácz family's apartment. After a while, Bereményi decided to go home; the parents told him to turn left upon leaving the building. He turned right instead, came to the deserted square, and saw dead bodies and blood on the ground. The shooters had left; the ambulances had not yet arrived. Then he noticed, through the fog, a few living bodies among the corpses; a woman called out to him, "What are you looking for here, little boy? Go away." He saw someone he recognized, walking around just like him; approaching him, he recognized his math teacher. They greeted each other formally, making no mention of what had happened. He headed home; climbing back into his apartment he scraped himself. His parents, upon returning home, neither noticed his scrapes nor mentioned the demonstration or shootings.[6]

Cseh's life was also directly affected by the 1956 Revolution, but differently. According to Cseh, the uprising, though far away, brought an unfamiliar exuberance to Tordas. People were laughing and smiling. Toward the end of October, the head teacher of his school asked him to cut the Rákosi crest out of the center of a large Hungarian flag, with the entire village watching. (Mátyás Rákosi—an ardent Stalinist and Soviet ally—was the de facto leader of Hungary from 1949 to 1956, a time of purges, show trials, and run-of-the-mill repression.) Cseh recalled trying to cut as perfect a circle as possible while the crowd grew impatient. Finally he completed the task; the people lifted the crest-free flag up, fastened it to the iron rod of a truck, and drove into Budapest singing.[7]

This event illustrates how abruptly Hungary's official ideology could change. The objective of the 1950 curriculum (during Rákosi's rule) had been to teach students "to become conscious, disciplined citizens of the People's Republic, who are loyal to the working class and build Socialism." Ideological instruction began in the earliest years of school and continued through the university. Ideology permeated every subject: for instance, the objective of the physics curriculum was to help a scientific world view "to evolve and by so doing laying down the foundation of a dialectical materialist worldview. Fight against idealistic view of life." Specific textbooks were mandated and compliance inspected and enforced.[8] According to Csengey, schoolchildren at this time lacked the joint and benevolent influence of school and family; instead, school and family exerted "mutually opposing" influences on each other, as children learned cheery, vulgarized Marxism by day but went home to poverty and skimpy meals. Parents and grandparents would react to their children's dutiful recitations with quiet horror: "Old women would make the sign of the cross, quietly moaning, when their ten-year-old grandson stood before them and said there was no God."[9]

Like many others, Cseh's family experienced abrupt changes at the time of the 1956 Revolution. For some time, they had been living in separation, through necessity; his older sister attended a high school in Budapest and lived with their aunt; the father also spent some time in Budapest, and Cseh lived in Tordas with his mother. In November 1956, they were suddenly all able to move together into an apartment on Villányi Road in Budapest; a colleague of Cseh's father had decided to emigrate and quietly handed over his apartment to them.[10] This became the place that Cseh would consider home from then on, even in adulthood when living on his own.

In June 1961, Cseh graduated from the Attila József Secondary School, now the Saint Imre Secondary School. Around this time, he received his first guitar, a seven-string Russian guitar that his grandmother had bought for him. He had never held a guitar before but had become fascinated with the instrument when watching a local band. Because of his guitar's wide neck, he had difficulty even holding it properly; he began by playing on one string, which he plucked with a matchstick. It was at this time that he wrote his first song. His grandmother taught him *tercelni*, which he instantly learned: that is, the practice of singing at the interval of a third above or below the instrument or other singer.[11]

During the 1960s, both Cseh and Bereményi began to find their way into their art, in the midst of simultaneous freedom and restrictions. The freedom lay in solitary work and in a lively artistic underground, where Western music and literature were overtly or covertly spread, and where numerous artistic collaborations took shape. Yet with the ever-present censorship and surveillance, a sense of despair pervaded and was often expressed through (and exacerbated by) alcohol consumption. Cseh commented in an interview with Sándor Fodor that "when a man drinks, he is almost always seeking suicide in it" and that some of their friends had died from alcohol: it poisoned them, or they died in an accident, or killed themselves and that "alcohol was always there in the background."[12]

After Rákosi, the leadership of János József Kádár—who had been put on trial by Rákosi's government and imprisoned for three years, and who rose to power during the 1956 Revolution—seemed relatively permissive and lenient, particularly in comparison with other Soviet satellite states. Having taken measures to crush the opposition that had gathered force during the Revolution—according to a CIA document, he "either acquiesced in or ordered the execution of [Imre] Nagy," who served as prime minister from 1953 to 1955 and led the Revolution—Kádár initiated an era of reconciliation based on the slogan "he who is not against us is with us," as well as a new economic policy intended to stimulate growth. He rehabilitated former victims of Rákosi's Stalinist regime and offered rewards to those in the intelligentsia who played by his rules. Yet those who refused to play the political game, or who stayed outside of it, were not only denied privileges but in some cases risked arrest. Many ventured the risks; a new political, intellectual, and artistic opposition began to burgeon. Young people, aware of other ways of life outside of Hungary's borders, lived in furtive or overt opposition to the regime.[13]

In the 1960s, Cseh and Bereményi did not yet know each other. Cseh applied to art school twice unsuccessfully, worked for a while as a laborer, and eventually earned the credentials to teach art in schools. During this time he played music informally for friends. He took his first steps into the "Indian" lifestyle in 1961, when he and several friends, just graduated from high school, decided to fight each other in the manner of Native American Indians, in a valley of the Bakony mountains. Over time, this developed into a dedicated practice; Cseh considered himself an Indian for the rest of his life. His Indian name was *Füst a szemében* ("Smoke in His Eyes").[14]

In the summer of 1965, just a few months before Cseh obtained his teaching diploma, Péter Bacsó released his romantic comedy film *Szerelmes biciklisták* ("Bicyclists in Love"), for which Cseh performed both the theme song and another song. Set in the region of Lake Balaton, this film expresses a whimsical way of life in the midst of nature, far from the cares of the capital but laced with anxiety. Cseh's playing was also featured in his 1967 film *Nyár a hegyen* ("Summer on the Mountain"), in which an artist, a teacher, and a doctor purchase a property at a quarry near Balaton, only to discover—well, the doctor already knew—that it used to be an internment camp. The idyllic surroundings and sounds set the backdrop for difficult and surprising confrontations with the past.

The relative freedom of the Balaton microculture during this era was later conveyed in Cseh and Bereményi's song "A hatvanas évek" ("The Sixties"), to be introduced in the next chapter. The first two lines are telling: "In the sixties, toward summer, the youth problem came to a head." According to historian Sándor Horváth, this "youth problem" was a topic of discussion at the time, in contrast with the events of 1956, a taboo subject.[15] Thus the very mention of the "youth problem" (*az ifjúsági probléma*) in the song suggests that it was in the air. The irony here is that this "problem" consists of an idyllic lifestyle of boating, dancing, and reading.

In a curious way, it was precisely the conditions of their generation that allowed Cseh and Bereményi to meet. Csengey describes how, at the start of the Beat era, "almost an entire generation moved into rented apartments" that had been created to accommodate the population after World War II. They moved away from their villages and towns and into cities, separating themselves from their parents and grandparents.[16] When Cseh and Bereményi met in 1970, Cseh was living in a sublet on Iskola Street; Bereményi had been moving from one place to another. Cseh was now teaching; Bereményi had worked in book advertising, then film dubbing (two rather monotonous jobs). Thus there was nothing holding either of them back from following the new direction that presented itself on that day in 1970 when they wrote their first two songs together. Bereményi moved in with Cseh and remained his roommate for a year and a half. Cseh continued teaching for a while, then left his job when the songwriting and performing took over.

Artists of that time—or rather, those artists who chose not to seek official approval—faced a narrow set of choices, none of which led to material rewards. They could emigrate, testing their luck abroad but giving up their home. They could resist official dogma and directives, risking various kinds of trouble at every turn and often creating troubles of their own, through drinking and other self-destructive habits. They could attempt some kind of truce, surviving in the system somehow without embracing it. Or they could let themselves be destroyed entirely, from the outside or from within; according to some estimates, in the vast majority of the years from 1960 to 2000, Hungary had the highest suicide rate in the world.[17] Let us take a look at a few artists who took each of these directions.

An icon of Hungarian popular music of the 1960s was János Baksa-Soós (1948–2021), founder of the inimitable band Kex, which recorded one EP (lacking government support, that was all they could manage) and gave rambunctious, spontaneous concerts before Baksa Soós's emigration in 1971. Their performances came with surprises: once they performed the Beatles' "Ob-La-Di Ob-La-Da" thirteen times in a row, each time in a different style; on another occasion they acted as if they were going with the audience on a trip. Some of these concerts involved political protest and parody, drawing the attention of the authorities; on one occasion, the police arrived with dogs, to which Baksa-Soós rejoined that "It is odd that the dogs are wearing caps and the police are barking." The music of Kex varied richly from psychedelic rock to dance music to their poignant classic "A család" ("The Family"), which, entwined in ornamental cello melodies, reminisces about a time in the past when the family still lived together.[18]

After a jeep of military men swerved onto the sidewalk in an attempt to hit Baksa-Soós—a murder attempt ordered from above, according to András Kisfaludy, the band's founding drummer and the director of a documentary film about the band—he decided to leave the country. He had already lived in East Berlin for several years and spoke German fluently (his mother was German); now he moved to Essen, where he studied graphic arts. In 1978, after obtaining a master's degree from the Düsseldorf Academy of Fine Arts, he relocated to West Berlin, where he spent the rest of his life as a prolific artist, musician, writer, and event organizer. His work was shown in several exhibits in Hungary after the regime change. He died in 2021 of a severe infection; in 2022 a memorial concert was held in his honor at Hungary's Ördögkatlan Festival (the name "Ördögkatlan," or "Devil's Cauldron," refers to a local folk legend). It was Baksa-Soós who first invited Cseh to play on stage, during an intermission in a Kex concert in the spring of 1971. Cseh played three songs on this occasion, his first time performing for a large audience.[19]

If Baksa-Soós epitomized those artistic rebels of Cseh and Bereményi's generation who left the country, János Gémes (1943–2002), known as "Dixi," epitomized those who stayed (in fact he never went abroad). Although there was no one like either of them, both illustrated the difficulties of the era for those who attempted some kind of freedom. Dixi, a poet, actor, spoken word performer, late night reveler, prophet of beauty and nonsense, improvisor, provocateur, and raging alcoholic, still figures in the lives of those who encountered his work and persona. Born of a Jewish mother and Christian father (who abandoned the family early on), he became a ward of the state and was raised by foster parents; he served in the army for one year but was dismissed as unfit. According to Tamás Szőnyei, he gave spontaneous performances in countless nightclubs, pubs, and cafés (from which he was often banned); an anonymous commenter adds that he had a reputation for finishing any drinks that customers left behind.[20]

In the photo-novel *Antoine és Désiré* (only loosely connected to the album of the same title) by Bereményi and János Vető, Dixi appears as Désiré (and Vető's close collaborator Lóránt Zuzu Méhes as Antoine); they appear on the streets and in bars in various situations, positions, and qualities of light and shadow. Dixi's large eyes, chiseled face, arched eyebrows, and top hat give him a dreamy yet comical appearance; at times he can look wild, at times absent, at times bemused. Dixi's actual poems seem to match these pictures well: for instance, his poem with a question mark as the title:[21]

?

one-eyed ringmaster
in a mold-dusty top hat
doorman
shallow-draft in a briny sea breeze
am I real in a dream
or am I dreaming in reality?
am I?

Mihály Víg described Dixi in a eulogy:

He was free when everyone felt like a slave, because no one had less tolerance for slavery than he. Wild, ecstatic, surreal, in a language no one spoke better, he hurled his poems into the wind with lavish richness. Stubborn, deeply determined, he tried to elevate sad, alcohol-sponged reality into the realm of poetry. Speech became an expression of aesthetics and spirit, language was used for its intended purpose, in that strange age when it was still easy to get a few slaps in the guardroom just because you had long hair.[22]

For a dim sense of Dixi's presence, one can watch videos of his improvisational performances: for instance, in 1999 in a park, as filmed by András Fiath. To an outsider he might look like a homeless madman, raving about the dangers of propaganda—but this was one of thousands of such performances over the decades. He was a mystical figure, always meaning a little more and a little less than might appear. A documentary about him by Lehel Oláh brings out the complexity of his personality and effect.[23]

Dixi's fate differed markedly from that of the singer Zsuzsa Koncz, one of his contemporaries. Eulogized in Cseh and Bereményi's comically poignant song "Ha Koncz Zsuzsával járhatnék egyszer" ("If Only I Could Go Out with Zsuzsa Koncz"), Koncz was admired and beloved for her rich, powerful voice, playful stage presence, and wry lyrics, most of them written by her close collaborator János Bródy (1946–), a key member of the bands Illés and Fonográf. Cseh himself played on several of her albums. Koncz sang (and still sings) for crowds around the world and has released album after album both at home and abroad; while she thus cannot be considered part of the Hungarian underground, she lived out many of the tensions of the Kádár era. The social critique in the songs sometimes ran afoul of the authorities; her 1973 album *Jelbeszéd* ("Sign Language"), composed and written by Illés, was censored after its release (its first printing sold out, but no further printings were allowed until 1983). The irony, play, and power of her performance—and the hidden messages in the lyrics—make her work intriguing and difficult to classify. (I could have focused on Bródy here but opted for Koncz, if only because she embodied and performed the songs.)[24]

If you watch a video of her performing "Ha én rózsa volnék" ("If I were a rose") with Bródy in 1986, before a large crowd of young people, many of whom are holding candles, you can sense how much she could convey through intense performance and coded language. The song expresses a yearning for integrity and openness to the world (and we fill in the blanks: in a country that is both closed off and dishonest with itself). There are moments when the crowd claps, recognizing a hidden meaning in the words; in the last verse they sing along. "If I were a street," she sings in the fourth verse, "I would always be clean. Every blessed evening I would be bathed in light. And if a sprocket-wheel were ever to step on me, the ground too would collapse, crying."[25]

Let us also consider the song "Majomország" ("Monkey Country"): Bródy's musical rendition of Sándor Weöres' poem by that title. Ostensibly a children's poem, this can be read as satirical commentary on a country that has spun into animalistic chaos: for instance, one stanza reads, in Edwin Morgan's translation, "Monkeyheroes rise and fight / in monkeyfield and monkeysquare, / and monkeysanatoriums / have monkeypatients crying there." Bródy, Koncz, and their fellow musicians recorded the song version in the 1970s but did not release it until 2019; in an interview, Koncz said she was not sure why it did not come out at the time, but doubted it was direct censorship. Nor did she recall which album it was intended for: the 1974 album *Gyerekjátékok* ("Children's Games")—which immediately followed *Jelbeszéd* ("Sign Language")—or the 1975 album *Kertész leszek* ("I Will Be a Gardener"). As for why they decided to release it now, Koncz remarked that upon hearing it again, she was struck by its freshness and relevance to the current situation in the country. The lighthearted ragtime texture of the song is betrayed by the insistent repetition of the word *majom* ("monkey") in the lyrics and Koncz's sassy, savvy intonation. The irony of the first line, "Jaj, de messze Majomország" ("Ah, Monkey-Country Is So Far Away") would not be lost on Hungarian listeners.[26]

An outspoken critic of censorship in Hungary today, Koncz has been criticized for claiming authority on this issue when she did not suffer like the "true victims" of the Kádár era.[27] The problem here is that many of these "true victims"—if the authenticity of their victimhood is to be measured by the gruesomeness of their fate—ended up dead and would not be able to speak today at all.

One of these was the pop singer Pál Szécsi, of Jewish and Roma origin, whose mother gave him and his two sisters to foster parents and fled the country during the 1956 Revolution. His father had been shot by Nazis in the last months of World War II, when Szécsi was barely a year old. When living with his foster parents, Szécsi attended school in Mezőtúr; he later became a ward of the state. He worked as a laborer at various jobs; at a work party, when he was sixteen, someone from the Divat Intézet ("Style Institute") noticed his charisma and offered him a modeling job. Soon afterward, he began to sing and take singing lessons; from there he rose quickly to stardom. Yet his life was filled with pain: he drank heavily, attempted suicide eight times unsuccessfully, and had tumultuous relationships with women. His relationship with the actress Edit Domján ended tragically with her miscarriage, their divorce, and her suicide. Szécsi's attempts at contact with his mother came to little; she told him not to come to the U.S. in search of her and did not take interest in his music. After multiple suicide attempts in which he asked for help at the last minute, Szécsi killed himself in 1974, at the age of thirty.[28] While Szécsi's music itself fell squarely in the pop entertainment category, he himself lived as an outsider—Jew, Gypsy, and orphan—whose early life was shaped by the world war and the revolution. Some of the details of his life and death are unknown, partly because of the reporting practices of the time; according to the journalist Márk Herczeg, because the government and press covered up singers' scandals, much information about him was conveyed only through word of mouth.[29]

Through these glimpses at several of Cseh and Bereményi's contemporaries, we see some of the complexities of an era that drove some to immigration, others to the edges of society, and still others to an ongoing dance between the establishment and its discontents. Yet whatever this generation experienced during the Kádár era was only part of its worldview, as it had also been shaped not only by the events and circumstances of the 1940s and 1950s, but by the older generation's silence around them, as well as the silence of the official press.

Bereményi wrote the screenplay for Ferenc András's 1985 film *A nagy generáció* ("The Great Generation"), which has since become a classic. Its plot runs roughly as follows: three male friends, Makai, Réb, and Nyikita, have decided to emigrate to the West. Of the three, only Makai and Réb's girlfriend have passports, so Réb steals Makai's and departs with Mari. Eight years later, Mari, having returned to Hungary, is working in a doll boutique with Nyikita; Makai is a radio DJ. A relationship has developed between Mari and Nyikita, unbeknownst to Nyikita's wife. Réb comes back with his and Mari's teenage daughter, Marylou, who does not know her mother; as it turns out, Réb hopes to succeed at a Hungarian version of the American Dream, whose secret rests with an elusive man by the name of Kálmán Vetró, whom he cannot manage to track down (the name Vetró, which originates from Italy, was Bereményi's surname at birth). The main characters' generation contrasts sharply in the film with that of their elders, who have lived through both world wars, and that of the younger generation, who bear the brunt of their parents' aimlessness and confusion, yet the film places no ultimate judgement on any of them.[30]

Why the title? In a 2012 interview, the director explained that he and Bereményi had used the term *nagy generáció* somewhat sarcastically here; moreover, that they had deliberately chosen the word *generáció* instead of *nemzedék*, because this generation could not really be called a *nemzedék* yet, and only life itself would tell whether it was great, small, good, or bad.[31]

To what extent does Cseh and Bereményi's work take part in and speak to this generational experience? To begin approaching this question, let us consider Dénes Csengey's insights, or a part of them.

Dénes Csengey's 1983 work ... *és mi most itt vagyunk* ("And We Are Here Now") examines the failures of Cseh and Bereményi's generation. He uses the word *nemzedék*, weightier than *generáció*, but in quotes (which give it some uncertainty and irony). According to Csengey, this generation emerged from the brutality of World War II and the Rákosi dictatorship into a kind of relative freedom that they largely wasted, relaxing into the fashionable aspects of the beat movement without taking on its responsibilities. Some of this was due to the restrictions of the era and the continued surveillance, some of it due to the generation's own choices. He points to several bands—Illés, Metro, and Omega—each of which, in his view, had tremendous talent and potential but chose an easier way. (He expresses admiration of Illés and the lyrics of Bródy but also criticizes his clichés.) In Csengey's view, only when the beat movement came to an end could something new emerge; this was nothing other than the music of Cseh and Bereményi.[32]

In Csengey's view, Cseh's first public performance, *A Dal nélkül* ("Without Song"), captured the tensions, contradictions, failures, and dreams of this generation, especially those who strove or yearned for some kind of resistance to the current status quo. Everyone had to choose whether to fit in or resist; Cseh's audience had primarily chosen the latter, or were simply incapable of fitting in. The songs of *A Dal nélkül*, bitter, ironic, yet tinged with romanticism, were actually non-songs sung by a non-singer (hence the title, as Csengey understood it). Understated, performed with an apologetic smile, they spoke to something the audience knew intimately.[33]

Csengey traces the development of Cseh and Bereményi's work from this concert up to *Frontátvonulás*, which he regards as the peak of their opus. (I take up *Frontátvonulás* in the fifth chapter.) He carries the reader through the work all the way up to the double ending, where first the character Vizi (performed by Cseh), then Cseh himself, as himself, says, "It's over, get it?" For Csengey, all of the equivocations, hesitations, lies, escapes of this generation (and not only this generation) have come to an end here: "The ceremonies of self-pity celebrated with drink, the flattery in the fallen hero's romantic pose, the rhetorically charged generational self-deceptions, the masterful tricks that turn helplessness and hopelessness into playful, grimacing jokes, the irony and self-irony leading nowhere, the evenings brimming with tepid nostalgia, the omniscient winks, the faith of waiting for a miracle ablaze with alcohol's flame, the deadly pathos of aborted destinies, the entire generational idyll is undeniably and irrevocably over."[34]

What, then, can succeed this—for this generation and for Cseh and Bereményi's art? Apparently nothing more, nothing less than action; anything else would simply continue the equivocation: "For Vizi, a young man capable of performing miracles (floating the glass in mid-air, i.e. defeating gravity), the next stage of his destiny cannot be anything other than a full-blooded, valid, followable action program. Or the madhouse."[35] Here is where Csengey's argument has not entirely stood the test of time. While sensitive to the nuances and playfulness of Cseh and Bereményi's work, he nonetheless views it as an expression of an unrealized political or social movement (which, he acknowledges, must take place offstage, in the world). Was the "Great Generation" capable of being galvanized politically, of breaking through its contradictions and stagnation? If so, to what extent would Cseh and Bereményi's work take part in this?

Everything points toward a negative answer to the first question. As Csengey himself observes, most members of this generation had chosen to acquiesce to the system or even use it toward their own ends. Of those who resisted—often in self-destructive ways—many lacked political inclination or distrusted politics altogether. Csengey—younger than this generation but old enough to know them personally—stood out in his political dedication.

Cseh said of Csengey that "he believed in the clarity of things; he likely didn't grasp that politics are different from the truth."[36]

As for Cseh and Bereményi's work, whatever its political undertones, it does not make political statements or propose political action. While the ending of *Frontátvonulás* marked a turning point in their collaboration (this was the last major work they composed together before Bereményi declared a hiatus from songwriting), the next step was not what Csengey had anticipated in his treatise. During the hiatus, they created the show and album *Jóslat* ("Prophecy"), for which the songs had already been written; to many, this seemed like a much weaker version of *Frontátvonulás*, or at least an abrupt departure from their apparent trajectory. But Cseh and Bereményi had always insisted on creating art on their own terms, which would match no one's expectations exactly and fit no agenda. To view their work as representative of a generation is to turn it, in a sense, into a spokesperson—but their work speaks to an expanding audience over a long stretch of time.

True, their work encodes and relates a generational experience. Even their shortest, simplest songs abound with references that someone outside the generation (or era) will miss. Yet as Csengey himself suggests, it is precisely the outsider who finds a home in them. Many of Cseh and Bereményi's listeners across the years are drawn to the songs themselves: the forms and genres, the language, the mixtures of pain and laughter, the secrets, the surprises, the sharpness, and the "non-song" quality. When high school students today give concerts in Cseh's honor, they do this not out of of historical piety but out of direct recognition; the songs are alive for them.[37]

Moreover, Csengey perceived and illustrated the stagnancy of the generation: its inability or unwillingness to act, its neglect of its own possibilities. Today many disagree over the nature of the Kádár era. Some look back on it with nostalgia: in their view, people were poor but could get by more easily than now; they were censored and watched but not killed for their views. Above all, they came together, talked with each other, spent evenings listening to music together. All of this makes the troubles of the era harder to define: they were not only external but internal. People coaxed themselves out of risks, perhaps without even realizing it. Many accepted the Kádár system and its relative permissiveness, reasoning that things could be worse; or else they rejected the alternatives.

Cseh and Bereményi's audiences of the 1970s and '80s must have perceived in the songs a rare liveliness, integrity, and life. The songs bring out a yearning; when listening, we might depart a little from who we have been. This is as needed today, and as rare, as it was fifty years ago. To be alive is to be shaken again and again out of habits and clichés (and yet to have them; life also requires some routine). In addition, audience members must have heard their own lives playing out: situations, phrases, characters so close to them that the recognition itself seemed to call for action of some kind. But what kind? Not necessarily political action; perhaps some kind of internal action, a shedding of false certainties.

Cseh and Bereményi famously described their songs as *helyzetjelentések* (roughly: "situation reports"). While this suggests that the songs refer to a concrete time and place, it does not imply exclusive, restrictive reference. For one thing, "situations" recur (in different forms); for another, the "report" in this case involves imagination and transformation. These "situation reports" evoke the specifics of an era but also create a reality of their own. As Cseh saw it, the songs conveyed reality swiftly (within a few minutes) to those whose sense of reality had been upset.[38] The songs' precision lies in their artistic transformation; in that sense they cannot be mapped, point by point, onto what we can name.

The songs verge on something barely perceived. They live not only at the edge of song forms, but at the edge of language: uncertainties, dim sensations and intuitions, the wind blowing the words, tipping them over a little. In our time, where "influencers" and others glorify self-certainty and snappy judgements, many of us yearn for and seek out this indistinct place where we can gather and listen to songs that we apprehend and love in hundreds of ways but will never pin down—and would not want to anyway.

Chapter 3

Levél nővéremnek ("Letter to My Sister"): Cseh and Bereményi's First Album

If you close your eyes and listen to the recording of the performance of *Levél nővéremnek* ("Letter to My Sister") at the R. Klub on March 25, 1976, you can imagine how strange the first few words might have sounded to the audience. After the piano introduction by János Másik, Cseh comes in with his unaccompanied voice: "*Ez egy levél...*" ("This is a letter..."). The song is about itself, but also about a letter; that is, the letter is the song, or the entire show, or our lives. The letter is the hero; the hero is the song. Often letters have been set to song—for instance, in opera—but rarely do they appear as protagonists. Here, the narrator, the letter-writer, mixes something like liturgical chant with conversation: he continues to describe the letter, in broken phrases that hint at something beyond the fragments.[1]

Let us now turn to the album, released in 1977, and listen to it likewise from the beginning.[2] (I will return to the concert recording later.) This time, a few lines in, we hear Másik in tandem with Cseh, repeating the words almost immediately after him. "This is a letter. / Its envelope is blue. / I bought the stamp for a forint. / The place and date: / Dated: Budapest. / All right, all right. / Let this be the scene... / The place and date... / Let there be scenery. / This is a letter. / This is a letter. / The place and date. / The place and date. / 1976 is the year. / 1976 is the year. / This is that year. / Let it be, let it be... / This much is known. / This is a letter. / I write to my sister. / Her name is Irén. / This much is known. / Right now it's winter. / A regular season. / All right, all right. / This is a letter. / Let there be a letter. / The place and date. / Let there be scene. / Let there be scenery."

The images are sparse, archetypal, abstract: letter, forint, stamp, date, sister, winter. The echoes (of one voice by another) and the repetitions within the lyrics give the sensation of something coming into being, hesitant, half-aware, undefined so far except for the basic facts (envelope color, year, place, addressee). This introduction ends in suspense: "Let there be scene. Let there be scenery" and instantaneous quiet, before the album rolls into the next song, "Budapest," with its tuneful, melancholic guitars, vocal harmonies, and cello pizzicato. As the album proceeds, the letter excerpts continue to contrast and alternate with the songs: the former hesitant, sparse, fragmented, the latter bound up in form.

"Budapest," one of the most famous songs in their entire opus, raises the question of whether to leave (the city? the country?) or to stay in Budapest—and although it answers, *maradunk*, "we will stay," the ambivalence or despair lingers. About this song, Anna Szemere writes, "The poignant debate between two voices, possibly within the subject's head, implies that there is a huge price tag on both choices."[3] The stakes are private and internal. The song evokes daily habits, snatches of conversation, but not a single street name or landmark. There is no mention of the Danube, or the hills of Buda, or a specific pub. Just as in the "Beginning of the Letter," the word "Budapest" gathers meaning quietly.

The melody repeats throughout the song, but with many variations. The refrain is sung like a question-and-answer dialogue, with Cseh singing the first two lines and Másik the second two. Over the course of the song, the voices alternate between dialogue, unison, and harmony; the guitar instrumentation ranges from basic to ornate.

In this translation I have preserved the rhythm and a semblance of the rhymes, while taking some liberties that do not disrupt the meaning. In the snatches of conversation, just as in the original, sometimes syllables have to be crowded into a beat. Otherwise the rhythm is self-explanatory.

Tell me now, tell me, what will we take as our home?
Shall we stay put or pack our belongings and roam?
Here is the city, we are its dwellers.
Here's where we'll stay, this is its name: Budapest.

Up in the morning, such is the custom of ours,
Off to the store for milk, János and Tamás,
Gaps in the houses, through them they clamber,
Into the passageways between houses, that's how they go.
[*Refrain*]

Up in the morning, such is the custom of ours,
Off to the store for milk, János and Tamás,
Looking in puddles, at themselves gazing,
Bits of tobacco deep in their pockets, that's how they go.

"If I might ask, is it time yet for *pálinka* shots?"
"Do you still know me, teacher, or have I slipped out of your thoughts?"
"Éva appeared before the abortion committee yesterday."
"I'm selling my winter coat, but no mortal will pay."

"A smile at our *házmester* might save our proverbial butt."
"Look at my forehead, the envelope didn't stick shut."
"I'm someone else, not the one you set out to find."
"Comrade Fáskerti, a favor, if you wouldn't mind..."

"A black hole is a nonexistent celestial orb."
"Three years from now, I won't have to serve any more."
"Do you still know me, teacher, or have I slipped out of your thoughts?"
"If I might ask, is it time yet for *pálinka* shots?"

Tell me now, tell me, what will we take as our home?
Shall we stay put or pack our belongings and roam?
Here is the city, we are its dwellers.
Here's our abidance, here we'll abide, we'll abide.

The snatches of conversation evoke an era with vignettes of humor, loss, survival, obligations, encounters, mistakes: a teacher who might have forgotten one of his students, a possible abortion, the self-preserving act of smiling at the *házmester* (the building superintendent who, during the socialist period, reported on tenants to the government), a need for money, a "black hole" (perhaps reference to past events that people do not mention or acknowledge), a mistaken identity, a favor asked, obligatory military service, a craving for alcohol. The song hints at political commentary while also eschewing it, insisting on messy everyday life. The bleak but evocative picture leads the listener to understand that home lies largely in routine and language, that changing one's country of residence would be futile, as it would mean being uprooted from these words themselves.[4]

The language of the song, the word play, the internal rhymes, the dexterous use of word order and grammar—all of this shows Bereményi's keen sense of the possibilities of the Hungarian language. For instance, the lines "*Házakon rések, azon kilépnek, / házak közt járat, azokon járnak, indulnak el*" ("Gaps in the houses, through them they clamber, / Into the passageways between houses, that's how they go") has the internal assonances and alliterations of *házakon* and *azon*, *rések* and *kilépnek*, and *házak*, *járat*, and *járnak*; it plays with singular and plural (the plural *rések* followed by the singular *azon*, then the singular *járat* followed by the plural *azokon*), all for a pleasing and intricate clambering effect.

The next letter fragment—where the letter itself begins— places its writer in an espresso bar (where hard alcohol is among the offerings). He sings urgently and rapidly, with sweeping piano in the background.

Dear Irén!

Please forgive the long silence, the delayed letter. This letter, I hope, finds you in good health. I'm fine, writing from an espresso bar, thinking of you as I lean over paper, sweet sister, my dear sister.

So, yes, a *presszó*. The noise is great here, the shouting. A man has just caught my attention, a woman next to him, a glass before him, containing an evil drink, he talks and asks, and what he says, I write down on paper:

The following song, "Presszó," relates what this stranger says and asks (of his interlocutor, the pianist in the espresso bar, sung by Cseh and Másik, respectively). The song takes surprising lyrical and musical turns within a subdued cabaret style; let us look at it verse by verse. In Hungarian, *eszpresszó* and *presszó* can refer both to the drink itself and to the establishment that serves it. As for the stranger who haplessly winds up there, Bereményi comments, "I knew a man who was like a part of me. Who strives in vain and sinks into the night. Into large, soft nothingness. ... Who is eaten up, digested by the era. And yet you like him. He tries everything and then gives up."[5] Here we see him out of sorts, bewildered, scrambling for a scrap of meaning.

What is this?
It's an espresso.
And you?
I'm the pianist.
And me?
You are a guest.
Hm, how fine. Classy place. Hm, how fine. Classy place.

These few words have set the scenery: a "classy" espresso bar, a piano, a guest who can't stop talking, who seems impressed with the place even though he doesn't know at first what it is. The music is halting, piano chords starting and stopping with the phrases, like the introduction to a song in a musical, until the waltz-like "*Hm, de finom. Príma hely,*" which they sing together. The questions and answers each end on particular notes of the scale: the questions on the supertonic and the answers on the dominant (and later on the tonic as well).

And... if I may ask, couldn't I instead...
No. Because it's an espresso.
And... tell me, couldn't it...
Are you thinking of the glass?
Yes, couldn't it be taken from my sight?
No... no... because this is an espresso.
Hm, how fine. Classy place. Hm, how fine. Classy place.

Now the pianist has begun finishing the guest's sentences and thoughts; we find out, moreover, that the guest is in a bit over his head, trying to regain control of himself but unable, as the establishment itself makes this impossible. Here the waltz-like motif begins not with "*Hm, de finom,*" but with "*Nem... nem....*" ("No... no..."), as though the very rules and restrictions were what made this a "classy place." Then the pianist and guest come back together for "*Hm, de finom,*" after which the questions continue:

And if I may ask... there's no closing time here?
None... It's that kind of espresso.
And if I may ask, couldn't this lady be taken from my side?
No. She belongs to herself.

Just look at her, a fine little lady, look at her luminous hair.
Fine lady, classy lady. Fine lady, classy lady.

In the above verse, the dialogue changes slightly: after singing "No. She belongs to herself," the pianist goes on to praise her and her hair; then the two come back together for "*Finom nő, príma nő.*" The anguish of this verse—the guest wanting the woman to be taken away, just as he wanted with the glass—is masked by its playfulness, so that the next verse comes as a surprise: a burst of despair sung in a rapid three-four time with guitar, in a folk style, with rhymed couplets (the translation below takes slight liberties):

Don't let me touch the lady, please don't let me...
don't let me touch the glass, please protect me.
I think you know me, I'm Szeberényi, the famous
economist, don't let me live like this, there's creative
work awaiting my talent, but with no closing,
there's no one to pull it off, no mind so imposing.
This fancy lifestyle, I'm afraid it would corrupt me,
the constructive work of the community confronts me.
In the new mechanism I was the head,
and now I end up in an espresso bar—dead!

The astonishing, almost tragic (but wry and satirical) revelation then succumbs to the waltz motif, the piano, and the atmosphere, as the piano starts to take off, and the pianist sings, followed by the guest:

Piano... nice little place... Classy ladies... Fine ladies.
Piano... nice little place... Classy ladies... Fine ladies.

Then, inevitably, the guest gets drunker and drunker, and his speech more fragmented, as the piano motif slowly appears to ascend:

Ha-ha-ha! But of course!
Ha-ha-ha-ha! Nice little place.
They're playing the piano.
Ha-ha-ha-ha!

That's how it goes, it's that type.
Nice little place.
Ha-ha!
Of course. But of course.

Now the dialogue resumes; at first the guest tries to repeat what he has already said before. The dialogue then begins to refer to the song itself, as the pianist reveals which chords correspond with the dialogue. The song ends up being about music, music that has no end, but within that, a little play about drunkenness, folly, pride, and confinement, about the extreme constraints of the era, the collapse of an economic system, all of this in a little espresso bar, in a song.[6]

My name...
I know, Szeberényi.
You know...
You can't live like this.
My badge of honor is on the table, in the glass!
Pin it on... hm, hm, hm, how nice.
And diplomas too!

At this point the song becomes self-referential, speaking of its own chords and the pianist's playing. Szeberényi realizes that there is no escape, because without a closing time, he will never leave (a closing time would force him to stop drinking and go home, but there is none).

What is this?
It's an espresso.
And this?
It's D major.
And E minor.
There won't...
There won't be a closing time.
Why?
Because I'm playing the piano.

[*Piano solo.*]

Ha-ha-ha-ha-ha!
But of course!
Ha-ha-ha-ha-ha!
But of course, they're playing piano!
Of course!
Ha-ha-ha-ha-ha-ha!
Oh, this is great!
Ha-ha-ha-ha-ha-ha!
Ha-ha-ha-ha-ha-ha!
Ha-ha-ha-ha-ha-ha!

So ends the song, on a note of maniacal laughter and the piano trailing off. Here the album has still only barely begun, but its unique genre is already apparent: dialogues, songs, stories within a letter to Irén (shown in pieces), a letter than finally ends and gets sent off into uncertainty. As the album continues, the stories have to do with heartbreak, memories, difficulties (of the sixties and seventies, with one glance back at the fifties): an alcoholic father who destroys others' lives in addition to his own; memories of youthful summers on Lake Balaton, before they had a sailboat; contemplation of a possible meeting with former love who emigrated and has returned to Hungary; a train ride to Kraków; a dream about meeting with a married woman; a ceremony; a memory of a class field trip; a story of almost moving but ending up staying; a state of drunken reverie after a concert, with Mozart and alcohol on the breath, memories of holding hands, a doorbell being rung, an imaginary name next to it. In the final song of the album, "Kézbesítés" ("Delivery"), the letter-writer wonders, at the end, "An important ceremony, who knows where it comes to a halt? / Irén doesn't answer, because she has to take care of the kids. / Sealed in an envelope, who knows where it tosses about? Tell me, Irén, where does this all come to a halt?"

The letter excerpts do much more than connect the songs; they mark out the territory of the album, which stretches from confession to wordlessness, stuttering, incomplete thoughts. They delve into personal memories, mention family members, reflect incoherently on themes that cannot quite be gathered up, and speak of the letter itself. They bring out the album's ironic yet direct and personal tones. Musically they chant freely or sing within the strictures of a melodic form and rhythm. Some songs have no letter excerpts between them, and some letter excerpts sound like songs, so that the boundaries blur here and there. Nonetheless, most of the letter excerpts are distinctly recognizable through their E minor key, their chant, and their invocation of Irén.

In the third letter excerpt (immediately after "Presszó"), the narrator asks Irén not to meet with their father, who has been a "nobody" ever since he abandoned their mother; he is a "troublemaker," a heavy drinker, a seducer. The narrator then claims that his own first marriage came to an end because of the father; this woman, "poor Ida," a "good wife," still looks him up. "She was a flag," he writes; because of her, he fell apart a little. "Well then, well then," this excerpt concludes. "That's how I am, / that's how I was too. / That's how I am." In a few brushstroke lines this excerpt conveys broken lives running through generations; yet Irén, though part of the family and beloved by her brother, seems untouched somehow, or at least not destroyed. If Irén is a part of the narrator, as Bereményi has suggested, then a part of the narrator likewise remains intact. This comes through only subtly, through the invocations of Irén and the gentleness of the chant.

A different kind of letter fragment comes after the next song, "Apa Kalapja" ("Dad's Hat"), the first song on the album in a major key. Here it is all fragments, and brief, with something like the sound of wind in the background: "A memory, a memory... / The date and time... / The years follow each other in a curious way, / dear Irén. / The date and time..."[7] Cutting back into E minor, this fragment resets the mood of the album, as if reminding us where we are.

Still another kind of fragment, or letter-moment, occurs halfway through the album: here, instead of the chanting, the fragment has a song rhythm and a ceremonial tone, as if the letter were turning a corner: "You see, dear Irén, / the letter is halfway through. / Is it writing itself, / or do I write it sovereignly? // No matter, I must go on, / the family awaits a sign of life. / Tell mother, dear Irén, / that I send her a kiss." The same melody and rhythm recurs at the very end of the album, after the completion of the letter, in "Kézbesítés" ("Delivery"), which ends with the sound of a cello bow bouncing on the strings. These two moments in the letter's life—the halfway point and delivery—could be thought of as the meta-letter; instead of containing the letter's text, they report on it from the outside, as does the very beginning of the album, the "Levél kezdete" ("Beginning of the Letter"), which in fact has nothing of the letter's contents (beyond the place and date), but rather announces its existence and describes its basic features.

Sometimes the boundary between letter fragment and song is blurred, as in "Költözködés" ("Moving"), which sounds like a fragment but has no mention of the letter or Irén. Unlike most of the other letter fragments, where the voices of Cseh and Másik are staggered or in unison, this song is broken into two parts, each one sung by a different person (or half of a person), one of whom is moving away, the other staying. Thus the song (or excerpt) echoes the ambivalence of "Budapest." Because of its chanted style, it sounds like an internal debate.

I'm moving.
they're carrying all my stuff to my car,
I'm leaving,
this flat will no longer be my flat to me.

I'm moving,
I have a signout and a sign-in sheet,
I'm leaving,
the old flat I'm leaving here.

He's moving,
my old friend is moving away,
I'm staying,
I've decided it'll be good for me.
Let him go,
let them carry all his stuff to the car,
I'm staying,
this has happened before and will happen again.

I would like to introduce three more songs from this album, "A hatvanas évek" ("The Sixties"), "Nincsen más" ("Nothing Else"), and "Tanulmányi kirándulás" ("School Trip"), before returning to the concert recording and concluding with some thoughts. I have chosen these three not only because they are treasures in the Cseh-Bereményi canon, but because they hold some of the range of the album: "A hatvanas évek" capturing an era, "Nincsen más" expressing a kind of existential simplicity (combined with specific social commentary), and "Tanulmányi kirándulás" offering both a charming story and an artistic surprise.

"A hatvanas évek" tells in dreamy, fragmented images of the summers on Lake Balaton in the 1960s, when the Beat movement was in full swing under the early Kádár era, and young people plunged into their newfound, short-lived freedom. Anna Szemere provides important political and historical background for this song; to supplement her observations, I will focus more on the song's structure and progression. This is one of the most beloved songs at Cseh sing-alongs; Cseh's son, András, includes it regularly in the events that he leads. It has a repeated refrain, a melancholic, lilting mood, and some lovely harmonies for those willing to try them. The lyrics are filled with allusions that listeners and singers may recognize.

While the translation below takes liberties, it preserves all the details needed for the present discussion. The acoustic two-guitar introduction, which establishes the melody of the chorus, has a beautiful counterpoint; in one of the musical phrases, the one guitar ascends and descends, while the other ascends; this ascending and descending suggests something like the gentle waves of the lake. The first verse establishes the pattern of verse and chorus:

> Back in the sixties, with summer approaching,
> the youth problem swelled into bold display.
> I think back on how we would cross from Almádi
> to Siófok boatwise day by day.
>
> Oh the old, oh Lake Balaton,
> olden summertone,
> though we had no sailboat of our own.
> Oh the olden, olden terrace chairs,
> where we sat and stared
> all the way across old Balaton.

In the verse, Cseh and Másik sing in time together, in harmony; in the chorus, Másik follows behind Cseh in the "Oh" lines, with the result that we hear a succession of "ohs." The first verse ironically mentions the "youth problem," which, as Szemere explains, refers to the influence of rock music and Western media on youth culture, which experienced increasing government surveillance.[8] The irony (as I see it) lies in the contrast between this notion of a "problem" and the tranquil activities described: taking a boat from Almádi to Siófok (that is, crossing the lake). Lake Balaton is far longer than it is wide; the passage from Almádi to Siófok crosses a plump section of the width. Thus we can infer that, in the chorus, the staring "all the way across old Balaton" means gazing to the visible opposite side. (If you look across the lake lengthwise, you will not see the other side at all.)

The lack of a sailboat, mentioned in the chorus, has special importance because sailboats were for the privileged, yet even without privilege or money, one could live out a Balaton way of life, later to be gathered up into memories (which suffuse the song). The subsequent verses show these memories in a dim collage.

Films too were made, and hitchhiking youngsters
stared down at us from the glowing screen.
They gazed at the mirror of water and wondered
what all those babbling bubbles might mean.

Oh the old, oh Lake Balaton....

Back in the sixties, the world came together
under a loose theoretical tent.
In Kafka and Sartre, in faraway wisdom,
it gazed at itself in astonishment.

Oh the old, oh Lake Balaton...

The widening rings of consolidation
rolled from Balaton every which way.
I think back on crossing from Bélatelep
to Révfülöp one summer day.

Oh the old, oh Lake Balaton...

The second verse ("Films too were made...") has to do with the creative projects that took place in the Balaton area, the hitchhiking, the livelihood in the air; the third verse, with the ideas being read and disseminated; and the fourth, with "consolidation"—government initiatives taken to soften the blows of the 1956 Revolution and aftermath. Like crossing from Almádi to Siófok, crossing from Bélatelep to Révfülöp involves a short path, not a long one. Yet both of these short trips are treated as memorable—perhaps because of the lack of a sailboat, the lack of luxuries that would make such crossings ordinary. The song is unabashedly nostalgic; one of its hidden messages, perhaps, is that those days cannot be retrieved, except in memory: a harder time has set in, people have aged, and Balaton itself has changed.

While the song teems with political innuendo, it also has to do with memory itself: how it might consist of a fleeting image or an abstraction, or even the lack of something (such as a sailboat). There is something irrational and whimsical about its details, the lacunae conveying as much as the words or more.

Something similar can be said for "Nincsen más" ("Nothing Else"). Szemere interprets the song as "a harrowing statement about the housing crisis Hungarians faced and its dramatic effect on couples who could not afford to separate as a result."[9] This meaning may be apparent to those who lived through the era, but to those who did not, the song with its quiet, rumbling, fingerpicked guitar could convey a moment (and an existential state) when a way of life comes to an end but nothing takes its place.

I made the translation as bare and sparse as possible, keeping some of the basic rhythm. Because the word "délelőtt" ("late morning") has no precise equivalent in English, I translated it as "a morning almost gone." I made a few other adjustments as well; for instance, in the third verse, I added the phrase "speaking truly," and in the fourth, the inversion of "leaned, begging" and "begged, leaning."

> There's nothing else in this song,
> nothing else, just a street
> where I lived once upon a time
> and a morning almost gone.
>
> That was the morning when I figured
> I'd throw Éva out the window.
> Éva bending in the foyer,
> packing dirty clothes away.

And she shouted, and I shouted,
and outside the tram rattled
on the street, and speaking truly,
I don't know what happened next.

Out the window—I remember—
out the window I leaned, begging,
privately I begged, leaning,
Lord, give me another place.

Well, this song has nothing else,
just the third day of a heat wave,
and Eva, and another street,
and a morning almost gone.

Well, this song has nothing else,
nothing else, just a street
where I lived once upon a time,
and a morning almost gone.

Slightly reminiscent of Leonard Cohen's "Famous Blue Raincoat" but without the suggestions of sordidness, the song marks one of the tendencies in the Cseh/Bereményi canon: toward simplicity and plainness, lack of ornament. The song asks to be taken as it is, while also hinting at hidden layers.

The final song to consider here, "Tanulmányi kirándulás" ("Educational Field Trip"), brings out another special aspect of Cseh and Bereményi's work: its sheer delight, its way of enchanting an audience. This song is also remarkable for its musical properties: alternation between jaunty country-style verses and a slow, hymn-like chorus that sparkles with mischief.

In Hungarian education during this era (and beyond), a *tanulmányi kirándulás* was a particular kind of field trip involving a lesson: in this case, a biology and geography lesson. The date—1962—suggests a somewhat thawed, relaxed atmosphere and a bunch of young teenagers; moreover, this was the year when a new geography curriculum was published with the aim of making the subject more interdisciplinary and experiential.[10] Bereményi was sixteen in 1962, but the boys in this song—the school is single-sex—seem around twelve or thirteen, in early puberty. It is quite an expedition: the principal, the homeroom teacher (the *osztályfőnök*), and the female geography teacher all take part. It is because of this female geography teacher that the song undergoes a transformation.

I will translate the country-style verses literally, since they have a flexible rhythm and no rhyme; for the idyllic choruses, I will convey both the rhythm and the rhyme. I have put the chorus in italics to distinguish it from the rest.

> Our best field trip
> took place in 1962,
> up at the Lajos Spring
> the class had a good laugh.
>
> We weren't coeducated yet,
> the class was made up of boys,
> among the sunspots shining on the path
> I and all the rest.
>
> With:
> *Mr. Csányi, our class teacher,*
> *Mr. Csőke, the school leader,*
> *for geography, Ms. Vértes*
> *in a nylon blouse was there with us.*

The "With" preceding the chorus allows the rest to proceed in rhythm; in Hungarian, "with" is conveyed through the instrumental case ending, which in turn provides most of the chorus's rhyme.

So far, the picture presented is recognizable across times and cultures: a class trip that the students take as a great adventure. With three teachers present—including the principal of the school (who, in the Hungarian system, also teaches), one can imagine a rather large class, or maybe more than one class.

> Observe its complexity!
> the female teacher said,
> holding up a lovely shiny-backed
> beetle for us to see.

We observed maple trees
and tall oak trees,
and made the distinction between pistils and stamens
all along the way.

Female geography teacher,
Vértes in her dark-brown sneakers,
blue bra peeking through her clothing,
fingers yellow from nicotine.

Here we have to play a little with the word stresses to make the rhythm work, but this fits with the playfulness of the song. "Female geography teacher" sounds a bit odd in English, but this is justified here; in Hungarian the *-nő* suffix emphasizes that the teacher is indeed female. This verse and chorus edges into boyhood sexual fantasy: first, the teacher holding up the beetle and telling them to "observe its complexity"; then the distinction between pistil and stamen, and finally the image of the teacher herself, blue bra, nicotine stains, and all.

For the last verse and chorus, the verse is shortened by half and the chorus doubled, giving a sense of eternity to the final idyllic image, which begins just when the female teacher closes her eyes.

In a clearing, during the break,
Vértes, the female teacher
lay down and closed her eyes
among many stamens.

Grassy glade bedecked with flowers.
Blue, red, yellow, all these colors.
All those geography teachers
fallen eyelids, outstretched sneakers.

Mouth filled with the taste of walnut,
chilly, chilly swigs of water,
dreamy geography teachers,
fallen eyelids, outstretched sneakers.

I reintroduced the "sneakers" here for the sake of the rhyme; I believe it contributes to the image. In this last, doubled, chorus, time seems to stand still; the teacher multiplied, the flowers, the sleeping give the sense of an infinite, heavenly place, with a boyish twinkle: a crush on a female teacher who dresses somewhat revealingly, smokes, but also shows the children the wonders of the natural world. Her subject, geography, matters here too, for, as mentioned earlier, geography was already being taught as a comprehensive, multidisciplinary subject with elements of history and science. Thus a geography teacher had the ability to give students a view of the world (and, in this song, a glimpse of her own body).

Having considered six of the songs of this album, along with several of the letter fragments, let us now return to the concert recording from March 25, 1976, to see what more it reveals. The concert has songs that do not appear on the album, and vice versa; the sequence is also somewhat different. Besides these differences, and differences of musical arrangement within the songs, we can hear the audience's coughs and laughs. While the album has many instruments, the concert is a duet between Cseh and Másik alone; the sparseness suits the music well.

No definitive laugh can be heard until "Presszó," where people chuckle or roar at almost every line. There is a particular burst of laughter at "My badge of honor is on the table, in the glass! / Pin it on... hm, hm, hm, how nice." After this song, the next fragment is conspicuous for its lack of laughter; thus, from now on, we can hear not only the laughter, but the audience's silences and seriousness; no laughter can be heard again until "Álomfejtés" ("Dream Interpretation"), followed by a stunning, eruptive letter fragment absent from the album. In addition, we can sense the small room, the attention, the unusual nature of this evening. The rendition of "70 vagy 60" ("70 or 60"), later renamed "Jóslat" ("Prophecy") and included in the *Jóslat* performance and album, has a captivatingly raw quality, with a rattle shaking out the beat. The duet of guitar and piano in "Jutalomosztás" ("Reward Distribution"), which also draws laughter, has Másik accompanying Cseh on the higher keys at first, then plunging into a march-like, somber (but witty) section followed by a coda. The concert has the lively, eerie, thrumming "Feljelentés" ("Denunciation"), which does not appear on an album until *Utóirat* ("Afterword") in 1987. Some of the songs are performed quite differently from the album version; for instance, in this version of "Költözködés" ("Moving"), Cseh's and Másik's voices alternate frenetically. The concert has one song that mentions Antoine and Désiré, "Egy Bogár" ("A Beetle"), later to become a beloved classic in the *Antoine és Désiré* show and album. Two of the songs, "Filmszínház" ("Movie Theatre") I and II, comically describe a movie-goer's experience, then (dreamily) the walk home. The concert as a whole bursts with possibilities: fictional characters, situations, mixtures of song genres and musical styles, and myriad subtle jokes.

Those attending the *Levél nővéremnek* concerts (or listening to the album for the first time) must have encountered something unfamiliar and bold: melancholy, wit, subtle satire, and a way, it seems, of pulling songs out of thin air. Political and nonpolitical, funny and dead serious, these songs convey something even to a listener who knows nothing of the language; taken together, they form a letter addressed to Irén but swiftly delivered to us.

CHAPTER 4

Antoine, Désiré, and Other Characters

A song can resemble a story, play, or film; it has room not only for action and scenery, but for characters of all sorts: dignified, silly, familiar, vague, eccentric, ordinary, funny, tragic. Anyone listening to Cseh and Bereményi's songs for the first time might wonder: Who are Antoine and Désiré, so often mentioned in the songs? How did they come into being? Who are the other characters of Cseh and Bereményi's songs and shows? This chapter will explore some of these figures.

Songwriters across styles and eras have brought characters (personae) into their songs. This allows not only for storytelling, but for recognition and return; we come to associate a character with a song, a group of songs, or the songwriter or performer. For Cseh and Bereményi, the characters take on a life of their own: not of heroism, but of seemingly trivial (yet secretly weighty) actions, thoughts, and arguments. We come to know them as though they walked on our streets, disappeared around our corners, and popped into our pubs.

In addition, a character wedges some distance between the songwriter and the subject matter; we stop assuming that the song is directly "about" the songwriter or performer. This gives imaginative freedom to the writer, performer, and listener alike. We can take in the songs without forcing any literal correspondences. At the same time, we can see any of the characters as a part of ourselves.

The characters of Cseh and Bereményi's work take several forms. First, there are the recurring characters: in particular, Antoine and Désiré, Vizi and Ecsédi, and Irén, the addressee of the letter framing *Levél nővéremnek* ("Letter to My Sister"). Next, there are incidental imaginary characters: for instance, Comrade Eagle in *Frontátvonulás* ("Frontal Passage") or Szeberényi in the song "Presszó" (*Levél nővéremnek*). Then come the fictionalized cultural figures, from Ádám Balogh to Arthur Rimbaud to Lee van Cleef. Finally, we encounter fictionalized versions of people Cseh and

Bereményi knew, from a former teacher to the legendary Zsuzsa Koncz.

This chapter will focus primarily on Antoine and Désiré, the protagonists of several albums and shows and of numerous songs. After that, it will briefly consider other recurring characters (Vizi and Ecsédi, whom I take up at greater length in the next chapter), incidental fictional characters, and incidental characters from the so-called real world.

It is hard to imagine Cseh and Bereményi's songs without Antoine and Désiré; after all, the two characters came into being with the very first song they wrote together, "Az ócska cipő" ("Shabby Shoes"). Just how these names and essences occurred to him, no one knows, but I can imagine them being inspired by the melody that Cseh played for Bereményi, which he (Cseh) described as *franciás* ("Frenchy" or "French-ish").[1] In any case, Antoine and Désiré had come to stay; later they would become the protagonists of the stage show and album created in their name.

The 1978 album *Antoine és Désiré* constitutes only part of the larger Antoine and Désiré story that Bereményi and Cseh created in song, show, story, and picture. On this album, Cseh is the sole composer and stage performer and Bereményi the lyricist. The musicians Gábor Kecskeméti, Győző Lukácsházi, István Mártha, János Novák, Péter Román, and Ágnes Szakály accompany Cseh on the album. At concerts, in between and around the songs, Cseh told many tales written by Bereményi and sometimes partly improvised; these texts are absent from the album. (In concert, Cseh tended to perform these songs and stories solo; by the time of the album's release, he invariably did.)[2]

An insert in the album provides the fictional biographies of the protagonists; in addition, Bereményi and the photographer János Vető later wrote a photographic novel about them (twenty-five of its photos appear on the *Antoine és Désiré* album cover).[3]

Just who Antoine and Désiré are remains a mystery. Some listeners associate Antoine with Bereményi and Désiré with Cseh; in interviews Cseh and Bereményi denied any direct identification, but Cseh suggested that both he and "Dixi" (János Gémes, described in the second chapter), had a little bit of Désiré in them; moreover, that the banter between Antoine and Désiré reminded him of the way he and János Másik used to converse before their falling out (they reconciled many years later).[4] Beyond that, Antoine and Désiré play out a conflict that exists in each of us.

Antoine and Désiré are near-opposites, despite their shared adventures:

Antoine adheres to rules, conventions, and norms, while Désiré lives on the fringes, not only of society, but of language itself. Dénes Csengey described their friendship as on the one hand unbreakable, on the other "not free of tension." In Csengey's interpretation, they represent the two possibilities of their generation: conformity and outsiderness, both of which result in featurelessness. To what extent is such featurelessness tragic, to what extent comic? This, Csengey suggested, depends on the particular concert and context. Bereményi commented in 1980 that he tended to laugh at the two characters while Cseh took them seriously, but that "the genre was composed of these two [perspectives]."[5] While one can appreciate the songs without knowing the characters' backstories, a brief introduction to their lives gives a glimpse of the larger work.

According to the biography in the album insert, "Antoine" (fictional real name: Antal Tóth) was the teacher's pet and later took an interest in public affairs; he married Irén Vetró, the love of Désiré's youth, but cheated on her sometimes. He had a degree in law; he liked drinking, but not to excess. In 1987 he caused a mortal car accident (killing Désiré, we glean from the latter's biography); after serving his jail term, he regained equanimity and was well respected by others. He died in 2002 in a hunting accident.

"Désiré" (fictional real name: Dezső Balogh) was born in 1944 in Chemnitz, where the war had swept his parents. In 1946 the family returned to Hungary and moved to Gyömrő, where he attended elementary school and played with his classmate Irén Vetró. He began high school in Budapest but was soon kicked out for frequenting various dance halls as well as for "cosmopolitanism, rock and roll and other debaucheries, existentialism, and cowboy pants." He moved back to Gyömrő, took on manual labor, and finished high school through evening courses. At age twenty he started frequenting Budapest again and met Antoine. People considered him sensitive because he once played with a beetle all day long and took interest in history and physics; yet his biographer—that is, Bereményi—comments that "if his influential friend Antoine had not propped him up by the underarm, Désiré would have sunk still deeper." In 1987 he died in a car accident caused by drunk driving; "naturally he was not the one drunk (but Antoine), nor was he the one driving (but Antoine)."[6]

In the albums and shows, however, Antoine and Désiré do not take part in a large story arc (unlike Vizi and Ecsédi). Rather, the stories surrounding them are momentary vignettes, infinitely recombinable, always allowing for something new. Throughout all of these, Désiré is the understated hero, the one in the dim spotlight (more songs have to do with him than with Antoine), but Antoine plays an indispensable role in Désiré's life, as does their friendship in Cseh and Bereményi's work.

I will give a brief description of the album *Antoine és Désiré* as a whole, song by song, with an eye to the two main characters, and then focus on three of the songs: "Antoine, Désiré és a szél" ("Antoine, Désiré, and the Wind"), mentioned in the first chapter; "Egy bogár" ("A Beetle"), and "Demonstráció" ("Demonstration").

The album begins with the comically urgent "Antoine, Désiré és a szél" ("Antoine, Désiré, and the Wind"), in which Antoine, Désiré, the narrator, and the song itself are being blown and tipped by the wind. The next song, "Désiré és az eső" ("Désiré and the Rain"), sung in a country style, is self-referential from the start ("Désiré and the rain / is the title of the song / that I have been humming for thirty years."); it turns into a dialogue between Désiré and Antoine about whether the rain will take away everything that Désiré has, including his hopes. The third song, "Désiré apja" ("Désiré's Father"), also in a country vein, has Désiré describing and praising his father's work; his father is a heater, and it is thanks to him that the trains move. The fourth song, "Antoine és Désiré történelemkönyve" ("Antoine and Désiré's History Book") has something like a Slavic or klezmer feel; it cheerily but ironically salutes some of Hungary's *kuruc* warriors of the seventeenth and eighteenth centuries (Balogh, Tyukodi, Bercsényi, etc.), then proceeds into a dance, then into the Lakota language. This song is a beloved number at Cseh sing-alongs; its darker meanings are not lost on the participants. In the fifth song, "Désiré és a múlt" ("Désiré and the Past"), Désiré, alone at home with his grandfather (his grandmother has gone to the movies), decides to interview him about times of yore, specifically about the Hungarian defeat at the Don, and to record this on tape; he ends up with a recording of gurgles and other internal sounds, which he calls "hieroglyphics of the past." The singer concludes, "I believe we can follow Desiré's path; / may all generations reach out to each other."

In the following song, "Egy bogár" ("A Beetle"), to be described in more detail later, Antoine and Désiré come upon a beetle in a glass; it becomes the object of their observation, but they cannot figure out how to go about it. The next song, which goes through a number of swift musical changes, tells of Bea, who is arriving by suburban train; the only problem is that she doesn't know of Désiré's existence, he doesn't know her either, and because both are "underinformed," both remain unhappy. It concludes on an exuberant note nonetheless (with thick political ironies). The last song of the first side, "Az ócska cipő," the first song that Cseh and Bereményi wrote together, has Désiré staring out into the bleakness: the mud, his shabby shoes, the landscape—and then remembering something that Antoine said, and continuing onward.

The second side of the album opens with "Amikor Désiré megérkezett Budapestre" ("When Désiré Arrived in Budapest"), which has been rendered in film by János Szász (in his short film *Utóirat*, "Postscript," described in the eighth chapter), played and sung in a murky tango style, describes Désiré getting a sublet, then getting into a fight and longing to place an advertisement for a better apartment, which would allow him to bring Irén Vetró to Pest. It ends with a jazzy explosion of nonsense syllables. The next song, "Háromnegyed 1 van" ("It's a Quarter to One"), rumbling with piano and evocative of Hungarian folk songs, tells of Antoine sitting alone in the Aranyhíd guesthouse, a tune in his ear, when Désiré comes in, likewise with a tune in his ear, a political song, a song of many troubles, a tune that spills out into the street. The next song, "Désiré bottal üti a saját nyomát" ("Désiré Blazes His Trail with a Stick"), returns to a lively country mode and tells of Désiré's teenage escapades. Next we have "Demonstráció" ("Demonstration"), to be discussed shortly, in which Désiré goes out into the street wearing nothing but a sheet, which strikes Antoine as highly suspicious. The next song (another favorite at Cseh evenings), "Amikor Désiré munkásszálláson lakott" ("When Désiré Lived in a Workers' Dormitory"), tells of Désiré and his companions tying several sheets together and descending to the ground floor, where they pick up a woman named Ica and hoist her up to the fourth floor (that is, the fifth), who then receives praise from the police, who take her down and away, leaving a sad mood in the dormitory. The next song, "Tangó," a favorite of Cseh's, calls upon the addressee to be a child again and play with the singer.[7] "Let's play that we're afraid again, / let's play that we're playing again, / that time has become a blur, / that the tango is in style." The penultimate song, "Antoine nagy kísérlete" ("Antoine's Grand Experiment"), the only song told from Antoine's point of view, has Antoine reaching into his pocket and pulling something out that he then inflates: this turns into a woman, Aliz, who flies away but then comes back, proving Antoine's experiment a success. The last song, "Désiré megnémul" ("Désiré Falls Silent"), introduced in the first chapter, returns to Désiré's voice, where he tries to put his finger on a memory but cannot.

From all of this we glean that Désiré is indeed the protagonist, Antoine coming into the foreground only rarely; that the songs, mostly humorous, have moments of wistfulness and pain; that the music ranges in style from country to freestyle narration to tango to klezmer to traditional Hungarian folk, making for fluency of song; and that the stories, taken together, seem to tell almost nothing, but an "almost nothing" that holds the world.

Why does Désiré occupy center stage as the subject and often the narrator of the songs? Perhaps the songwriters' sympathy lies mostly with him, though they laugh at him too. Perhaps he reminds them (and us) of ourselves, if we have ever had trouble fitting into our environment or finding our proper place. Perhaps he also reminds us of others: people who live with idiosyncratic delight and despair and can neither succeed in the world nor quit it entirely. Cseh said of "Désiré megnémul" ("Désiré Falls Silent") that sometimes it was very good to sing, sometimes terrible, because he could not be indifferent to it.[8] In the 1970s, when Cseh and Bereményi wrote these songs, many of their generation had been pushed, like Désiré, to the peripheries: some committed suicide, some emigrated, and some sank into alcohol. The circumstances and political context have changed, but probably each of us knows a Désiré or two. That said, through their playfulness (and sometimes sheer silliness) the songs keep any direct associations loose and tentative.

Let us now look more closely at "Antoine, Désiré és a szél" ("Antoine, Désiré, and the Wind"), mentioned in the first chapter; "Egy bogár" ("A Beetle"); and "Demonstráció" ("Demonstration").

The first of the three, "Antoine, Désiré és a szél," can immediately be recognized by its percussive nonsense refrain, *"Tűrüpp, tűrűrüpp, türűrümm."* There are two distinct accent marks on the letter "u": the umlaut (ü) and the "hungarumlaut" or double acute accent (ű). This "hungarumlaut" indicates a longer vowel than the umlaut; here it occurs in the stressed syllables (the first syllable of *"tűrüpp"* and the second of *"türűrüpp"* and *"türűrümm"*). The song, with a brisk guitar rhythm, speaks obliquely of songs themselves; Antoine and Désiré are being blown by the wind, and they sing, and the song itself seems to "tip over a little." The narrator also hums, leaning forward because of the wind, and the song "also leans forward / a tiny bit along with me." Antoine and Désiré's coats are flapping; "I'm already afraid they'll fall over." He becomes afraid: "What if, at some point / we end up leaning too far forward?" But the song comes out of his mouth, "useful airflow for support"; they sing facing the ground, "lest we lean too far forward." Antoine and Désiré, "lined with wind" come over; the wind stops, and, with a slow tempo, Cseh sings, "My God, just now, now let us not topple forward." The song ends with the refrain sung ten times at the previous tempo, after which the guitar's final chord fades.

The language of this song is like the wind itself, blowing nothingness. Bereményi is ingenious at filling a phrase with space or trimming it down; here he deliberately breaks the writers' rule of eliminating all unnecessary words, doing precisely the opposite, for sheer fun. Consider, for instance, the second verse: *"Dúdolok én, / s mert fúj a szél, / előredőlök hát én is, / és ez a dal / előredől / énvelem együtt egy kissé"* ("I'm humming, / and because the wind is blowing, / I tip forward too, / and this song / tips forward / with me too a bit"). The word *hát* (approximately "well") adds nothing but character; the repetitions of *én* ("I") are superfluous (and not required in Hungarian), especially *énvelem* (an emphatic and archaic variant of *velem*, "with me")—yet this inflation of the syllable count does much more than pad the lines: not only does it create wind, but the repetition of *én* suggests playful insistence: I exist, I declare, even though the wind is tipping me over. The entire song is filled with such inflations and emphases, which, combined with the *Tűrüpp, türűrüpp, türűrümm* refrain, give the sense that a song can be made of anything at all, or of close to nothing. At the same time, something is at stake: this risk of tipping forward can be taken as the danger of expressing an opinion, or following an emotion.

"Egy bogár" stands out for its sheer silliness and play; it too demonstrates the possibilities of songs. The premise seems trivial: Antoine and Désiré, having discovered a beetle in a glass, set about to observe it but get caught up in the complex choreography of such observation. It seems that Désiré is the one who can't get it right; Antoine, exasperated, complains that "I can't get anywhere with you" and starts to take off. Désiré tries to persuade him to stay and try again ("Antoine, Antoine, hold on!"), but Antoine does not stop. Then Désiré just stands still and cries, "Antoine, Antoine, Antoine," at which Antoine at last turns around. For the rest of the song, Désiré tries to figure out how it will work. This part displays some of the wonders of the Hungarian language: "*Mondjuk én ideteszem, te meg most odaállsz, aztán én állok oda, de akkor te meg ideteszed... aha... hogy is? ...hogyha én ideteszem, akkor te odaállsz, mikor meg én odaállok, akkor te már mindig idetetted....*" The prefix *ide-*, meaning "over here," joins with *teszem,* "I put it," forming *ideteszem,* "I put it over here"; likewise, the prefix *oda-*, "over there," joins with *állsz,* "you stand," forming *odaállsz,* "you stand over there." Then the *ide* and *oda* get switched, some of the action shifts into the past, and things get utterly confused, and Désiré's speech breaks into fragments, ending the song: "*nem... nem, nem most teszem oda azonnal... hova is... egyáltalán... nem... majd én eldöntöm... így... vagy nem... majd ő... majd ő dönti el... sőt... persze... há' egyszerű... idébb... idébb... és akkor ti hova teszitek? Megnézem... áhá*" ("no... no, not now, I'll put it there right away... where... not at all... no... I'll decide... like this... or not... then he... then he'll decide... in fact... of course... it's simple... more this way... more this way... and then where will you two put it? I'll see... aha"). The "*ti hova teszitek*" ("where will you [plural] put it") comes as a surprise, since until now this seemed to be an exchange between Antoine and Désiré—but at some point Désiré involved the beetle's decision too ("then he'll decide"), so they have become a jumbled trio.

"Demonstráció," whose rumbling guitar evokes Leonard Cohen (but whose lyrics do not), begins with Désiré asking his mother for some clothes, because he lost the ticket he had received at the laundry service and is thus left with no clothes at all. She tells him that only a sheet is left and recommends that he wrap himself in it. He does so and ventures out into the street, where he meets Antoine, who asks him, "What's the big deal?" Désiré outlines the situation, but Antoine suspects him, because of his garb, of making some kind of public demonstration. He expresses this suspicion through the onomatopoeic (and exquisitely sung) "*Hohohó-hó-hoho-hohohohohó*" and "*Ahahaha-haha-hahahaha-ha.*" In response, Désiré spits at him and tells him, "I already told you what the big deal was." He— or perhaps the narrator—continues with his own "*Ahahaha-haha-hahahaha-ha,*" "*Ohohó-hóhohoho-hohohohohó*" and says, "This spit, if possible, is an even better demonstration!" which he follows with a cornucopia of *Hmhmhm*'s and *Ahaha*s. (The word *demonstráció* can mean a political protest, an academic presentation or proof, or an attention-commanding action.) Antoine and Désiré keep running on and disappear around a corner; the narrator concludes, "*Ohóhoho-hohoho-hoho-hó! /*

This disappearance is the very best demonstration! / *Ahahaha-hahaha-hahahahaha.*"

This whimsical, comically paranoid song—which brings Nikolai Gogol's "Nose" to mind—hints at bureaucracy, nudity, and demonstrations, but none of these takes over; instead, the song becomes about the syllables and everything they can do and express, and about the song itself, which finally "disappears" along with Antoine and Désiré. Nonetheless, the final words, "This disappearance is the very best demonstration," hint at an existential (and possibly political) meaning and might leave you with an odd ache.

Antoine and Désiré are by no means confined to this album (and its corresponding stage show); they also appear as the protagonists of *Jóslat* ("Prophecy") and *Jóslat a metrón* ("Prophecy on the Subway"), released in 1984 and 2003, respectively. A dialogue between them provides the structure for the stage version of *Fehér babák takarodója* ("White Dolls' Curfew"); this dialogue is absent from the 1979 album. In addition, they crop up on various other albums: for example, Désiré is mentioned in passing on *Mélyrepülés* ("Flying Low" or "Deep Dive"), the 1988 album that Cseh created with Dénes Csengey) and is memorialized in "Désiré Mauzoleuma" ("Désiré's Mausoleum," which appears on the 2004 album *A véletlen szavai* ("Chance Words") in which Antoine also appears as a character). There are probably scores of unpublished Antoine and Désiré songs as well.

Let us now briefly consider some of Cseh and Bereményi's other characters, beginning with their recurring pair, Vizi and Ecsédi, the protagonists of the 1983 album *Frontátvonulás* ("Frontal Passage") and the 1993 album *Nyugati pályaudvar* ("Nyugati Station"). More will be said about them in the next chapter; suffice it to say here that they resemble Antoine and Désiré in their playful yet tense friendship, but differ in that their routines have come to a breaking point, prompting Vizi to seek a new life. The tension between their desires—Vizi seeking a new life and Ecsédi seeking Vizi—propel the story of *Frontátvonulás* through a series of encounters and songs. The story line is tighter and the stakes higher than with Antoine and Désiré, but at the end we do not know for sure whether anything changes.

Like Antoine and Désiré, and even like Irén and the narrator in *Levél nővéremnek*, Vizi and Ecsédi can be understood as two tendencies in the human soul: the one desiring a break with the past, the other, a reunification with a friend (and, along with that, a reliving of the magic they have experienced together). When we watch or listen to *Frontátvonulás*, our sympathies might tilt now toward Vizi, now toward Ecsédi; they unite at the end, but tentatively, without resolution.

Incidental characters in Cseh and Bereményi's work can be divided twice: into patently fictional characters on the one hand, and, on the other, characters based on cultural figures or contemporaries of Cseh and Bereményi; and, for an additional splitting, characters that figure prominently in a given song as opposed to those that simply pass through. Of the patently fictional characters, we have nearly everyone in *Frontátvonulás* and *Nyugati pályaudvar* and many of the characters in *Antoine és Désiré*; of the characters based on known figures, we have the subjects of nearly all the songs on the aforementioned 1979 album *Fehér babák takarodója* ("White Dolls' Curfew") and the 1981 album *Műcsarnok* ("Art Gallery"), as well as elsewhere. Many of the songs of *Fehér babák takarodója* are dedicated to fictionalized versions of actual women, some of whom Bereményi knew personally; in *Műcsarnok*, most of the songs have to do with a writer, a film actor, or a form of art (Sándor Petőfi, Endre Ady, Lee van Cleef, Fyodor Dostoevsky, a film, a song, and more). In both cases, the songs play with their own possibilities: what they can be about, what they can make of "reality," and how they can become reality themselves.

Some characters appear in Cseh and Bereményi's songs just for an instant: for instance, in the song "Budapest" on the album *Levél nővéremnek* (discussed in the previous chapter), János and Tamás head off to the store for milk; a former teacher is encountered on the street; "Éva" appears before the abortion committee; someone tries to sell his winter coat; a favor is asked of a certain Comrade Fáskerti; and more. The aforementioned "Amikor Désiré munkásszálláson lakott" ("When Désiré Lived in a Workers' Dormitory") has a number of transient characters: Feri and Imre Bíró, who help the narrator hoist Ica up to the fifth floor; the police who rescue her, and the collective *munkásszállás* ("workers' dormitory"). In "Lee van Cleef," on the album *Műcsarnok*, the characters Barleycorn, Charley, Hombre and Dick are mentioned in each of the choruses but none of the verses. Thus these transient characters often provide a backdrop for the main ones; they often appear as the multitude against whom the individuals can be perceived.

Songs about historical characters may be at least partly about something else entirely. The cunning "Dal a ravaszdi Shakespeare Williamről" ("Song About the Cunning William Shakespeare"), from the *Műcsarnok* album, contains a few barely concealed political jabs. Here is an English translation of the opening verse, with minor liberties taken for rhythm and rhyme:

> Long, long ago, in the land of Denmark,
> lived a king's son who, one lovely day,
> hiding a secret with a bad ending,
> decided—oh horrors!—a fool to play.
> Living thus sane in a world of madmen,
> one day he fell onto a poisoned sword;
> the throne was then taken by tranquil barons
> who dwelt in the realm between peace and war.
> But still this prince died with such aplomb
> that they gave him a magnificent tomb.
> And this very same tomb—alackaday—
> can even be seen on the stage today.

Then the chorus:

> In this lovely country, show me just one
> trickster as great as Shakespeare William!
> In this lovely country, show me just one
> trickster as great as Shakespeare William!

The verses proceed to speak of the "Moor" Othello and his murder of Desdemona, then the "hunchback" Richard III, whose hump has become the shape of the contorted world, but lest we think this has nothing to do with us, it then circles back to the present:

> And our mirror with all its scattered shards,
> Shakespeare glues up, Shakespeare repairs.
> We're standing here, mouths open and mum
> at everything known by Shakespeare William.

The song then returns to the chorus, which it repeats, ending on a slow

"William, William" with glorious chords. Yet all along, the song is pulling our leg. We know, from the start, that its events happened not so long ago, nor necessarily in Denmark; regicide, uxoricide, contortions are alive and well.

There is much more to explore in the characters of Cseh and Bereményi's songs than this chapter can touch on, but some general tendencies become clear. First of all, the pairs (Antoine and Désiré, Vizi and Ecsédi) recur many times in their work; these fraught friendships hold together against all odds, at least for a while. The members of the pair help each other by contrasting with each other (thus giving each other definition): Antoine knows how to survive in the world, but Désiré makes such survival meaningful, or at least captivating. Vizi has some form of ambition, a desire to move on, but Ecsédi (at least in *Frontátvonulás*) manages to persuade him to stay within their game and believe in it just a little while longer. In the lives of Antoine and Désiré, each episode is a self-contained fable; for Vizi and Ecsédi, the episodes tie together into a larger tale and motion. In the case of both friend-pairs, the language that fills their dialogue is endearingly simple, often breaking down into fragments and stuttering.

The other characters of Cseh and Bereményi's work play a panoply of roles and are rarely what they seem. A seemingly implausible character may come out of an episode in Bereményi's life; a famous figure may pop up where least expected. Nor do they represent what we might think at first. We might be saying good morning to the brigadier Ádám Balogh (in "Antoine és Désiré történelemkönyve," "Antoine and Désiré's History Book") and to a series of other historical heroes, but as Dénes Csengey suggests, the song actually grimaces at them and their disasters.[9] We might be hearing Lee van Cleef gallop by (see Chapter 7), yet the song is ultimately neither about the actor himself, nor about any specific character he plays, but rather about someone and something close to us. All the same, these songs stand out not for their allegories, but for what they do within their few minutes and chords and across the larger works. Combining, breaking apart, and recombining, the characters make simple magic, where the strange and the familiar trade places so quickly and so often that they become one and the same.

Chapter 5

Frontátvonulás ("Frontal Passage"):
A Masterpiece of Repetition and Ending

No, Ecsédi, I'm not the slightest bit ill. I just want to say that I've had enough of this. I don't know how many times we've done it, two hundred, three hundred times: we meet on the street and act like it's a coincidence. Then we go up to my place, drink the cognacs, coffee liqueurs, mixed drinks, and then I come down here to the train station and pretend I'm surprised that no trains are leaving here. And you make a ruckus all over town. Enough of this, Ecsédi.

Toward the end of *Frontátvonulás* ("Frontal Passage"), Cseh and Bereményi's 1979 stage show and 1983 album, Vizi reveals that he and Ecsédi have been playing out their own play again and again: that the events of the story are partly their invention, and that for Vizi they have become routine. This may surprise a first-time listener, as there has been little or no hint of this repetition until now. Thus *Frontátvonulás* raises the questions: At what point does invention become routine? What mysteries does repetition hold? What is the relation between repetition and creation; what does it mean for an event to repeat? What form do these questions take in a contorted world where no trains are running and no one is going anywhere—that is, where freedom is squelched from the start?[1]

Reveling in narration and song, *Frontátvonulás* tells of friendship and loss, stasis and freedom. About its protagonists, Miklós Vizi and (Tamás) Ecsédi, we know little except that they are friends and former classmates.[*] After a drunken evening at home, Vizi heads off in search of a new life; Ecsédi, upon waking and finding him gone, runs out in search of him. Both

---

[*] Ecsédi's given name, Tamás, appears nowhere in the text, only in external sources.

end up at Keleti Station, where all travel has halted and where desperate, raunchy characters have been playing out their routines for ages: a female ticket clerk, Vizi's drunken father, a suicidal man, one of Vizi's former classmates, an eighty-seven-year-old man, the bathroom attendant ("Mommy of the World"), and others. At the end, Vizi and Ecsédi perform a breakthrough: they drive a locomotive through the glass façade of Keleti Station and go on a victory jaunt around Budapest. They later watch the festivities at home on television; Ecsédi falls asleep, and Vizi pulls his hair and yells into his face, then addresses the audience, repeating his last three words in slightly different form.

Below this burlesque plot lie ironies, allusions, and emotions, simple meanings, and something mystical and unpinpointable. The story and songs are supremely silly yet poignant and dark; but as *Frontátvonulás* progresses, it turns into something else entirely: an elegy perhaps, or a tribute to the imagination.

The premiere of *Frontátvonulás* took place on October 18, 1979, at Budapest's Castle Theatre, four years before the album's release. Here and elsewhere Cseh performed it solo, telling the tale, singing the songs, and entering each character as he went along. He used one standing microphone and stood in place while impersonating the characters and action; thus this and subsequent shows combined concert and theatre. In its musical and lyrical richness and its special genre, *Frontátvonulás* exemplifies Cseh and Bereményi's creative collaboration. It also marks a breaking point: their last musical collaboration before Bereményi's seven-year songwriting hiatus.[2]

From the beginning, *Frontátvonulás* was recognized as a masterpiece. The poet and translator Grácia Kerényi, who attended the 1979 premiere, praised its artistic excellence: "The performance, exciting at the dramaturgic level—I didn't mention Różewicz, *Mrożek*, Ionesco by accident—is also musically outstanding, with parodic references ... and also holds its ground on the poetic plane." Kerényi also heard, below the text, a possible debate between Cseh and Bereményi about whether or not to continue.[3] That is, at moments, *Frontátvonulás* may be about their art and about art in general.

Frontátvonulás not only survived over the years but has recently taken on new life. In 2024, graduating students of the University of Theatre and Film Arts created a version for the stage in which six actors clamber up, down, and around a two-tiered structure and play multiple characters and instruments, trading off so seamlessly that the peripheral and central actions interweave continually, every element contributing to the whole, every actor coming forward at times, receding at others. Faithful to the original work yet profoundly original, the production earned critical acclaim and toured Hungary and Romania. The group continues to express gratitude for this reception and the resultant opportunities. In late 2024 they formed a theatre company, SICC Production; since then, they have continued performing *Frontátvonulás* within their growing repertoire.[4]

Here I will describe *Frontátvonulás* itself and then the SICC version, examining the questions of creation and repetition that arise in the work. I had the opportunity to speak with both the director and the musical director of SICC about their approach to *Frontátvonulás*; the later part of this essay refers frequently to these interviews.

If there is a single image associated with *Frontátvonulás*, it is that of Vizi holding up a glass and releasing it. This happens twice, near the beginning and near the end, but we learn from Ecsédi that Vizi has done it hundreds of times. The glass, according to the story, floats in the air. On stage you can see and hear the glass fall and shatter, but the mental image of the floating glass captures the imagination and at times seems more real than the falling and shattering. At least the ambivalence can be felt. *Frontátvonulás* itself is about the imagination, but how? The question will not be settled.

Frontátvonulás abounds with tensions: between motion and stasis, passion and indifference, continuation and ending, floating and falling, imagination and reality, dream and waking, attention and distraction, repetition and newness, routine and ritual. A miniature epic, it takes place mainly within an infernal microcosm, Budapest's historic Keleti Station, a majestic, eclectic edifice with an arched iron-and-glass façade.[5] Various would-be travelers and workers go through their motions; it appears that they have been doing this for years. Vizi and Ecsédi ultimately break out of this confined world, only to unmask this feat as another iteration of their own routine (perhaps). Everything happens, yet nothing does; through its paradoxes and musical variety, *Frontátvonulás* releases a cascade of interpretations.

Most of the characters have a song to sing; the musical styles range from lullaby to tango to ballad to chant, yet arise organically from the story, as though song were everywhere. Some of the songs are both spoken and sung. Several end in humming or onomatopoeia (*dumdumdum, dididi, tratara,* etc.), suggesting that they could go on forever. The lyrics and narration are so unusual and prickly that they might surprise you even after you have heard them many times over. They bring out some of the everyday glories of the Hungarian language; even a passing phrase can leave you in awe.

The story combines mundanity with mystery. One mystery of the story revolves around the aforementioned miracle of the floating glass (Cseh performed this with an actual glass, which would crash onto the floor and break). Another mystery is found in the double ending: after all is said and done, and Ecsédi has fallen asleep, Vizi yanks him by the hair and shouts into his face: "If you yell women's names at me here one more time, and street addresses, it's over, get it?" The album ends with Cseh addressing the audience: "It's over. Get it?" We are left wondering what is over and whether it has truly come to an end.

Frontátvonulás moves through several stages, each stage revealing at least one of the tensions of the work. In the first stage, Vizi, dissatisfied with his empty life, decides to take off and start anew; he leaves the apartment while Ecsédi is still sleeping. Ecsédi, dismayed at finding his friend gone, goes out in search of him, but finds the pedestrians on the street indifferent to his plight. In the second stage, Vizi, reaching Keleti Station, encounters all sorts of languorous, seedy characters, none of whom intends to go anywhere (except for the suicidal man, who believes he is initiating a "movement"). No one seems interested in helping him leave; instead, they try to draw him into the ongoing activities (the endless, dreary festivities in the restaurant, where Vizi's high school classmates are still celebrating their graduation, from years ago). Here we see not the tension not only between the overall stasis and Vizi's desire for motion, but between various calls for sympathy and nostalgia and his rejection of such sentimentalities.

Slowly it dawns on Vizi that no trains are leaving at all; at this moment (the third stage), Ecsédi finds him, but Vizi wants to end their entire game (it seems that they were just playing all along). Ecsédi, dismayed at the thought of ending it, since he has enjoyed it so much, asks Vizi if he could do his trick with the glass again. The mention of the trick brings Vizi around; he performs it again, and once again the glass floats in the air. In the fourth and final stage, they board and steer a locomotive through the glass wall of Keleti Station and all around town. All of this comes to an end where it began: in the apartment, with Ecsédi slumped over a chair. Vizi's stern warning, yelled in Ecsédi's face, is then repeated to us.

Many have interpreted the words "It's over. Get it?" as a signal of an absolute ending, emphasized by the repetition itself.[6] But Vizi does not tell Ecsédi that it's over for good; he says that this will be the case *if* Ecsédi yells women's names and street names ever again. That is, he's giving Ecsédi one more chance, as friends often do—and we don't know how many last chances he has given or will still give. The sternness of the double ending is counterbalanced by the rather silly condition given by Vizi and the uncertainty over how many times this has played out. In addition, we know that *Frontátvonulás* itself has come to an end many times—and been performed again. The play is truly over *for now.*

Let us now look more closely at the play, with particular attention to the tension between repetition and creation.

Any discussion of *Frontátvonulás* must acknowledge the album's limitations in comparison to the performances. Some songs in the performances are absent from the album; moreover, the album cannot capture Cseh's expressions or the audience's reactions.[7] Nonetheless, there is enough here for a listener to enjoy and absorb and to understand differently with each iteration. Even those who do not speak Hungarian can appreciate and enjoy *Frontátvonulás* if familiar with its premise.

Since the album itself does not have track divisions, the track numbers cited here match those listed on the *Frontátvonulás* page of the Cseh Tamás Archívum website; the link to this page as well as the link to the album on Spotify, can be found in the endnote to this paragraph. The quoted text throughout this section matches that on the Cseh Tamás Archívum website. Most of the quotations will be in English translation only; song titles will be named in both Hungarian and English so that the reader can find them easily. The songs highlighted in this chapter are included in the playlist at the beginning of the book.[8]

The front cover of *Frontátvonulás* displays a wry, melancholic black-and-white photograph of Cseh (taken by Miklós Gáspár). Cseh performs the album solo; the sound effects and musical accompaniment were presumably added by Péter Péterdi, the musical director. Cseh, Bereményi, and Péterdi are credited on the back cover, along with Károly Peller as sound engineer, Gáspár for the photo, and József Szurcsik for graphics.

The title word has a meteorological meaning: according to a Hungarian geographical glossary, it refers to "the passage of a weather front over an area, causing weather changes and affecting the human body as well." It also connotes the passage of an army; thus, audiences might associate it with the Soviet Army's supposedly temporary occupation of Hungary, or perhaps with attempts at resistance or revolt. The word arises only once within the work (beyond its title). In context, it suggests some kind of human movement, a disruption of the usual order of things—and on the other hand stasis and occupation.[9]

The beginning reveals Ecsédi's and Vizi's disorientation and separate quests. In Cseh's spoken narration, Ecsédi is running around with a photo of his old classmate Vizi, at the intersection of Bajcsy-Zsilinszky and Arany János Streets in Budapest, asking pedestrians if they have seen him anywhere. Instead of answering, they just stand around. One of the pedestrians asks another if he knows who this person is; the other replies that it is Ecsédi, that he is harassing people, and that it is already in the news. He presses a newspaper into the other's hand, in which a text appears in "italics, that is, cursive letters." This text is the first song of the album, the wistful, incantatory "Vizi és Ecsédi találkozott" ("Vizi and Ecsédi Met Up") (track A1). This stands as an example of the surprising ways that narrative can lead into song in *Frontátvonulás*: in this case, the song arises as the *italicized* text of a news article. The dreamy singing contrasts with the seemingly silly lyrics (which play a key role in the whole). Here is a translation (with minor liberties taken for rhyme and rhythm).

Vizi and Ecsédi met up yesterday,
and giving each other a shipload to say,
sailing their phrases through stories of yore,
drank up two liters of coffee liqueur.
And since nothing else in the place could be found,
guzzled some cognacs down to the ground.

Ecsédi, near midnight, cried out in distress,
yelling out women's names, street addresses.
Places where he had lived some other time,
then something glimmered within Vizi's mind:
There's still some mixed liquor left from yesterday.
Remember, we loved it! – he gushed fervently.

[Whistling]

We loved it, we loved it, he gushed to himself,
we drank just mixed liquor, just that, nothing else,
Shout away, go ahead, shout women's names,
I'm off to the kitchen for more of the same.
With these words Vizi left the smoky room,
and back in the kitchen he found himself soon.

For a glimpse into the extraordinary language of this song, the phrase "he gushed fervently" is a translation of a single Hungarian word, *lelkendezett*, which recurs in the following line. *Lelkendezett*, a verb based on the root *lélek*, "soul, spirit" conveys enthusiasm and a certain talkativeness. The irony here is that this enthusiasm—about the dregs of mixed liquor—will come to a quick end.

Vizi makes his way to the kitchen, gets dizzy, and wonders where he is: "How did I get here? I didn't prepare for this. What is this here, where I am? What sort of train am I on, who booked the ticket?" This disorientation leads into the second song, "Úristen, hol vagyok?" ("Lord God, Where Am I?") (track A2), and sets the mood for what is to come. It is significant that Vizi invokes the image of a train, for the trains will presently come to a halt, then, at the end of the album, break into motion again.

The song moves gradually from speech into melody and rhythm. In contrast with the previous song, where a short melody repeats, this has a longer melodic shape, spanning the entire song. It is a brief, unified expression of being physically and existentially lost—along with a theatrical motif, since Vizi suggests that someone else is playing the illusion that this is he. Here again, the translation takes minor liberties.

Lord God, where am I?
Lord God, where am I?
When did I book this ride so I'd
go rumbling away with a train?
Lord God, where am I,
Lord, what did I end up inside?
When on earth did I get stuck here,
where there is only half an I.
Half, half, half an I,
I am not here, not I,

since someone other than I,
someone else is playing the lie
that this, this am I.

This crisis of identity catalyzes one of the miracles of the story, for now Vizi declares (in Cseh's spoken narration) that he has to make a change, since "if I stay, it's the end of me." He realizes that he has been procrastinating with his life, just like everyone, but now will procrastinate no more. "Let's do an experiment!" he decides. "Now it's possible, because now I want it." He goes to the kitchen table, where, among lots of unwashed dishes, he finds a glass. He takes the glass, "like this" (Cseh demonstrates with an actual glass), lifts it up, "like this," and lets it go (the glass shatters). Cseh tells us, "Vizi's glass stayed there in the air. The glass floated in the air, Vizi looked at it and knew that from this moment on, he was capable of everything; he could accomplish everything." In performance, Cseh would hold up an actual glass and release it; the glass would drop and break, but according to Kerényi, the power of suggestion was such that one could sense, along with Vizi, a moment of intuition. Cseh commented in an interview that this was mesmerizing for him too; at moments he wondered what would happen if it actually stayed in the air.[10] This glass-dropping miracle will recur later, toward the end, and will give clues to the whole.

Vizi makes his way into the train station—encountering outside the building a young man who warns him against entering because of the scandal going on inside, and then, inside, the female ticket clerk, and within the restaurant area, the *dizőz* (diseuse, or nightclub singer) and then his former classmate Halmos, accompanied by their other classmates, the "banqueters." (In Hungary, graduating seniors hold a banquet, with alcohol, after finishing all their exams; teachers are invited, and they all feast and drink together.) Halmos sings a cheerful-sounding yet trenchant song in a folk-troubadour style about how many lives have gone under ("Hányan kipusztultak," track A7): "How many have been destroyed, / and not the worst of all, / but above their potsherd-covered heads / the sun rises all the same." Later on, the song reaches a moment of poignancy, where Cseh pauses: "and here I say the song, / that this is ungracious, / ungracious weather for youth, / cloudy weather left and right, and then rain, / a rain that smites everything down, / it seems everything thus comes to an end, / that there will be rain, it will smite everything down..." From here, Halmos starts to go around in circles with his words, until he breaks into humming *dududum* and *dididi.*

Vizi, oblivious to the tragedy of the song, loses patience with him, telling him, "Halmos, cut out that didi-ing and dodo-ing, I didn't come here to whine with you. I didn't come to whine, Halmos!" But if he seems heartless, he then points to the banqueters and says he has had enough of them, a reasonable sentiment, for who wants to be stuck in a graduation celebration his whole life long?

Halmos directs Vizi's attention to the eighty-seven-year-old man in the corner, who takes no offense at being stared at, but just smiles and sings a gentle, dreamy song (track A9) with a rough yet slightly outlandish story: about fighting in two wars, about leaving some thirty-nine women and being left by about twice as many; about pissing in tank traps and eating horse cadavers and still surviving. His son, he sings, has become a neurotic, unable to take the changes; when he looks at his grandson, he sees a weak thing. Will they survive? He sees something falling apart; and he wonders, in a hundred years, who here will know Hungarian? When he looks at the people there in the room, not one of them is hard as concrete—"if you fly on the first wind, what will come then, I ask?" Vizi (not realizing that the question applies to him) rejects the entire discussion and insists on knowing when the trains are leaving. Here, as in his response to Halmos's song, we see Vizi ignoring all information and wisdom that does not pertain to his immediate purpose: to leave. Yet the narrator seems to sympathize with him, because he earnestly wants to go (anywhere at all) but is trapped.

Now Ecsédi, still running around with the photo (and similarly obsessed), keeps asking if anyone has seen his friend. By coincidence, the narrator tells us emphatically, he ends up outside Keleti Station. Making his way through the crowd, he falls and the photo falls from his hand. He crawls around trying to recover it; as he does so, a "goyzer-stitched shoe" steps on his hand, a shoe so shiny he can see his own face in it. Ecsédi recognizes this shoe from somewhere—"Hey-ho, hey-ho, hey-ho! Let's get a grip," he tells himself—and addresses Comrade Sas ("Eagle"), the owner of the shoe. Sas questions whether Ecsédi is in his right mind, Ecsédi starts asking about Vizi, and Sas lets it slip that Vizi is causing us "a commotion, a scandal; he's doing a circus act." (In Hungarian this is particularly funny: "*a felfordulást, a botrányt, cirkuszozik.*") Ecsédi, gleaning that Vizi is at the train station, cannot contain his delight, but Sas keeps ranting about the dangers and the scandal, and about how Comrade Sólyom ("Falcon") has gotten angry (after being informed by Sas of the goings-on), and does Ecsédi really want this to reach Comrade Karvaly ("Sparrow Hawk")? Sas continues in this manner—but Ecsédi, oblivious to the nature of these warnings, presses on, asking if this actually means that Vizi is at the train station. Sas takes him by the shoulders and tells him to relax, then reaches into his pocket, pulls out a candy and puts it in Ecsédi's mouth. Now Comrade Sas, who according to the narrator has sung beautifully until now, starts to "sing at an even more exalted level"; the next song—"Sors elvtárs dala" ("Song of Comrade Fate," track B2), puts Ecsédi in a trance.[11] This song, which Cseh sings with great relish, playfully lampoons the saccharine optimism and paranoia of Hungarian officials (at various levels of the echelon) while also pointing to something more disturbing: the pervasive surveillance. Ecsédi then snaps out of his trance, realizes Vizi is in the train station, and runs off to find him.

He enters Keleti station, where we have just left Vizi asking whether there are any trains departing at all. This moves us into the second phase of the story: assembly and stagnancy. Vizi approaches the ticket counter and discovers his own drunken father burying his head in the ticket clerk's hair. After Vizi looks up at the ceiling and sings the devastating "Jó év volt" ("It Was a Good Year," track B3), about being no trouble to anyone when he was born—more about this song later—someone grabs his arm with great force and turns him around. It is the female restroom attendant, who reveals that she has been waiting for him since time immemorial, and that everyone here calls her *mamika* (Mommy). Promising to reveal a secret to him, she begins to sing her song, one of the funniest and most poignant of the album: "A világ mamikájának dala" ("Song of the Mommy of the World"), With rumbling fingerpicked guitar and a dreamy lullaby lilt, this song reveals one of the essences of the *Frontátvonulás* worldview: that everyone here belongs to one immense, trapped family, mothered by the only person who seems to know what is going on (or not) and who has possibly the dirtiest, humblest job of all.

> Since I had no husband to make me pregnant,
> I gave birth to a train station, travelers within it.
> I make my many infants vomit and burp,
> and I watch as they kick their lives to the curb.

Türű-rű-rürű-rüm, türű-rürű-rüm.

Since I had nothing else, just scores of latrines,
in the end I became the world's mama queen
in a train station, birthing this whole fray and you,
so listen to my song, kiddie-poo:

I, mommy of the world, whisper in your ear
that no trains whatsoever are leaving from here,
everyone's pretending, parading their druthers,
but they stay here with me—I am their mother.

I'm the mommy of the world, just letting them play
that the idling trains will depart here some day.
I know they need starter games, how could I not?
I know every one of them; they are my tots.

But nobody's moving, they just stand around lazy,
and among them you're one of my little boys, Vizi.
I'm the mommy of the world, and with you I'll level,
no trains are departing, there's no hint of travel.

Astounded, Vizi dashes into the restaurant, jumps on a table, and asks the crowd whether it is true that no trains are running, that this is an "pseudo-station" (the Hungarian word is the wonderful *álpályaudvar*, where the prefix ál- means "pseudo"). A silence falls over the room. Then people start shouting out: about Vizi's father, about the eighty-scven-year-old man, about the man who has just hanged himself, the banqueters—about how, for ages and ages, nothing has changed. Hereupon, the *dizőz* tests the microphone and begins to sing about the train station "where everyone's related, / where there's nothing besides / just waiting and waiting." Everyone has joined in by the time that Ecsédi enters.

Upon seeing Ecsédi, Vizi wants to call off the whole routine, he says they've done this some two or three hundred times already: met up on the street, pretending it was by coincidence, then going over to Vizi's place, drinking cognac, making their way to Keleti, and then pretending to be surprised that no trains are running. Ecsédi protests that it has been good and begs him to do his trick with the glass once more. Vizi consents with a weary smile, picks up a glass, lifts it up, and releases it. As before, the glass floats in the air. Ecsédi and Vizi begin to consider the physical implications of this phenomenon. After some absurd calculations, Ecsédi concludes, "So we have ten to the minus two in our hands," to which Vizi replies that it is not in their hands, but will be "in the train, in the train, in the train, in the train!" Both of them, apparently, have been seized by the exuberance of the miracle, which unites their opposing desires.

These opposing desires, after all, inhere in art, especially theatre and music, which require not only repetitive practice, but repetitive performance. To some extent, Vizi and Ecsédi have written their own play, which apparently they play out every day. At what point do the writers, directors, and performers (in this case Vizi and Ecsédi) decide that they have had enough of it and that it is time to move on? To what extent can something new be found in each of the repetitions? How can an old piece suddenly become new again?

Where is the border between routine and ritual, and between ritual and rite? Could there be a spiritual or mystical aspect to the repetition? The miracle of the glass holds the play together at its two poles; it is this miracle that brings Vizi back into temporary union with Ecsédi. They come together for a short interlude that seems by all counts blessed and glorious. Perhaps this miracle, or quasi-miracle, makes every repetition new; perhaps each iteration is new in that it dangles the possibility of a miracle.

One must not pose these questions naively, with ignorance of their context: Vizi and Ecsédi's daily play (if indeed they play it daily) meets with indifference, passive admiration, and suspicion from the outside world. Only at the end does the miracle dazzle the crowd and propel the two to victory and celebration. A locomotive bursts through the glass wall of Keleti Station and starts gallivanting around the city, past a series of landmarks and historic figures (who wave at them) and over the Chain Bridge. Vizi and Ecsédi are the conductors; the loudspeakers proclaim: "Long live Vizi, long live Ecsédi!" Flowers, confetti—and Ecsédi, who has climbed off of the locomotive, begins to give a proudly self-effacing poem-speech. In fact, he becomes the hero: it was he who believed in their game and in Vizi; it was he who persuaded Vizi to return. Then comes the aforementioned ending: Vizi and Ecsédi watching the festivities on TV at home, then Vizi yelling at Ecsédi that if he yells women's names and addresses again, "it's over, get it?"

The stage show and album end with Cseh addressing the audience: "It's over. Get it?," as if snapping us out of our state as well. Thus it starts and ends with endings: it begins with Vizi starting a new life (and presumably leaving his previous one) and ends with him threatening to end his friendship with Ecsédi, and then with Cseh declaring an end to the show. In between, the trains have stopped; travel has come to an end. Yet ironies multiply; Vizi's new life is not all that new; the trains are partly figurative; and the breakthrough at the end leads to something like a repeat of the beginning, with Vizi and Ecsédi drunk at home. Even Cseh's final words play against the continuation of *Frontátvonulás* as a performance.

The audience may understand the ending and the entire work in many ways. The work evokes a particular experience in Hungary: perhaps of the "Great Generation," perhaps of several generations at once, but in any case of an era where not only travel but self-realization was thwarted. Yet the intensity of *Frontátvonulás* for people of different ages, as well as non-Hungarians, suggests that it bursts through time and place, evoking our own conflicting desires to repeat our favorite rituals and to break with them—even the ritual of watching *Frontátvonulás*.

From June 2024 onward I had the joy of watching (on fifteen occasions and counting) the aforementioned reworking and performance of *Frontátvonulás* by graduating students of the University of Theatre and Film Arts in Budapest, who have since formed their own theatre company, SICC Production (the actors also play in numerous productions outside of the company). Directed by Vilmos Krasznai and musically directed by Kristóf Fülöp, this version of *Frontátvonulás* features six actors (Ágoston Liber, Dávid Kerek, Péter Turi, Atanáz Vatamány, Zoltán Sas, and Fülöp) dressed in bathrobes of different colors and playing multiple roles and instruments—guitars, bass, keyboards, violin, accordion, trumpet, toy xylophone, and kazoo—as they make their way up, down, and around a cramped two-tiered structure representing not only Keleti Station, but the characters' entire world. The action is carefully coordinated and calibrated, with actors passing instruments to each other, changing places, helping each other up and down the structure, or handing each other the microphone; at the same time it has a relaxed, lackadaisical feel; the actors respond to the moment and to each other.

At an outdoor performance at the Marczibányi Téri Művelődési Központ on June 25, 2025, just after Halmos (Turi) asked, perturbed and uncomprehending, "Te, Vizi, elutazol valohová?" ("You, Vizi, are you traveling somewhere?") a bird flew squawking over the premises. The squawking sounded like mockery: *you, Vizi, aren't going anywhere!* Everyone heard it, including the actors; they waited just one second to take it in. Then we all laughed together. (In every performance, the characters laugh over Halmos's question, but here the laughter took on a different timing and meaning.)

From the start of this project, even before rehearsals began, Krasznai and Fülöp determined that they would expand *Frontátvonulás* theatrically: that is, take the musical material on the album and translate it into theatre, creating a dramatic arc through the musical arrangements and staging. It was Krasznai who knew *Frontátvonulás* backwards and forwards; together they worked out the changes of tone and mood, both within and across the songs. Thus one song might have a rousing feel, another slightly childlike; or after a loud part, they might bring in some quiet. By finding these transitions and contrasts, they were able to give the play the emphases and meanings they wanted. This, according to Fülöp, was "step zero"; they worked out these ideas and details before approaching the others and continued to refine them from there.[12]

From the beginning, according to Krasznai, they conceived of all the actors playing all the way through, but the stage design itself—thanks to a university grant—evolved from a cube-like structure into multiple tiers and compartments, which allow them to rotate positions and progress through stages. The actors assemble the stage set together before each performance; this in itself looks like an intricate dance, as they hand each other tools and pieces, connect the electrical cords, amps, and speakers, put all the instruments in their proper places, and consult with each other along the way. Fülöp has compared the play (cautiously) to a religious ceremony, because of the way all the different parts work together, carrying the story through its various stages until the end, which resembles the beginning.[13]

With playful melancholy— for instance, with Vizi (Liber) swinging outward from the upper tier as he sings "Arthur Rimbaud elutazik" ("Arthur Rimbaud Departs," track A3), the *diseuse* (Sas) raunchily stretching out "her" fishnet-stockinged leg and flouncing her boa as she sings her tango of death (track A6), and the suicidal Loop Man (Turi, who also plays Halmos) bursting into a tap dance rendition of "Életem utolsó gesztusa" ("The last gesture of my life"), a Cseh-Bereményi song not part of the *Frontátvonulás* album or text but included in some of the performances—they bring the songs and story into us.

Their show starts with slow notes building on each other: a relaxed overture played by many hands on the same keyboard, then with trumpet added, then violin, all leading up to the play's first word, "jaj," an exclamation of lament. The progression was composed by Fülöp to match the Cseh-Bereményi song "Jaj, mit mondok majd" ("Ah, what will I say") from their *Utóirat* album, not originally part of *Frontátvonulás* but added by SICC to the end of the play. According to Fülöp, the melody at the beginning has the quality of instruments tuning to each other, playing their own melodies; at the end, the song leaves questions open. For Krasznai, this song raises questions important to the entire endeavor: on top of those posed by the play itself, it asks: *What will I say about all of this? How will I understand it?* They sing this song as themselves, not as their characters, thus ending the play in a personal and intimate way before the final words of the narrator and Vizi.[14]

Back to the beginning: after the prelude, the play bursts into speech, preserving the text of the original. Ecsédi (Kerek) calls out to the crowd, asking if they have seen Vizi, and the narrator (Vatamány) gives the background to the story. Then a pedestrian (Fülöp) calls out, *"Ki ez uram?"* ("Who's that, sir?") and immediately starts into tongue-trilling (SICC calls it "mouth balalaika"), which the others join one by one. Another pedestrian (Sas) replies (in a fiendishly raspy voice) that it's someone named Ecsédi who has been running around and harassing the passers-by. He shows the first pedestrian an article in the paper, the text of which is the very first song, sung by the narrator and Vizi, through which the trilling continues. Even now, I cannot pinpoint the exact moment of enchantment: the first note? the first trill? the sight of all the characters huddled together in the upper right corner of the structure? Whenever it happens, it seizes the audience.

The alternating parts and instruments create magic of their own. The song "Vizi és Ecsédi találkozott" ("Vizi and Ecsédi Met Up") goes through a dramatic change of mood and location. It is sung by the narrator (Vatamány) until it quotes Vizi's thoughts; then Vizi (Liber) sings until the word *lelkendezett* ("he gushed fervently"), which the narrator sings. Then Vizi begins to whistle, and in the background, Turi lifts his right hand high into the air, curves his index finger downward, and plunges it onto the keyboard, turning the song into throbbing rock, with everyone joining in.

Vizi and Ecsédi (Kerek) have a fight, slapping each other with tortillas that break and fly from their hands (Fülöp calls this the *buli rész*, or "party part"—a break from Cseh's musical world). Then, still within the rock mode, Vizi shouts his next words into a microphone, hands it to the narrator, who shouts *lelkendezett!* and makes his way with his violin to the kitchen, at this moment the upper left quadrant of the metal structure. In the midst of the change of music, scene, and mood (between the two instances of *lelkendezett*), we discover that Vizi has entered not only a new room, but a new state of mind. According to Fülöp, Vizi is tired of the drinking and the party; this is why he leaves for the kitchen. Thus the actors and directors pick up on a transformation in the song and bring it out both musically and dramatically; this allows us to believe Vizi when he says, in the kitchen, "What have I done up to now? Nothing. Nothing. Nothing."[15]

Or consider "Sors elvtárs dala" ("Song of Comrade Fate"), in which Comrade Eagle (Fülöp) puts a kazoo in Ecsédi's mouth (in the original *Frontátvonulás*, it is a candy, but as Fülöp points out, in both cases the goal is to keep Ecsédi quiet) and has him sing *ollálá* after him, which puts Ecsédi in a temporary trance. Here Comrade Eagle becomes a mad conductor and the rest of the cast the chorus, singing *ollálá* at his command as Ecsédi haplessly kazoos along. This *ollálá* becomes more and more feverish, until it transforms into "lálálá," careening into a series of musical quotes from pop songs—including Naughty Boy's "La la la" and ATC's "Around the World"—chosen on the basis of their *lalázás* ("la-la-la-ing") and chord progressions, though in fact, according to Fülöp, anything can have *lalázás*.[16] This transformed song evokes the *tárárá, dididi,* and *türürű* of the other songs: a fevered reverie that could go on forever.

Skipping ahead in the play: in the aforementioned song "Életem utolsó gesztusa" ("The Last Gesture of My Life"), which originally appeared on Cseh and Bereményi's 1987 album *Utóirat* ("Postscript"), the suicidal man, or "Loop Man" (Turi) sings that he will throw his hat into this evening ("bom-bom-bom, bo-bo-bom-bom" goes the refrain), then go home hatless, turn on the gas, and then, when asked what he is doing, will reply that he is ruining the suicide statistics.The Loop Man tap dances as he sings, whisks himself up onto the stage structure, then jumps down again, circles around to the background, and dances his way offstage, followed by a procession— a nod to the director János Szász, who includes a similar procession in his film rendition of the song (discussed in the eighth chapter).

They make their way unnoticed to the back of the auditorium, where they surprise the audience by joining in with harmonies in the last verse of "Jó év volt," sung by Vizi (Liber) and his father (Kerek, who also plays Ecsédi). Without realizing it, we have been brought into matters of life and death, and maybe the worst human condition of all: being born into the world to stay still. Here is a translation of the song (with minor liberties).

A good year it was,
when I came into the world,
there were potatoes and bread,
and everyone was overjoyed.

A good year it was,
my father had just been discharged,
my sister was well again,
and my own birth wasn't hard.

A boy they wanted, three
point one four kilograms,
they all took joy in me,
just my raving mad
uncle said that:

He has a good voice,
that's not a cry but a song,
come on, folks, hear what I hear,
hear his song.

He will carry on
everything you began,
and he will never believe
that he's alien.

He'll be a good boy,
don't fear anything strange,
the fact that he was born
doesn't mean any change.

He's singing:
A good year this is
of my coming into the world,
there are potatoes and bread,
and everyone's overjoyed.

A good year this is,
my father's just been discharged,
my sister's recovered, and
my own birth wasn't hard.

I will carry on
everything you began,
and I will never believe
that I'm alien.

I am a good boy,
don't fear anything strange,
the fact that I will exist
doesn't mean any change.
Hm-hm, hmm-hm-hm-hm, hm-hm...

What this translation cannot convey is the exquisite timing of the syllables in Hungarian, particularly the line "*Jó év volt*" ("A good year it was"), where *Jó* and *év* have three beats each, and *volt* six. That elongation gives the song a melancholy that the SICC arrangement and performance enhances. Also, many of the words in the song are so evocative in Hungarian that their translation is only a shadow. For example, the word for "potatoes" here is *krumpli*, an informal and homey word (the formal word for potato is *burgonya*). The song creates an atmosphere that at once intimate, cold, and lonely, where Vizi is welcomed into the world as a repetition of what preceded him (and where, by implication, a departure from the past would pose a threat).

Then the "Mommy of the World" (Vatamány, dressed in a white bathrobe and cap, as he has been all along) sings to Vizi in a bass voice; Vizi rushes back into the Keleti Station restaurant, meets with derision when he asks whether it is true that no trains are leaving at all, and ends up joining the *dizőz* on violin, losing himself in the repeated melody. Ecsédi catches up with him, and we know the rest: Vizi wants to call it all off, but Ecsédi persuades him to do his trick with the glass. This opens up into the rapturous and heartbreaking finale, with the soaring music (reminiscent of the opening), Vizi and Ecsédi hugging each other with all their might, and Ecsédi's proud and humble speech-poem. All the characters form part of this final picture and sound, preparing us for the goodbye; the SICC version brings everything around full circle, returning even to the initial "jaj," this time by bringing in Cseh and Bereményi's song "Jaj, mit mondok majd" ("Alas, what will I say"), which SICC renders with gorgeous bareness. Vizi's words at the end resemble a glass falling and breaking—twice, leaving us to drop it a third time by heading out into the world.

According to Fülöp and Krasznai, Vizi's statement that he and Ecsédi have played this game hundreds of times gives a twist to the story but does not resolve it definitively. The question is left open for the viewers. Since there is no hint earlier in the play that either Vizi or Ecsédi is running into familiar people or situations (with the possible exception of Vizi's father), Vizi's revelation at the end, according to Fülöp and Krasznai, does not contradict the apparent newness of the events throughout the play. That is, while the events are going on, they are completely new; but then it appears that they have been played out hundreds of times. Krasznai says that he himself is not sure how many times Vizi and Ecsédi's routine has repeated, if at all; it might be entirely new yet familiar, or it might happen every evening. Fülöp connects this question with their own repeated performance of *Frontátvonulás*: it stays alive for them no matter how many times they perform it, because they let their walls down and create it together in each moment, responding to each other, not insisting on following the script millimeter by millimeter, but letting it take its own form and direction.[17]

This question of repetition connects with that of the glass: according to the story, it falls on the ground and breaks but remains floating in the air. Krasznai said that the floating glass parts were even more challenging to work out than the stage set: they had to figure out what kinds of metaphors and images they want to create through this. They considered many ways of rendering them, with different kinds of glasses. They finally decided to represent the glass in two different ways, one at the beginning, the other at the end. In the beginning, there is an actual (plastic) glass that Vizi drops; the Narrator is standing below him, holding out a bucket, and the glass usually falls inside it. (Vizi has his head turned so that he cannot aim precisely.) At the end, there is no physical glass; all the characters are holding imaginary glasses in the air, and when Vizi releases his, a shattering sound can be heard—created by keyboards—but all the characters gaze out at the glass as if it were floating.

As Krasznai explains, the ensemble wants the audience to consider the questions: do we believe in miracles, or do we not? Is there a miracle or not? Or perhaps is there a miracle at some moments or not at others? According to Krasznai, the text of *Frontátvonulás* suggests that we might believe in miracles that fly in the face of reality, or else understand the miracle itself as reality, freeing us of all laws, including physical laws, so that everything is questionable and malleable.[18]

The SICC version of *Frontátvonulás* brings the problems of Vizi and Ecsédi right into our midst; not only do we sympathize with Ecsédi as he goes looking for his friend, or with Vizi as he starts a new life, but we watch with familiar horror as everyone around them goes to seed, and the only one with a sense of "initiative" plans to take his own life. None of this is alien to us; in fact, we may know the themes all too well but find little room to bring them up. To Krasznai, *Frontátvonulás* is the work of great creators and relevant to all eras and stages of life: it brings up questions of solitude, lostness, the will to act, the inability to do so, the condition of being surrounded by negative suggestions, and, most important of all to them, a friendship that overcomes everything. For Fülöp, some of the familiar themes have to do with a desire to find a path: deciding to do something with your life after looking at it and realizing you have accomplished nothing; or in Ecsédi's case, wanting nothing other than to find his friend. Both of these, according to Fülöp, are noble desires; both are recognizable.[19]

In way after way, *Frontátvonulás* plays with the question of repetition, enticing us into the same. We lovers of *Frontátvonulás* come to see the play again and again, thrilling in it just as Vizi and Ecsédi thrill in their locomotive ride. We become them, in other words, but we are also left with their unease. What do we lose when we repeat an activity over and over? What do we lose when we give it up? Vizi sees his life going to waste; Ecsédi, hearing that Vizi wants to end the routine, reacts with dismay; why end something that has been good? Both of these attitudes respond to a deeper question about the imagination. Does our imagination die when we create or hear the same stories over and over? Or does it come to life each time?

Or is the act of imagination itself reality? *Frontátvonulás* does not give an answer, but when watching SICC's *Frontátvonulás*, even for the fifteenth time and beyond, I know that this short stretch of time holds an infinity. Krasznai himself speaks of how the work keeps changing in meaning for him. Even while he is busy handling technical matters in the back of the room, a certain phrase might strike him in a new way.[20]

If we define *routine* as a repeated action that may or may not have meaning, *ritual* as a repeated action with meaning, and *rite* as sacred ritual, we can see that Frontátvonulás plays with all three and rises, over the course of the story, to the level of rite. *Frontátvonulás* itself is the floating glass: through the play, we live out the kind of imagination that breaks barriers. It is also a ritual, and ultimately a rite, of loss and letting go: Ecsédi losing Vizi, Vizi letting go of his former life (or trying), we ourselves leaving the play behind. Throughout the play, the loss is delayed and suspended; at the end, it becomes ours. But because rites are meant to be repeated, the words "It's over, get it?" suggest their opposite: by leaving now, we can return later. The dark auditorium makes way for our lives, and our lives for the next show. To come back to it, we must let it go; anything that matters must be let go in some way.

Nothing can bring back the astonishment that Cseh's audiences must have felt when they saw him perform *Frontátvonulás*, enacting every character, singing all the songs, with nothing but a guitar for an instrument and a glass for a prop. But the work has continued in new forms, bringing new astonishment. Who knows what versions of *Frontátvonulás* may lie ahead, how many hundreds of times it may be performed still, how many thousands of people it may reach. Or how it might come back to mind all of a sudden: a raspy voice, a wisp of a song turning into more and more.

For all its absurdity, *Frontátvonulás* grapples with essentials. It shows a microcosm filled with apathy, decadence, surveillance, and despair; breaking its rules, two young men set out on separate, urgent quests that ultimately bring them back together (briefly). Everything burns with newness; everything has been played out hundreds, thousands, of times. It is silly and urgent, mundane and astonishing. Where is our place in this mixture? We yearn to find it, we discover it in the play (a melody, a gesture, a moment), and once that is over, we seek it again in the world.

CHAPTER 6

Jóslat ("Prophecy"):
Looking Forward by Looking Back

Is Cseh and Bereményi's *Jóslat* ("Prophecy") a failure or a treasure? I argue for the latter; but to tackle the question, one must distinguish between the stage version and the album, both of which appeared in 1984. The stage version is one of their strangest works, the album one of their most beautiful; taken together, the strangeness and beauty become part of the same phenomenon. But should they be taken together?

In none of Cseh and Bereményi's other works do the stage and album versions differ as widely as here: the former largely absurd and frenetic (at least on the surface), the latter dreamy and gentle. Both versions surprised those who had expected this work to follow upon *Frontátvonulás* in some way—yet if *Frontátvonulás* hinted at a break in their collaboration, *Jóslat* took it as fact. Both the stage show and the album look forward by looking back; the songs (written between 1970 and 1981) span the years of Cseh and Bereményi's collaboration before the latter announced that he would write no more lyrics. The story itself is structured as a retrospective that turns into prophecy.

In the stage version of *Jóslat*, a citizen named Désiré wakes up disoriented, having slept in his coat and dreamed two songs, and sees a woman in his apartment, who is leaving for work at that very moment. He thinks she might be his wife; upon encountering an older woman cooking eggs in the kitchen, he tries to ask her about the younger one, but instead of replying, she reminds him about his appointment with Antoine that morning, at the Blaha Lujza Square metro stop. (Most of the story takes place in metro stations and on metro trains.)

Antoine and Désiré meet up; before Désiré arrives, Antoine realizes that he is receiving "metacommunicative signs"; "I know something," he thinks,

"I just don't know what." (This brings to mind Vizi's similar realization in *Frontátvonulás*.) A little later, upon discovering that he can affect people with his eyes; he works himself up into performative frenzy (difficult to translate, but literally, "Have an effect, have an effect, my eyes!" and more expressively, "Go to it, go to it, eyes of mine!"). He has such an effect on a young news vendor that the latter tosses away one newspaper after another, triggering a mass scramble for free copies. The newspaper vendor throws himself at Antoine's feet and asks him to be his leader. At this point Désiré arrives. (From Désiré's waking to his meeting with Antoine, four more songs have been sung.)

Désiré discovers that when he stares into Antoine's eyes, two drawbridges appear; he takes the one into Antoine's right eye and finds himself back in childhood. Then he takes the other one, into his old age—but the story picks up from there; we barely get a glimpse of what he saw.

Now they hit upon their game: beginning in the current year of the story, 1974 (one decade before the premiere), Désiré will prophesy forward, year by year. Antoine commands each prophesy, and Désiré responds with a song. While this is happening, they run into various personages: the teenage news-vendor, who later in the story becomes rich and takes on the moniker the "King of Körút" (körút means "boulevard); one of their former teachers, who attempts to tell them what is what; numerous passengers getting on and off the train, sometimes recognizing and calling out to each other; and in the end, a little girl, the "person of the future," whose words quote from a poem by Sándor Petőfi.[1] Just before the end, when the "King of Körút" asks Antoine to prophesy about 1985 (the future for everyone at the time of the premiere), Antoine goes blind and sings "Pridem," a mysterious song about mistakes and false measures. The little girl, whose mother is in the hospital, goes home and hums one of their songs to herself: "A vidéki rokon" "Country Relative"), which now has a different meaning from before.

What can we make of a strange tale like this—and of its complete absence from the *Jóslat* album? At the time of its premiere and record release in 1984, *Jóslat* puzzled some of its listeners while enthralling others. The previous performance and album, *Frontátvonulás*, had struck many as a masterpiece and promised an even greater artistic breakthrough ahead. Some critics, attending *Jóslat* or listening to the album, were stunned by the songs. The journalist Attila Michnai recalls: "I don't know how many times, but it's certain that I heard it many times, since whenever I drove Tamás to his performances of this show out in the provinces, I listened to the full performance. And it's a miracle, because not for a second could I get bored, even after the umpteenth show; I always discovered more and more wonders in a song or a string of songs."[2]

Not everyone was entranced. Grácia Kerényi wrote that the character Désiré of this production was "more passive and primitive" than the Ecsédi of *Frontátvonulás* and nothing like the Désiré of yore. Of the text itself—that is, the narrated story around the songs—she wrote that those familiar with Cseh and Bereményi's work may find that "this prose, with its ramblings, witticisms, flights of fancy, and self-repetition, seems more routine drudgery than inspired work." The writer, poet, songwriter, and translator Péter Fábri bewailed the absence of some of the better songs from the performance (although, as he noted, some of these had been listed on the poster for the opening night). He went on to call *Jóslat* "the songwriting pair's saddest work yet."[3]

I hear the *Jóslat* stage performance as elegiac prophecy filled with wit and play. For all its madcap activity and surreal events, it leads to a quiet catharsis. Looking forward by looking back, the work's prophecy, crowned by the final song, "Pridem," involves recollection, anger, sorrow, and purgation; the girl at the end grasps with simplicity what is important. To hear what *Jóslat* holds, one must take it on its own terms: not as a fulfillment of the promises of *Frontátvonulás*, but as a gesture toward peace in a frenetic world.

Readers of this essay can watch the video of the final stage performance of *Jóslat,* read the text—available in Bereményi's 1993 volume *Kelet-nyugati pályaudvar* ("Keleti-Nyugati Station")—and listen to the album. These are not identical; the album seems remote from the text and performance versions, which are close to each other. However, the poster for the opening night (at the József Katona Theatre on March 15, 1984) suggests a show similar to the album: according to the poster, eight of the songs included that night are also on the album (but we cannot assume that the song listing on the poster matched that of the actual show).[4]

Subsequent shows closely matched the text of *Jóslat* as it appears in Bereményi's *Kelet-nyugati pályaudvar*—and shared only four of the songs with the album. Not a single song on the album mentions either of the main characters, Antoine or Désiré, nor does the album include the narrated text or any hints of the overarching story. Their later album *Jóslat a metrón*

("Prophecy on the Metro"), released in 2003, includes much of the text of the original *Jóslat* show, but with certain changes and updates; in addition, most of the songs are different. Thus there is more than one *Jóslat* to consider.

This essay will first consider the stage version of *Jóslat*, in which Cseh performs solo; then the *Jóslat* album, on which Cseh is accompanied by a number of musicians. The lyrics are all by Bereményi except "Az égboltsapkájú" ("The One in the Sky Cap"), for which both Bereményi and the poet Sándor Weöres are credited.[5]

Like *Frontátvonulás* but with greater frenzy, *Jóslat* combines absurdity and meaning, magic and mundanity: Antoine commanding his own eyes to have an effect, commanding Désiré to prophesy year by year; the many passengers entering and exiting the subway car, again and again; the subway car doors opening and closing, opening and closing; and the hallucinatory transformations—Désiré traveling into each of Antoine's eyes, the vendor becoming a millionaire, Désiré becoming a clock. Yet the tension of this strange hyperactivity finds release at the end, in Antoine's blind "Pridem" and the girl's humming of "A vidéki rokon" ("Country Relative"). "Pridem" is *anagnorisis*, confession, and warning: Antoine recognizes that he has gone too far, forced too much. The Petőfi-allusive girl, in contrast, affirms that Antoine and Désiré's efforts are being carried on, that the songs matter. We have no idea how she learned the melody of "Egy vidéki rokon," since the song appeared in Désiré's dream, not in the lucid part of the story (if there is one). Perhaps the whole story is the girl's dream, or Désiré's. Or perhaps songs have a special way of traveling.

In Désiré's prophecies, commanded by Antoine, each year (and each song associated with it) comes with a theme; as a whole, this could be seen as a satire on societal trends and passions, or as a kaleidoscopic view of Désiré's personal life. Several songs precede the prophecy section; not every year has a song. All of the songs were actually written between 1970 and 1981 but do not appear in the order of their release. Thus 1974 is "the very worst year" (with "A hetvennégyes év," which appears on the album as well); 1975, the year of revolution (with "Soltész baba," which appears on the 2003 album *Jóslat a metrón*); 1976, the year of making money (with "Hajdútánc," which appears on the 1987 album *Utóirat*, or "Postscript"); 1977, the year of the family (with "Biblia," which appears on the *Jóslat* album); 1978, prophesied by the newspaper vendor, the year of passions;

1979, the year of knighthood; 1980, apparently a year of lostness (with "Hát a régi úton tovább," which appears on no album, only in a recording of the last *Jóslat* performance); 1981, the year of knowing more than others; then a few years are skipped, and Antoine and Désiré sing a recap of "Jóslat"— which Cseh now chants in a speaking voice, his voice rising to a shout. As mentioned before, 1985 (the true future in relation to the time of the performance debut and album release) becomes the year of blindness, with Antoine singing "Pridem" (which appears on *Utóirat*).

Let us consider the songs "A vidéki rokon," "Jóslat," and "Pridem" (the first two of which appear on the album as well). "A vidéki rokon" and "Jóslat" represent two dreams that Désiré had at the very beginning of the story. "A vidéki rokon" has a lively foot-tappable syncopated beat, an infernal landscape, and an anxious mood. Cseh sings it reflectively and confessionally, with a smile here and there, inhabiting the voices as he goes along, as though recalling a painful memory; my translation (which takes slight liberties) is as follows:

I wish someone else would wake up in my empty bedroom,
and that sideways hail would smash what I just witnessed,
the taste's in my mouth, some kind of taste, it won't go away,
I sit up in bed, take off my coat, toss it away.

In a town, if my memory's right, I lost my reason,
three men in a kitchen grabbed me, became my prison,
I had wings, they flapped free, the ceiling they found,
I beat this way and that, and down to the ground.

And down there the three of them called: don't be meek now.
You've got it wrong, weren't we thinking where you should sleep now?
A feather fell out of my wings and somewhere outside
a car drove silently by with a relative of mine.

This was the one I thought I could depend on,
the very same one who left me undefended,
He buzzed away in the car, a pillow-soft night,
but he's the one I'd have told the source of my fright.

In a town, if my memory's right, I lost my reason,
three men in a kitchen grabbed me, became my prison,
I was freezing, the one who seized me had fingers of fire,
And far away I could hear a road-ripping tire.

Lie down in bed, you look tired, be careful Laci,
you don't have to choose bed so promptly, promptly, promptly.
Sleep now, what's the matter, it's already dark,
What are you shouting, what, what, what, what, what, my poor lark?

What car, what kindred, what road, what's all this you say?
I knew it would finally, I knew, I knew, I knew,
I knew it would turn out this way.
Careful, he's jumping up, hold the kid down.
What do you want to eat, what, what, come now,
explain, a tiny, tiny, tiny *tójáslepény?*[*]

Later let's have a drink when the scare's behind us.
You want me to give you a kiss? I was so frightened.
We cut it off there, but where?
Laci, tomorrow we'll go, go, go, go buy tickets at the square.

In a town, if my memory's right, I lost my reason,
three men in a kitchen grabbed me, became my prison,
A feather fell out of my wings and somewhere outside
a car went silently by with a kindred of mine.

The song moves from melody into mania; its delirium and fever evoke childhood illnesses, when the world swirled around us in a room. At the end it picks up its former melody and rhythm, recapitulating some of the earlier lines. What is this song? Who is the country relative? Is this the tale of a nightmare, or of life? Whatever the answers, the song has to do with utter alienation, where the kindred, the one who might have understood or

---

[*] A *tójáslepény* is a Hungarian breakfast dish or appetizer, similar to an omelet or frittata. It is typically folded over and filled with meat and vegetables. I kept the word in the original because none of the translations conveys it properly; also, it lends itself well to rhyme.

helped, simply passes silently into the night (or is carried away). Yet the ending of *Jóslat* transforms the song; the girl, returning home alone, with no one there to greet her, reflects on meeting Antoine and Désiré and continues thinking about them in bed. "Who is this Antoine and this Désiré?" she asks herself. "They sang, that's the important thing, that they sang." Then she hums, "A feather fell out of my wings and somewhere outside / a car went silently by with a kindred of mine." The story ends with her falling asleep. A strange poignancy mixes with the ironies. For the girl, the "kindred" in the song could be her mother or the song itself; in any case, the lines seem to offer comfort, not terror. The girl does what we all do to some degree: she finds herself in a song, brings new meaning to it, and carries it into her sleep and life.

The second song of Désiré's dream in the story—the title song—appears as the first on the album. It contains two obvious oddities: first, it states that the year is 76 (whereas we learn shortly later that it is 1974); second, it refers to a woman named Irén, presumably Irén Vetró, who does not appear elsewhere in this album. An "Irén" is the addressee of the letters in *Levél nővéremnek*. Here, Irén seems to come from nowhere or from a foggy past, yet the song itself sounds fresh, nearly awake, with an incantatory melodic pattern, and a percussion beat that Cseh beats on the body of the guitar. (In fact, this song was originally part of their *Levél nővéremnek* show, as early as 1976; in that context, the speaker is likely telling himself to write all of this to Irén, his sister.)[6] As usual, my translation takes some liberties:

> Seventy or sixty
> now seven and sixty.
> A faceless year this.
> Go tell Irene this.
> Write, tell Irene this:
> the years of the eighties
> cap-wearing, fading,
> Write, tell Irene this.
> Ten are their places,
> slow are their paces,
> caps they are wearing
> shaded their faring,
> caps pulled downward,

all the ten faces'
foreheads are covered,
ten noses covered,
all ten mouths covered,
ten standing covered,
eyes fully covered,
caps ten in number,
sticks ten in number,
beating a clearing,
not with their clubbing,
just with their swinging,
stumbling and tripping,
knocked by the sticking,
Tell her the latest,
years of the eighties,
Write her the latest,
years of the eighties.
Nothing they rave at,
nothing they gaze at,
nothing alarms them,
hide here, my darling.
Ten sticks are hiding
inside my eyelids,
beating the land out,
see what I am now.
Beating the land out,
ten sticks that stand out,
here is the new noise,
here is the new noise.
White sticks approaching,
pelting the roadway.
Tell Irene numbers,
gang with ten members,
Tell Irene one thing:
I'm scared of nothing.

The last line then repeats, with small variations, until the end.

The song conveys an era in which people look into the void but beat out a new rhythm, a new path, with ten white sticks (*tíz fehér bottal*), and the speaker is afraid of nothing (*semmit sem félek*). The song's poetry is especially interesting, with repetitions and changes orchestrated so that despite the repeating rhythm, phrases, and melodic line, the language is continually new. The music, too, though nothing more than a repeated chant and beat, evokes both an archaic past (when poetry was recited in this way) and a bare, unknown future. Kerényi points out that the repeated "I'm scared of nothing" at the end (which in Hungarian is unambiguous—literally, "I don't fear anything"), contrasts with the Désiré of several albums ago, who was frightened of all sorts of things.[7] The song could be heard as uplifting or terrifying: uplifting because of its suggestion of newness and fearlessness, terrifying because this fearlessness may come from oblivion.

As for "Pridem," the last words and song of Antoine in the stage performance, this song was released on vinyl only later, on their 1987 album *Utóirat* ("Postscript") but holds part of the key to the *Jóslat* story. In the final stage performance (and probably in earlier performances), Cseh sang it with his eyes almost closed. *Pridem* is Latin for "before" or "earlier"; the full title of the song on *Utóirat* is "Pridem XVI századi énekekből" ("Pridem from Sixteenth-Century Songs"). The word *pridem* occurs in a number of Hungarian folk songs, such as "Megholt feleségem," in which half of each line is in Hungarian, the other half in Latin, and the first two lines have the end-rhymes *quidem* and *pridem*. The style is somewhat reminiscent of Hungarian *virágénekek* ("flower songs," that is, love songs) of the sixteenth and seventeenth centuries.[8] Yet there is no way to pinpoint "Pridem," with its rumbling guitar, chanted confession, archaic language, syntactic fragmentation, and cry of *hajahajhaj*. I offer the following imperfect translation, keeping the word "pridem" as it is:

I shout to you,
poor catches,
thirsty fishermen,
running hunters.
Your herd is cursed,
in duty and drought
it brings no profit
to deaf Hungarians.

This is the rumble,
I shout to you.
Bottomless sacks,
big wise falsities.
Haj, hajahajahaja. Pridem,
I have gone blind.
In every broken home
I was a wrecker.
It was and is not,
this was my shouting,
leave it and take it,
and I didn't hear.
My idol-worshipping
fighting noblemen,
full of false vows,
evil enemies.
So many false measures
so many false measures,
so many false measures,
so many false measures,
hajahajhaj. Pridem,
I have gone blind.

After the song, the mood changes abruptly. Désiré splits in two, and when the hands of the clock come together, he becomes whole again. He asks King for another beer and repeats the process: breaking in two, becoming whole. This continues, faster and faster. Antoine shouts out the count, the teacher gives grades to the mannequins, the mayhem continues, and at this point the girl arrives and asks everyone to quiet down, since her mother is sick. From here the story moves into the ending. Even within this mayhem, "Pridem" is not easy to forget. It sounds like the true prophecy of the album, or one of them, for prophets speak not only of what will happen, but of what already has and no one has dared to see. Antoine's accusations turn outward, then bend inward toward himself, the homewrecker, the one who has gone blind and perhaps was blind long ago (hence "pridem").

There are thus at least three prophets in the stage version of *Jóslat:* Désiré (who does most of the prophesying), Antoine (who delivers the final and most devastating prophesy), and the girl (who hints at what this all might mean). Each of them prophesies for different reasons and in a different way: Désiré unwillingly, upon command, Antoine in a burst of remorse or confession, and the girl by way of recollection. To a lesser extent, the news vendor and teacher prophesy as well.

Prophecy abounds, prophecy is song—but prophesy does not lull itself to sleep, except in the case of the girl. The repeated chant in "Pridem" of "so many false measures" feels like a tolling bell. The "false measures" here apply not only to society, not only to the political system, but to the distortions in the mind and heart. Hidden inside the silliness and strangeness of *Jóslat* is a warning: We may all be blind; we may all have gone blind long ago; our pursuits may be leaving us poor. Beyond this, "Pridem" seems a response to the aforementioned "Désiré megnémul" ("Désiré Goes Silent") of the *Antoine and Désiré* album. Désiré goes silent, Antoine goes blind—so not only do they end up as equals, but they have both faced something that cannot be described in terms of the senses. "Pridem" could be a kind of apology that never gets spoken, that has to cover its mouth and eyes.

Criticisms of *Jóslat* remain valid: the narrative is both hectic and repetitive, much of the text taken up with such activities as people entering and exiting the metro car over and over again, or a character repeating a word or phrase. But even such repetitions have more to them than may appear. In each of the songs mentioned here, repetitions take the form of a chant or refrain (and, in two cases, a reprise); the spoken repetitions take part somehow in the larger, more mysterious incantation. *Jóslat* hints at personal loss—of what kind, we cannot know exactly—and a dim, mitigated, but nonetheless hopeful reminder, in the thoughts of the little girl, that "they sang, that's the important thing, they sang."

This comforting conclusion mixes with questions and ironies. The girl has seemingly forgotten about her ill mother, for whose sake she asked the revelers to quiet down. We have no idea how she ended up hearing the song that she hums, or when she might have heard Antoine and Désiré singing together. The song she hums has a more disturbing meaning than she seems to realize; if it were applied to her, the "country relative" here could be her mother, who is not simply ignoring her but going to the hospital.

It is also unclear whether we have seen a prophecy or a retrospective, and whether the two have something to do with each other. Everything seems to tilt toward prophecy. First of all, as mentioned before, the title song is sparse and filled with momentum, suggesting a clearing of the past, a forward movement. Second, even though all but one of the years of prophecy occur in the past in relation to the audience's frame of reference, they nonetheless move forward and ultimately cross into the future. Third, as in many ancient and Biblical tropes of prophecy, the prophet sees when he goes blind. Prophecy here is not a prediction of the future but rather a startling insight into—and release of—what has happened until now.

In that sense, the album may have more in common with the stage performance than appearances suggest. Haunting and dreamy (with only a few livelier numbers), and featuring an array of instruments and sounds, the album takes the listener from the title song all the way to "A furulyás ember" ("The Flute-playing Man," or, more precisely, "The Recorder-playing Man"), whose flute-playing—in words— takes up most of the song. "*Csak fújja, fújja, meg fújja*" ("He just blows, blows, and blows"), Cseh sings over and over, with growing intensity verging on rage, until the very end, when he sings, "*És én elmegyek újra*" ("And I leave again"). If "Pridem" has to do with going blind, then "A furulyás ember" hints at a break with words. Both in the stage performance and on the album, song and music outlast most other things: historical eras, human vanities, prophecies themselves. Both versions of *Jóslat* end with a departure: the girl's departure from the crowd and into sleep, and the speaker's departure from the album.

For the sake of adventure, let's see what happens if we interpret the *album* as the girl's dream, after she has returned home from her encounter with Antoine and Désiré. There is no justification for this, except that listeners are at liberty to experiment. Suppose she dreams that she encounters Antoine and Désiré again and that they sing the album's songs for her. She hears the beat of a drum and draws near; she finds Désiré singing "Jóslat" and is entranced.

She then sinks back into the sweetness of "Glong-glong-glong," which I imagine Antoine and Désiré singing about sitting down together under the trees until noonday softens. The nonsense syllables "*Glong-glong-glong-glong-glong, hej!*" convey pure and temporary freedom. The song also harbors sadness; according to Bereményi, it was written when he had already reached an understanding with Cseh that he would write no more songs. For Cseh, the song evoked a time when he, Másik, and Bereményi sat under a walnut tree together, in Kővágóörs (a village in Veszprém County) and "there was a lot of wine on the table."[9]

Suppose, furthermore, that this girl was born in 1974 (which would make her ten years old in the frame of the *Jóslat* story). The next song, "A 74-es év" ("The Year '74") would then pertain directly to her, just as Vizi's "Jó év volt" ("It Was a Good Year") in *Frontátvonulás* tells of the year of his birth. This girl, we can imagine, has seen her share of misery, so the song's words, cast in a waltz-like, nostalgic lilt, would come to her as no surprise ("The year '74, / '74 is a cursed year, / the worst of the worst of years, / I hope there will be no more like this"). I see the girl nodding along, even smiling, as the string instruments soar. Then comes the ironically titled "A legjobb viccek" ("The Best Jokes"), in which the speaker is at the table with his family, whose members shout the "best jokes" in his ear, until he finally exclaims, *Ismerem* ("I know [this joke]"), which astonishes the family, and which he has been repeating ever since. The song ends memorably with a stream of repeated *ismerem* and *ismerem ezt* ("I know this"), and finally, "and at last I dare to say that / I recognized these long ago, I know, I know this!" I imagine the girl singing along with glee.

Then comes the dreamy "Gyerekkorom" ("My Childhood"), one of the most haunting songs of the album, with Péter Gallai playing moog and piano along with Cseh's guitar and various other accompanying instruments. The singer describes his childhood as hiding in a hole under a rock; he asks it to come out. The song is musically intricate yet soft-spoken, with a vocal pause before each instance of *gyerekkorom* after the first occurrence. The middle section, with its more robust rhythm, feels like the first stirrings toward awakening, or like childhood coming out from under the rock; then, with a fading sound effect, it drifts back into sleep.

The next song, the boisterous boogie-woogie "Biblia" ("Bible"), one of the most popular songs in the Cseh-Bereményi repertoire, plays with the notion of marrying the Virgin Mary and raising Jesus "our redeemer" together. The song describes idyllic family life that abruptly changes when the Redeemer is taken away—but the narrator and the Virgin Mary go back in the house and set themselves to having another child. The political allusions—to dissidents and their fate—might be lost on the little girl as she listens, but not the essential meaning; she knows what it means to have a family member taken away, as her mother is at the hospital.

The following song, "Az égboltsapkájú" ("The One in the Sky Cap"), which in places closely resembles Weöres's extraordinary poem "Az ég- sapkájú ember" ("The Man in the Sky Cap"), has a melody and texture reminiscent of Hungarian folk songs, with magnificent whistling by Cseh and harp-like strumming of the guitar. In the girl's dream, perhaps the Weöres poem and the song mix together—that is, perhaps the Weöres poem, which she might have heard, comes to her in the form of this song. Both the poem and the song have to do with outsiderness: a person who has been shouted at and told that he was born at the wrong time, who then sets out into the world with the sky as his cap, heading through alleyways and finally making his way to a meadow where he loses "the border of borders" (literally, "the border's border"); from here he can go anywhere, and no one knows him. Listening to the song, the girl might hear her solitude in it. (In an interview with Sándor Fodor, Bereményi said that he identified perfectly with the Weöres poem.)[10]

The next song, "Az első fénykép" ("The First Photograph") carries the solitude further. Rumbling and melancholic, it starts with someone looking through family photos: a photo of himself, with a glass of wine on the table; then a photo of his father, whose glass sparkles as he brings it to his mouth; then a picture, perhaps accidentally taken, of his mother filling a glass; then one of a meadow right after a storm; then one of a lively trip, maybe four years ago. Through the transformations of the song, these all become pictures of him: in the last verse he is the one in the first, second, and third pictures, but the meadow and the trip remain unchanged.

We then come to the achingly happy "Pécs," with free, languorous rhythm and long organ (moog) strains. The speaker tells of going to Pécs in a car and how maybe that was the good thing that happened in his life. Bereményi comments that he used to hitchhike to Pécs to see a woman, and once he got a ride all the way to her place, and that he does not ask for more than this.[11] One can sink into the atmosphere of the song and glean its meaning without understanding the words. In the girl's dream, this might have been a part of transition, a slow, almost timeless passage soon to be broken by time.

Let us move along a little more quickly now: I have already discussed "A vidéki rokon" ("Country Relative"). The following song, "Sohase láttam..." ("I have never seen...") is in a rousing blues style; the inspiration came when Bereményi was reading the book *Mi a jazz?* ("What Is Jazz?") and found, in the section on blues, the line "*Sohase láttam ilyen időt*" ("I have never seen such weather").[12] The song describes a time out of joint, where yellow has become green and green red, where it is raining and the ground is dry, where the body freezes and burns at once. Then the album drifts into an idyllic vision with "Fűszálszobám" ("My Grassblade Room"), in which the speaker imagines a blade of grass as its home. Perhaps the girl dreams that she is leaning on a blade of grass and that it starts to float in the air, holding her like a hammock, from which she can see endless grass, with light shining through and bringing out the many shades of green.

The album ends—and here I imagine the girl drifting out of sleep—with "A furulyás ember" ("The Flute-playing Man" or "The Recorder-playing Man"), in which the flutist plays on and on, through the lyrics, which, after the introductory lines, consist of "*csak fújja, fújja meg fújja*" ("He just blows, blows, and blows"), over and over, with different moods in each repetition, ranging all the way into something like triumph and rage, and finally, at the end, a bare "*És én elmegyek újra*" ("And I go away again") and celestial, dissonant organ sounds that suddenly die into silence. The song brings new meaning to the girl's words in the stage performance: "They sang, that's the important thing, that they sang." Here, too, the flutist blows on and on, but we sense that it takes everything he has; it requires resisting the world and living on with the instrument.

The girl, upon waking, tries to put her dream together, but there is no one to tell about it, and even if there were, she would not be able to explain it. It can only be told in these songs, so she goes through the day, humming them as they come back to mind. Some of them scare, some delight her; some seem as though they could be her own. She will carry them through her life.

By imagining the album as the girl's dream, we can bridge it with the stage performance in a way that seems curiously fitting. At the same time, I assume no one intended the album this way. The album likely resembled the premiere performance of *Jóslat*, but without the narration; subsequently, the stage performance was likely adjusted and different songs included. If this is so, then there is a unity to these versions after all: they came from an original source, in which "prophecy" has to do with looking back, a concept that is paradoxical only on the surface.

Prophecy—"speaking forth"—is not limited to predicting the future. Biblical prophets and the prophets of Greek mythology and literature told of the past and present as well; that is, they communicated a divine view, which ordinary humans were unable or unwilling to see. The prophecy of the stage performance of *Jóslat* works directly with time, moving forward year by year until it breaks through to the actual future. In contrast, the album seems mainly to have to do with the past: its idylls, terrors, and yearnings. Instead of divine, its message is human; its somnolent texture draws us into a deep alertness, an awareness of when we have been happiest, or most frightened, or pushed to the brink. Within this "we," each of us wanders to different memories and associations. To understand *Jóslat*—both the stage performance and the album—I must walk away from the crowd, even the crowd of my thoughts, go into a quiet room, and listen to them again, and then take them in my mind out to the meadow, where I lose the border of borders.

CHAPTER 7

"Lee van Cleef":
A Syllable That Turns Into the World

In the 1970s, images and legends of the Wild West swept across Hungary in new forms. Those who had grown up on the novels of James Fenimore Cooper (in translation) now had access to a plethora of Western films.[1] Many Hungarians not only absorbed but longed for these stories, whether on the page or on the screen; Hungary itself, in their eyes, had become something like a ruthless West, but with few heroes. Through evoking the West and playing "Indian," many sought to capture some kind of heroism and purity.

Since the beginning of the eighteenth century, the "outlaw" (*betyár*) has figured prominently in Hungarian lore. Peasant gangs—largely formed after Ferenc Rákóczi's War of Independence—lived in nature and robbed and killed passers-by. Some of the famous outlaws became the subject of stories, novels, biographies, songs, and films; within these, an "Eastern Western" or "goulash Western" genre came into being.[2] One example is György Szomjas's 1975 film *Talpuk alatt fütyül a szél* ("The Wind Is Whistling Under Their Feet"), which combines cowboy Western and Hungarian folk motifs. Cseh himself played music in several films belonging to this broad genre, including Miklós Jancsó's 1972 film *Még kér a nép* (English title: *Red Psalm*), about a peasant strike in the 1890s on the Hungarian plains. The song "Mindig csak végig" ("Always to the End"), which that Cseh and Bereményi wrote for this film, has traits in common with the song "Lee van Cleef," the subject of this chapter, particularly the repeated "hey hey hey."[3]

The American West offered an imaginative terrain for Cseh and Bereményi's songs. Cseh's dedication to the "Indian" lifestyle and their shared love of (U.S.) Western films and legends allowed them to use Western themes and images as allegories of their own place and time. The allegories were never direct or didactic but instead suggestive, open to interpretation.

In 2024, the Petőfi Literary Museum and the Cseh Tamás Archívum released *Western dalok*, an album of Cseh and Bereményi's Western songs, all of them performed by Cseh, with János Novák on mandolin in one of the songs.[4] Seven of these songs were previously unreleased; the others had been released before, but the versions included here are from remastered concert recordings and bootlegs, not studio recordings. The album includes, along with songs by Cseh and Bereményi, a Lakota prayer translated by Cseh, an Arapahu song, the folk song "Laredo" in Bereményi's translation, a song based on a poem by Edgar Lee Masters, and a cover of Jerry Lordan's "Apache." These songs—with their strumming, fingerpicking, whooping, and whistling—evoke the intimacy of Cseh's informal performances, among friends.

Of all the songs on the album, the most famous is "Lee van Cleef," which first appeared on their 1981 album *Műcsarnok* ("Art Gallery"). This song tells an elusive story of "Lee van Cleef" (the actor? One of the characters he played?) who goes through something like life, death, and resurrection, but with ironic twists and contemporary allusions. The song is known for its recurring *hej* ("hey"), which the song's Lee says in response to even the direst situations and which the narrator adopts as his own. Occurring both singly and in bundles (*hejhejhejhejhejhej*), it ranges in tone from amusing to angry to tragic to wistful—and differs markedly from the more melancholic "heys" of "Mindig csak végig" ("Always to the End") in Jancsó's *Red Psalm*.

Lee Van Cleef (1925–1989) was known primarily for his roles in spaghetti westerns, such as *The Good, the Bad, and the Ugly* (1966) and *Death Rides a Horse* (1967).[*] During World War II, he served in the U.S. Navy as a sonar technician. After his discharge in 1946, having taken an interest in acting, he began performing in off-Broadway stage productions. In 1952 he played his breakout film role in Stanley Kramer's *High Noon*; this was to be followed by scores of films over the following decades. He persisted despite overwhelming obstacles. In 1958 he broke his kneecap in a car crash; his doctors told him he would never ride a horse again, but he

---

[*] When referring to the actual actor, I capitalize the "Van" in his name, in accordance with the official spelling; when referring to the song character, I keep it in lowercase, in accordance with the song title and lyrics.

managed to resume his riding within six months. His manner, character, and appearance set him apart; to Sergio Leone, he resembled Vincent van Gogh, with "the same brand of hopelessness, the hint of genius, the same intense eyes, eagle-like nose and clear forehead."[5]

The song's verses and refrains have distinct musical modes: the verses are freer in their syllabification and melody (part spoken, part sung), the refrains more bound to the beat and tune (which sounds like a cross between a country song and a Soviet marching dirge). The guitar style varies accordingly: fingerpicking during the verses, and tight strumming in the choruses. On the album, other instruments can be heard as well, but these are inessential to the song, as Cseh performed it solo.

The song can be broken into three parts, each one with its verse and refrain (though the lyrics of the refrain change). In the first part, Lee is presented as a stoic hero who says "hey" no matter what happens (but gets shot and starts to die). In the second part, he gets dragged around behind a horse (and apparently dies, although this is ambiguous). In the third, a bunch of drunken men think they have spotted him, that he has become a photographer (but that can't be him, they think). At the end, they hear a horse approaching and think it must be Lee. Yet Lee remains elusive.

In translating the song, I took liberties for the sake of rhyme, rhythm, and certain nuances but tried otherwise to convey the meaning and details as precisely as possible. In the discussion that follows, I point out any major discrepancies between the translation and the original.

The first verse consists of four stanzas, audible in the song and visible on the page:

It's been four days that we haven't ate and
Lee van Cleef says nothing but: "Hey, heyheyhey, heyheyhey!"
Lee, he's that kind of guy.

When we crossed town and they shot at all of us,
he said nothing but: "Hey, heyheyhey, heyheyhey!"
Lee, he's that kind of guy.

In Oregon he was shot in the shoulder, fear flashed on his face,
but he just said:
Hey! Hey, hey, hey, hey!

Lee, he's that kind of guy.

Dying on a street corner, you still send four others into the fight:[6]
Hey! Hey, hey, hey, hey!
This only Lee could do.

So far, a reader can glean the following: the first two lines of each stanza are crowded with syllables, flexible in their timing (though they fit into the overall beat). The third line of each stanza comments on the previous two lines. The "heys" are all spoken by Lee van Cleef until the fourth stanza, when they seem to come from the narrator; even on the page, the varying punctuation and grouping gives the "heys" different tones. The verse portrays a stoic, inimitable Western hero getting killed by enemies. We don't know whether the song is referring to Lee van Cleef's own life, or to his combined roles, to his mystique, or to something else entirely.

The image of Lee with his back against the wall, dying, yet sending four others out, perplexes the listener. First of all, the image stands outside of the story line; it is as if several Lee van Cleef stories were merging here, as Lee should not be dying just yet. Second, what does it mean to send four others into the fight? The writer and blogger Bence Aradi observes:

This is an ambiguous line. It could mean that I send my four opponents to the afterlife in a hail of bullets, defeating them in a fair duel. However, it could also mean that I send four others forward into the hail of bullets instead of me, or even four of my comrades, while I remain behind. And since the work has four heroes in addition to the title character—the fan base, Barleycorn, Charley, Hombre and Dick—I would not completely rule out this interpretation either.[7]

If that last interpretation holds, then it could provide some insight into the role of Barleycorn, Charley, Hombre, and Dick, whom we will encounter shortly. Sending the four out does not necessarily imply cowardice; it could suggest foresight, as even on the brink of death, Lee sees that the fight has to be won.

In contrast with the verse, the refrain has measured syllables that align with the beat (the liberties in the translation do not distort the meaning):

We knew from afar that Lee'd soon be here,
it takes Lee Van Cleef to gallop that way,
Barleycorn, Charley, Hombre and Dick
and others join up and gaze the same way:
"Yeah, Lee Van Cleef, soon he'll be here.
It takes Lee Van Cleef to gallop that way.
Hey, hey, hey, it can only be Lee."

This refrain seems to go back in time to when Lee is still alive—or else to a timeless Lee Van Cleef, always galloping, always known by the sound of his horse, about to arrive any moment. We proceed to the second verse, in which it seems that Lee dies.

And one fine day we arrived, tied together,
in Fort Phil Carney[8], hey, heyheyhey, heyheyhey.
Lee was brought out front.

They struck his throat with the edge of their palms
and yelled in our faces, every one of them:
Hey, heyheyhey, heyheyhey. Look, look, Lee's leaving himself!

They had taken his pistol away, they dragged him behind
a horse with a rope, hey, heyheyhey, heyheyhey.
Lee left himself behind.

A curse on Phil Carney, that on that burning,
scorching day, hey, heyheyhey, heyheyhey,
Lee fell to the ground.

What I translated as "Lee's leaving himself" and "Lee left himself behind" (*"Lee hagyja magát"* and *"Lee hagyta magát"*) could also be translated as "Lee's giving up" and "Lee gave up"; "hagyni magát" can mean, idiomatically, "to let something happen to you." However, the more literal sense of "leaving yourself" seems richer here, as it can imply both giving up and dying.

The misspelling of Kearny in "Fort Phil Carney" is important to the whole—because it reflects a time in Hungary when access to foreign films was limited (though rapidly growing) and Hungarians picked up what they could. The misspelling of Kearny also adds to the song's mystery; even when a listener figures out the allusion to the place, it remains unclear whether it is supposed to evoke the place itself—Fort Phil Kearny, a U.S. army outpost in Wyoming and the site of the Fetterman Fight in 1866 and the Wagon Box Fight in 1867—or a range of Western films (such as George Sherman's 1951 film *Tomahawk*), or whether there is a specific film, with at least a scene at Fort Phil Kearny, in which Lee Van Cleef acted. A hunt for a specific reference will turn into a wild and aimless forage; the allusions evoke something more imaginary and more real than a particular role in a film.

In this second verse, even in the poem alone, without Cseh's performance, the tone of the "heys" has changed markedly. It is now spoken by the narrator three times and by the enemy once; it contains anger, dismay, violence. The refrain continues in this vein:

If you come from Carney, stay out of my way,
Lee Van Cleef stood there that scorched afternoon.
Barleycorn, Charley, Hombre and Dick,
If you came from Carney, they'd hunt you all down.
Carney's where Lee van Cleef ceased to be.
"Hey, hey, hey, tell me, where could Lee be?"

The translation "Carney's where Lee van Cleef ceased to be" gives *eltűnt* (literally "disappeared") a strong and specific interpretation. It would be more precise to say, "Carney's where Lee van Cleef disappeared." However, I like the identical rhyme of "be" and "be"; it suggests that Lee both is and is not.

One might wonder who Barleycorn is; there might be a vague allusion here to the English and Scottish folk song "John Barleycorn," or perhaps Robert Burns's 1782 version, which contains the stanza:[9]

And they hae taen his very heart's blood,
And drank it round and round;
And still the more and more they drank,
Their joy did more abound.

If the Burns poem is at all material here, then the allusion is ironic, for, while Burns suggests that Barleycorn attains immortality and glory through his death, Lee's ultimate "resurrection," suggested in the third and final verse, has tinges of humiliation, not only for Lee himself, but for those who know him.

Let us consider a few of the ambiguities in the song so far. We don't really know the attitude of Barleycorn, Charley, Hombre, and Dick; they seem to be Lee's devoted followers, yet they also view him from a distance, perhaps with some resentment. Moreover, we don't know whether Lee has died; it seems that he has, but he may have just disappeared; moreover, he may be eternally living, eternally dying. The third verse brings these paradoxes out.

We would drink far into the night, like ailing dogs,
just to get through a slushy winter, hey,
heyheyhey, heyheyhey, four ailing dogs.

We were hanging out on a street corner,
when Dick grabbed my arm and said,
"Hey, heyheyhey, heyheyhey. Look! Isn't that Lee?"

He's become a photographer, that's the word on the street.
We laughed when it came up: "Hey, heyheyhey, heyheyhey!
No way, that couldn't be Lee!"

We called after him, but he hurried away.
I never forgot that spiffy jacket of his.
Hey, heyheyhey, heyheyhey, it's all over now.

The phrase "*ennek vége van*" could mean "it's over" or, in certain contexts, "he's done for." Because of the way Bereményi uses the same phrase elsewhere, I opted for "it's all over now," which still carries the sense that it is over for Lee (and his world). At this point the song is clearly no longer about Western films, or Lee Van Cleef, or Fort Phil Kearny, but about something closer to home. Ákos Somos writes about it: "It spoke in and about an age when there were no such cursed heroes, because whoever wanted to be one was caught by the system, dragged through the city on horseback, and then either killed or turned into an obedient servant and informer. Gun heroes became photographers. But when that resounding western chorus comes in at the end, you feel like the gods are singing."[10] Here he refers to the final refrain of the song:

> His back to the wall, breathing his last,
> Lee Van Cleef was great at this feat.
> Barleycorn, Charley, Hombre and Dick,
> See how he stands alone on the street.
> They're waiting for Lee to come straightaway.
> "Dick, listen, isn't that Lee's horsebeat?
> Hey, hey, hey, that can only be Lee!"

Here I took liberties to convey not only the rhythm and rhymes, but the concurrence of different scenes: Lee standing on a street corner ("the street" in translation), and Lee heard on his horse in the distance. I created the neologism "horsebeat" to convey the sense of the original that "Lee's horse is pounding" and also to connect the "horsebeat" with a "heartbeat," thereby implying that Lee is still alive. Yet possibly Lee never comes; the sound of Lee's horse may be the sound of song and poetry.

The final verse and refrain suggest that this is not only a Western story, but also a story of socialist Hungary. Still, the song remains uncatchable, as does its hero in spirit; while Lee ultimately gets caught and killed, something of his essence makes itself felt even after his death, although the despair surrounding his death does not go away. The song's shifting time frames and perspectives, its ambiguity of life and death, and its rich nonsense syllables make this a song never to be figured out. Yet the "hey" itself is so elemental that it cuts through the mysteries, telling the listener that the song is somehow about us, even if we don't know exactly how. Perhaps there are Lee Van Cleefs among us: people who get dragged down for their excellence, who prevail but also perish. Perhaps we ourselves are gossips and onlookers, "ailing dogs" waiting for our Lee, the one who will save us even though we ruined him. If so, that message is not all. The poem and the song have a life that goes beyond us, a "heyheyhey" spoken by many voices, a syllable that turns into the world.

CHAPTER 8

"Váróterem" ("Waiting Room") and Its Film Rendition

In 1987, five years after Bereményi declared that he would write no more songs, he and Cseh released *Utóirat* ("Postscript"), a double album of songs they had composed between 1970 and 1982 but not included on any of the earlier albums. As far as they and anyone else knew, this was their last joint album, a farewell. The songs numbered among their favorites; the only reason for not releasing them earlier was that they did not fit any of the previous albums.[1] Many of them had been part of Cseh's stage shows. János Szász' 1988 film *Utóirat*, made while he was in college, casts nine of the songs from this album in cinematic form. (I recommend watching it on YouTube before reading further in this chapter.)[2]

"This album is sad and bitter," wrote the music critic Attila Kovács, "sometimes laughing itself to tears, sometimes sobbing into laughter." He goes on to describe "Életem utolsó gesztusa" ("The Last Gesture of My Life"): "The song bursts forth, the music bounces, and Tamás Cseh cheerfully sings that as the last gesture of his life, he will throw his hat into the Danube and then turn on the gas tap, thereby ruining the 'suicide statistics,' just as his parents did in their time."[3]

Such macabre exuberance makes way for the album's other moods, including melancholy: not the quasi-sorrow that we commonly associate with the word, but rather the kind that F. László Földényi describes in his treatise *A melankólia dicsérete* ("In Praise of Melancholy"), a melancholy from anywhere: "not only in unstrung, but in high-strung states; not only in sorrow or boredom, but in joy or ecstasy." It can "bring all kinds of things into relation that—in the eyes of the non-melancholic—have nothing to do with each other." It eludes definition: "if we name what it is, it is no longer that." It yearns, according to Földényi, for something beyond the present state of things, but does not have answers to its condition.[4]

Melancholy, understood in this way, fills Cseh and Bereményi's song "Váróterem" ("Waiting Room") and others and becomes the unstated subject of Szász' film. Just as on the album, melancholy mixes here with playfulness, morbidity, raunchiness, and boredom. That is, if we are trapped in a "waiting room" where nothing is happening, where nothing can happen, then the simple, subtle gestures are all we have. In a 1987 television interview, Cseh said that the songs suggest how to carry oneself in the world: they speak of everyday life, they are not calculating.[5] Szász' film departs from what Cseh saw as the "everyday" nature of these songs, bringing them into a kind of dream-realm, yet it is this very contrast of visions that gives the film its bold beauty.

Born in 1958 to Holocaust survivors, Szász worked from age 18 to 22 as a prop assistant at the Hungarian National Theatre; he later taught dramaturgy, then film directing at the Academy of Theatre and Film Arts. He was director of the American Repertory Theater Institute at Harvard University, as well as a faculty member there, from 2001 to 2003. His films—for instance, *Woyzeck* (1994), *Witman fiúk* ("The Witman Boys," 1998), *Opium: Egy elmebeteg nő naplója* ("Opium: Diary of a Madwoman," 2008), and *A nagy füzet* ("The Notebook," 2013)—have won numerous nominations and awards at international festivals and ceremonies. In 2023, according to his own account, he moved to Washington, DC in 2023 to escape the increasing harassment that he had been experiencing at home. In a recent interview he suggested that he would return in 2026, as he expected life in Hungary to change for the better.[6]

Utóirat (1988), initially a film for television and later released on DVD, places the main action in a mysterious waiting room in the remote countryside, yet the scenes morph from song to song, sometimes occurring outdoors, sometimes on a train. Nine songs, all but one drawn from the *Utóirat* album, come together in Szász' rendition: "Váróterem" ("Waiting Room"), "Ding-deng-dong," "Bányalég" ("Coal Mine Air"), "Benke és Pierre" ("Benke and Pierre"), "Egy képre gondolok, tudod" ("I'm Thinking of a Picture, You Know"), "Életem utolsó gesztusa" ("The Last Gesture of My Life"), "A 100. éjszaka" ("The Hundredth Night"), "Tépj rá a régi lányokra" ("Go After the Girls of Yore"), and "Kéne egy dal" ("A Song Is Needed").

The film begins with a jazz prelude played by piano and perhaps saxophone, then a car driving down a road in the countryside at dusk, stopping at the railroad gate that has been lowered for a passing train. The music fades; we see a boy; we hear a whistle. The train clatters by, unseen; the stationmaster lifts his lamp. Now an old man sitting inside the station comes into view; through the window, looking out from the inside, we see a long procession of people in long dark coats, carrying suitcases or rolling bicycles, as if leaving their homes for good. It is night now, indoors. A young seated woman lifts her eyes; a standing man in a top hat returns her glance. The waiting room is filled with people, each one quiet, self-enclosed, as though in a separate world, except for these flashes of eyes.

"Váróterem" ("Waiting Room") begins. The picture goes grainy at times, as though we were looking into the distant past. A fish appears (in a tank, it seems). Outdoors, someone drags an enormous suitcase or box on wheels. The door creaks. At last we see Cseh himself, sitting at a table, sitting, and smoking, joined by companions, one of whom brings beers for the other two. They talk pleasantly; they seem to be good friends. Around the waiting room, children sleep or half sleep; a woman applies mascara to her eyes; a teenager in a winter cap looks on with an arch, quizzical expression. A man seems to be speaking intimately to the woman we first saw earlier.

Then the song ends and fades into "Ding Deng Dong," where a man in hussar attire taps an intricate folk dance as five men and the boy, sometimes in silhouette, look on. The scene moves to a windowside, with Cseh singing alone; then he is on TV and "Bányalég" ("Coal Mine Air") begins—morbidly evocative of the Beatles' "Yellow Submarine"—with the stationmaster gawking at the blue, grainy image. Then "Benke és Pierre" takes place on a moving train car; the rain through the window carries into the snow and smoke of the next song, "Egy képre gondolok, tudod" ("I'm Thinking of a Picture, You Know") where Cseh is sitting outdoors, with the silent boy, in front of a fire.

Then footsteps clatter slowly on a bridge; a man waiting for Cseh's character behind a bridge truss greets him in a whisper, adjusts his (Cseh's character's) top hat, and joins him, dancing, as Cseh sings "Életem utolsó gesztusa" ("The Last Gesture of My Life"), to me the most startling song of the film in its cheery suicidality. Cseh and the man dance down the bridge, with the Mora Lisa band (made up of women) playing wind instruments behind them in a jaunty procession. He arrives home, hangs his hat on a peg, walks past a line of cooks into a bathroom where a naked woman stands in the bathtub, drapes a towel over her, proceeds into the next room, a classroom, where schoolgirls with Young Pioneer kerchiefs make solemn hand signals, then into a dining room where the trombonist of the band plays, lying on the table. Cseh goes back outside, followed again at first by the band, and heads through the smoky-misty air to the bridge, where he dances solo, receding into silhouette and smoke, his shadow falling all the way down the track. The lyrics (described at the beginning of the chapter) more than hint at suicide; the peppy rhythm gives them a sarcastic bite, and the "bom-bom-bom" refrain is so catchy (and easy) that you might end up singing along. Here is a translation of the song.

> This very evening, out on the bridge,
> *bom-bom-bom, bo-bo-bom-bom,*
> I'll throw my hat way over the ridge,
> *bo-bom-bom-bom, bo-bo-bom-bom,*
> That is, later I'll go home with no hat,
> *bo-bom-bom-bom, bo-bo-bom-bom,*
> my life's last gesture, let it be that,
> *bo-bom-bom-bom, bo-bo-bom-bom.*
>
> Once I'm home I'll turn on the gas…
> *bom-bom-bom, bo-bo-bom-bom.*
> "What are you doing?" If that's what they ask,
> *ba-ba-ba-ba-ba-bam, bo-bom-bom-bom,*
> to break it down, I'll put it this way,
> *bom-bom, bo-bo-bom-bom,*
> I'm blowing the suicide statistics away…
> *bam-bam-bam, bom-bom-bom-bom.*
>
> And since daycare has a claim on the kid,
> *bo-bom-bom-bom, bo-bo-bom-bom,*
> I'll lie down on his teeny-tiny bed,
> *bo-bo-bo-bo-bo-bom, bo-bo-bom-bom.*
> And there I'll remember Mom and Dad,
> *bo-bom-bom-bom, bo-bo-bom-bom,*
> who likewise made the suicide statistics bad,
> *bom-bom-bom-bom, bo-bo-bom-bom.*

And since—as we know well—gas smells rude,
bom-bom-bom, bo-bo-bom-bom,
And all the house stinks to heaven with food,
bom-bom-bom, bo-bo-bom-bom,
I'll inhale my lost love, oh what a buzz,
bom-bom, bo-bo-bom-bom,
and think about the bridge and how good it was,
bo-bom-bo-bom-bom, bo-bo-bo-bom.

'Cuz this very evening out on the bridge,
bom-bom-bom, bo-bo-bom-bom,
I'll take things out to a wonderful edge…
bo-bom-bom-bom, bo-bo-bom-bom.
I mean: I'll throw my hat in the stream,
bo-bom-bom-bom, bo-bo-bom-bom,
gestures like this were always my dream…

Pa-pa-ra-pa-pa-pa-pa-pa-pam,
hopp,
pa-pa-pa-pam-pi-pa-pa-pa-pam,
pi-pa-pa-pa-pam-pa-pa-pa-pam,
hupp,
tü-tü-pup-pap-pa-pam-pa-pa-pa-pam,
pa-pa-pa-pam-pa-pa-pa-pam…

The next song, "A 100. éjszaka" ("The Hundredth Night"), also known as "Amikor Désiré megérkezett Budapestre" ("When Désiré Arrived in Budapest"), appeared first under the latter title on *Antoine és Désiré*. The film shows people surreptitiously painting *VÁLTOZÁS* ("Change") in enormous letters on a wall; suspects perhaps getting arrested; mug shots, and what appear to be two police officers behind Cseh's character, as a film rolls and a bright light shines in the dark. He bicycles past the building, types on a mechanical typewriter, exchanges glances with women; near the end we see him still, not singing, his eyes filling with tears, before the last refrain, where he jumps off of a table, breaking a ceramic piece, and heads out into the street, followed by the police, then by a running crowd with a flag-bearer in the lead. At the end he walks back in the opposite direction with the boy, who carries the rolled-up flag, and ends up sitting next to a character played by Dénes Csengey. The lyrics begin, "Three people came to me / that night / my nose bone was broken / behind the museum // I need an ad on the wall of a house / maybe I'll get a better landlord / an ad, that's all I need / and I could bring Irén Vetró to Pest." The music alternates between a languorous tango, a country swing, and bluesy ragtime. The film proceeds to a rowdy dance scene for "Tépj rá a régi lányokra" ("Go After the Girls of Yore"), and then returns to the waiting room for the meditative, sad conclusion, "Kéne egy dal" ("A Song Is Needed") where the people in the waiting room and Cseh stand still as he sings and then fades out. The song ends, "See, here is a man who no longer sings, / well he knows: he has no home, his homeland does not call him. / And here is a song that cannot be hummed, / because it isn't songlike, isn't songlike."

This description only gives a fleeting sense of the film; many of its details appear in flashes, and many of its nuances are known only to a few. Yet it is enough that we can now return to the opening song, "Váróterem."

"Váróterem" tells, in a fragmentary manner, of memories of a "waiting room" where a couple is waiting together for their train to arrive. "They announced over the loudspeakers that our train is late," the song begins. "Train station, smell of oil, unpopulated waiting room. / Your head on my lap, you sleep with your face covered. / The neon light crackles, we wait for our connection." (For the time being, I will translate the lyrics more or less literally; an artistic translation will come later.)

The song ultimately highlights not this scene itself, but its persistence in the speaker's mind, even though it is made of nothing. This is one aspect of the song's melancholy: this "nothing" that will not go away. Another aspect is the physicality of this scene: the smell of oil, the empty train station, the announcement over the loudspeakers, the head on the lap. Anyone who has spent time in Hungary can picture this well; "waiting rooms" at train stations are often deserted places, with one or two people lingering late at night to catch a long-delayed train. This station can also be understood in existential terms: the people of this song are waiting for something to happen, some change, some connection, some departure. They wait not separately but intimately, their bodies touching, like a close couple or possibly family members.

"This midnight waiting room doesn't leave my mind. / You slept, I sat, that's how we waited for the connection. / There's nothing to this, but still it's on my mind a lot, / how we were stuck in a midnight train station." Here the waiting seems unnaturally long, and the darkness at its peak, yet the two people simply sleep and sit, two different ways of waiting. The narrator thinks back on it now; apparently the waiting is over, perhaps the relationship too, something has changed, but the waiting stands out in the memory.

"What sweet dreams did you have? I ask when you sit up. / No answer, you yawn, you stretch, you laugh at something. / I take off my coat, then put it on again, / I say something, and then once again you're asleep." Both of the characters alternate between actions or states: talking and silence, sleeping and waking, taking off the coat and putting it on. These repetitions convey sleepiness and a long stretch of time; they also stand out for their ordinariness, their apparent lack of anything special at all.

"This midnight waiting room doesn't leave my mind. / You slept, I sat, that's how we waited for the connection. / There's nothing to this, but still it's on my mind a lot, / how we waited for a distant connection." Here the partial repetition leads into a subtlety of the Hungarian language: in the second line of the stanza, "we waited for the connection" (*vártuk a csatlakozást*), but in the fourth, "we waited for a distant connection" (*vártunk egy távoli csatlakozásra*). The difference between *vártuk* and *vártunk*, the definite and indefinite past first singular plural forms of *vár*, "to wait," have to do with the difference between waiting for something specific (*the* connection) and something nonspecific (*a* connection). The song does not tell us whether a connection ever comes.

The final verse repeats. four times, "There's nothing to this, but still this alone is on my mind," (*nincs semmi ebben, mégis csak ez jár eszemben*), an intensification of the earlier "There's nothing to this, but still it's on my mind a lot." The waiting, whether hopeful or hopeless, has become the treasure of the song.

Musically, the song has a quiet, tender feel; in a three/four beat, in the key of A minor, and a melodic line that first climbs up and down, then descends, it is easily learned and sung. At Cseh evenings, even those who do not know the lyrics or have them on hand can join in for the last verse; thus an entire audience ends up singing together about something intangible that they know profoundly. It is as if we were all the waiting couple, one lying on the other's lap: so simple the singing, so memorable the "nothing," that we all join in.

The melancholy that comes through is not that of a lost love, or about times gone by, though this may seem so, but rather that of a moment in which nothing seems to happen at all, that does not even seem important, but that stands out among the rest. Or perhaps the melancholy of waiting itself.

Waiting has an inherent melancholy—in Földényi's sense of the word— because the thing we wait for is by definition absent and at least partly unknown. We wait with both hope and hopelessness: with hope because we think it will come (or we would not be waiting), but hopelessness because of this very state of waiting, of being confined to a place and a simple set of actions until this thing comes. We are caught between our immediate surroundings and something anticipated; as long as we wait, we can leave neither one. Waiting also borders on absurdity, since we never know for sure whether we are waiting for anything at all.

This waiting room can be understood as an era in which people sense something new around the corner, or at least long for something new—but to translate the song into a specific historical or political allegory would be a mistake. It could speak of many specific times, but it approaches something close to each of us, a state of mind where opposites almost come together: nothing and something, sleeping and waking, taking off a coat and putting it on, and a memory of someone's presence.

Szász clearly did not want the film to mirror the lyrics. Although there are people sleeping, and flickers of romance, we see, on the surface, nothing like the story of the song. Yet the film suits the song uncannily well, peering beyond the storyline (if it can be called that) into this waiting room itself. This waiting room of the film seems to hold many eras: perhaps wartime, time between wars, times of trauma, times of nothing happening at all, times of boredom, fear, friendship. At the center, or what seems like a center, Cseh sits with his cigarette and beer and two human companions.

To understand the film and its relation to the song, one must leave analytical approaches behind. The film works with the intuition, taking the viewer into the song's hidden layers. Everything seems to be happening (sleepily, languorously) in Cseh's midst as he sings and smokes—but perhaps all of these people come from different memories, different times and places; perhaps the speaker inhabits more than one of them. Time seems to have slowed down; everyone has arrived in this waiting room, but no one is going anywhere. Destinations, and therefore meanings, have been suspended, yet something persists: someone sinks into thought, someone greets a friend, someone looks up. Mihály Babits' words about Dezső Kosztolányi come to mind: "Life, in truth, is ungraspable."[7]

Let's see what happens when I translate the song not literally, but in a way that conveys the cadences. The word "csatlakozás" can mean "junction," "connection," and "joining"; it suggests both a train connection and a human connection. To convey this, I translated the pertinent phrases variously as "we wait for our transfer to come," "we waited to meet with the train," and "we waited for a distant connection to come." The combination of the three conveys the original sense. I took additional liberties as well, with the aim of rendering the original more sharply: for instance, I translated "*Nincs semmi ebben*" (literally, "There's nothing in this") as "A thing of nothing" (which evokes *Hamlet* and has a paradox to it). For this to work when sung, the word "thing" must receive the stress. Also, I translated "midnight waiting room" as "night-sunken waiting room" for the cadence and the vividness.

> The loudspeakers blared that our train was running behind.
> A station, an oil smell, a desolate waiting room.
> Your head on my lap, your face in your arms, you're sleeping,
> The neon light crackles, we wait for our transfer to come.
>
> The night-sunken waiting room doesn't depart from my mind.
> You slept and I sat as we waited to meet with the train.
> A thing of nothing, still it comes to me often,
> how we were stuck at a station deep in the night.
>
> What were your sweet dreams? I ask when you wake up and sit.
> No answer; you yawn and stretch, laughing at something within.
> I take off my coat, then drape it back over my shoulders,
> I start to speak up, but you've fallen asleep once again.
>
> The night-sunken waiting room doesn't depart from my mind.
> You slept and I sat as we waited to meet with the train.
> A thing of nothing, still it comes to me often,
> how we waited for a distant connection to come.

A thing of nothing, still my mind holds this one thing.
A thing of nothing, still my mind holds this one thing.
A thing of nothing, still my mind holds this one thing.
A thing of nothing, still my mind holds this one thing.

The melancholy lies in the paradox: that this memory is both present and insubstantial, both meaningless and intimate. Inflate it or throw it away—two great temptations—and it is destroyed. Such memory is not sacred, but its proper rendition requires a secular sort of observance: an ability to hold its dimensions and dimensionlessness, to see both at the same time. The waiting room expands into the whole of our lives and collapses in our palms.

The director Péter Pál Tóth writes about the film: "It's night inside, there's waiting and suffocation. We are *among each other*, there 'from within,' but filled with the *insolubilities* of our lives, pitying the ignoble agony of power on the brink of discredit."[8] What Tóth meant precisely by "power on the brink of discredit," I do not know—but the regime change was around the corner, and perhaps Szász, Tóth, and others sensed it. Perhaps the late train signals some kind of collapse or dysfunction. The songs themselves were written over a period of twelve years, from 1970 to 1982; their prophecy, all along, lies in their rendition of the reality that Cseh and Bereményi knew. "Váróterem," in essence, is reality: specific to a time and place, but also recognizable today.

We do not have to make superficial comparisons between the "waiting room" and the Covid era (for instance); the correspondences are more intuitive and enduring, stretching into the longer present. For instance, in our efforts to rank things in order of importance, we often go wrong, because it is those things almost without meaning that surge up in our minds without warning: a thread hanging from a button, a touch of the hand, the sound of footsteps, a few minutes by someone's side. How do you lift those moments up without making more of them than they are? How do you avoid sentimental kitsch while allowing for sentiment? Moreover, how do you remember the right things, and how do you know what they are? Is it that someone was sleeping on your lap, or that you were in a waiting room at midnight, or that you were waiting and waiting for your connection? Or is it the very act of remembering—a flash of something now gone—that becomes the center of the story, the "nothing" held in the mind?

CHAPTER 9

"Keresztben jégeső" ("Sideways Hail"): A Transformation of an Earlier Song

What do you do when you look in the mirror and see a lamb—or maybe a ship? When you don't recognize yourself and cannot convey the strangeness to anyone, even yourself? On the surface, "Keresztben jégeső" ("Sideways Hail") reflects the mood of Hungary's capitalist era, just as its earlier version, "A vidéki rokon" ("Country Relative"), reflects that of its socialist era, with imaginative transformations. But this rumbling song unrolls into solitude and friendship, humor and pain, and things that baffle the soul. The song is most easily reached through the intuition; still, I will try to elucidate it a little.[1]

"Keresztben jégeső"—first released in 2004 on the live album *Az igazi levél nővéremnek* ("The True Letter to My Sister") has long been a standard at Cseh events and gatherings. János Másik contributed to the composition of the music and performed it with Cseh on the album. Miklós H. Vecsei includes it in his song-play *Füst a szemében* ("Smoke in His Eyes"); Cseh's son, András, includes it in his Cseh sing-alongs; and Cseh himself performed it at his final concert, with Másik, on Bakáts Square on August 26, 2006, when he had already been diagnosed with cancer.

Both songs—"A vidéki rokon" and "Keresztben jégeső"—have the same melody, rhythm, and texture: stormy and syncopated, in D minor. The lyrics of both songs describe an infernal world; moreover, they have a verse in common, heard at the beginning of "A vidéki rokon" and the end of "Keresztben jégeső":

> *Kívánom másnak, hogy felébredjen üres szobámban,*
> *keresztben jégeső bombázza szét azt, amit láttam,*
> *számban az íz, valami íz és nem múlik el,*
> *ágyamban felülve levetem a kabátomat.*

Translated, with liberties:

I wish someone else would wake up in my empty bedroom,
and that sideways hail would smash what I just witnessed,
the taste's in my mouth, some kind of taste, it won't go away,
I sit up in bed, take off my coat, toss it away.

A literal translation reads, "I wish for someone else that he would wake up in my empty room, / and for sideways hail to blast to bits what I have seen, / the taste's in my mouth, some kind of taste and it won't go away, / sitting up in bed I take off my coat." There is something particularly resonant about the third line, "the taste's in my mouth, some kind of taste and it won't go away"—as if speaking of any time when the whole world does not sit right with us, when we are out of sorts not just with the surroundings, but with something larger.

The earlier song, "A vidéki rokon," describes a nightmare where the speaker is seized by two men and tries to escape, flapping away with his wings. During this time, a "country relative" passes by in a car. The song is peppered with chaotic dialogue between the two ad-hoc prison-guards, who try to calm their prisoner down, offer him a *tojáslepény* (similar to an omelet), and discuss buying tickets. The overall feeling is of confinement, isolation, and terror (as well as dark comedy). The "country relative," the one person the speaker could have talked to, is out of reach.

This song may allude to the kind of surveillance, prevalent in the Kádár era, where those who incurred even slight suspicion could be subjected to prolonged investigation and interrogation. Bereményi himself had such an experience with the police when, as a high school student, he traveled alone to Lake Balaton and participated in a prohibited activity: collecting glass bottles from a restaurant patio and selling them in Veszprém. Although he was ultimately cleared of charges (on the grounds that he had been coaxed into doing this and that his school principal spoke well of him), he had to spend many hours at the police station and—if his principal had not stood up for him—might have been expelled from school. Such incidents were not uncommon; young people frequently were arrested at Balaton, even for dancing. Cseh himself was banned from Almádi (a resort town by Lake Balaton) in 1962 for doing the "twist" and playing music to it.[2]

With "Keresztben jégeső," in contrast, the nightmare takes place not in confinement, but in the open world: the protagonist runs out of the room and into the street, in an unbuttoned coat, only to find no one who understands what he has lived or seen. The only hint of friendship is found in transactions: paying for a cognac, doing acrobatics on command. The dialogue is messy, whirling, and wild: the speaker looks in the mirror and is unsure whether he sees a lamb or a ship.

Let us look at the song stanza by stanza. In this case I will translate it literally to let the sense of the words come through as clearly as possible.

> One evening at dusk, before everything falls apart,
> And all objects are stripped of their outlines,
> It's good weeks later to leave the empty room,
> A single bang, let's go to the city, rotten world!

The vision is bitter and almost apocalyptic: we know from the start that leaving the confinement of the room and going to the city will bring no comfort, or if it brings any at all, this will soon come to an end.

> Whoever's crying after me, he can see me on the street in an open coat,
> He might be afraid of me, the way I'm running with my coat open,
> If he stands in my way, I'll keep at it, let's keep going!
> I'll get hold of the night, even if I am destroyed!

The problem with this newfound freedom (or the first of several problems) is that the person running out into the world has been through something that others cannot understand, something that makes him behave strangely; bent on encountering the night, he will risk destruction for it. The people apprehending him are not police but rather those who profess to care.

> He who saw me, what does he know of me, so hidden was I,
> What was I thinking in my empty room all by myself?
> Now I will be cheerful, I will be cheerful, even then I will be cheerful,
> Someone will perish, maybe I'll be the one, but still I'll be cheerful!

Here the song seems to be as much about the previous isolation as about the entry into the world, as if the two were mirror images of each other. Was the speaker confined by others? By illness? By his own thoughts? In any case, the pursuit of open air and night seems desperate and doomed. He promises to himself to be cheerful, but the repetitions of the phrase suggest how much effort this will take.

> You're going in, so go in, into the night,
> There's no end to it, even if you know how it ends,
> Go ahead boy, this is how I bolster my coat,
> When after weeks in the empty room, it gets out,
> Go ahead boy, this is how I bolster my coat,
> When, after weeks in the empty room, it gets out.

At this point the song veers into the surreal, with the speaker addressing his own coat ("Go ahead boy"), underscoring his isolation and his weeks of confinement. It is also here that we realize that the song cannot be followed logically; a different approach is needed. With the verses that follow, the song leaves logic even farther behind. Now it breaks into dialogue:

> You're going in, into the darkness, it's night.
> I'm you're best friend, pay me, if you've got it!
> What a world, what I see there stings, stings, stings my eyes.
> Pay me, I'll buy you a cognac!
> It's been a long time since I saw you, do you still love me, because I love
>   you!
> Come on boy, I know you've got it in you, jump over me!

Making sense of this verse would only distort it; we can only receive its impressions: an encounter with an old friend, a greeting and friendship expressed through payments, a declaration of love, an invitation to do an acrobatic trick, and beyond all of this: a place of estrangement, delirium, and craving. From here the song becomes still more bewildering and vivid.

> I've been watching you for a while, you don't belong here!
> That's good, that's good, that's good,
> That's good, that's good, that's good, that's good, that's good!

Then comes the most opaque verse of the song:

What's in the mirror? Look over there, because I don't dare!
Some lamb, some lamb, if I'm not mistaken!
Too good, don't you think? Yes, too good.
Well, is it a ship or a lamb? Not a lamb.
No? A ship.

As far as I know, no one knows for sure what this verse means. In a poem that responds to the song, Gábor Losonci-Kovács writes (in the third stanza), "A lamb disguises itself / As a ship in a mirror, / Which Tamás Cseh / Sings as Bereményi's / Lyrics, // But I still / don't understand." In the next stanza, the poet picks up on the word play: *hajó* sounds the same as *ha jó* ("if it's good"): "But now I see: / Yes, this for the lamb / Is too good a ship, / If it's good, then it's a swimming lamb, / And now I look too, / If you don't dare, / Because time will not pass, / Until sideways hail / Blasts to bits / What I have seen."[3]

Perhaps the connection between the lamb and the ship is this: a lamb (a Christian symbol) suggests goodness and innocence; therefore the object in the mirror is a lamb if it is good ("ha jó"); therefore it is a ship ("hajó"), also indirectly a Christian symbol. But more to the point: these lines laugh and scream; the brain cannot even name what the eyes see.

Now the song heads toward both a recapitulation and a further fragmentation, like the hail blasting everything to bits:

You're going in, into the dark, it's night.
What's up, what's the matter? Up? Matter? Problem?
Up? Matter? Up? Matter? Problem?
Up? Matter? Problem?
I'm your best friend… if you've got one!
How bright it is, it's pushing my sight to the brink.
Pay me! I'll buy you a stiff dark drink.

This verse plays with the word "van" (roughly translatable as "is" but used in particular ways). The question "Mi van?" repeats multiple times. It can mean, "What's up?" "What's wrong?" or "What's going on?"; I translated it into "What's up, what's the matter?" and then the words "Up?

Matter? Problem?" to convey the fragmentation. The phrase "if you have one" is "ha van" in the original (which relates somehow to "hajó"). I took some liberties with the last two lines; the "stiff dark drink" is a cognac in the original ("egy konyakot"), which rhymes in the original with "mit látok ott" ("what I see").

We now head into the final verse, which is the same as the first verse of "A vidéki rokon" (I translate it literally here):

I wish for someone else that he would wake up in my empty room,
and for sideways hail to blast to bits what I have seen,
the taste's in my mouth, some kind of taste, it won't go away,
sitting up in bed I take off my coat.

This needs no explanation, except that now this final scene in the room seems to hold past, present, and future, as does the act of taking off the coat. The last two lines are typically sung three times; the final time, there is a long pause before *kabátomat* ("my coat"), after which the piano takes over for a vigorous final stretch.

The song has something to do with a world where the individual does not belong, where identities break down, and where relationships are based on money (and entertainment and escape). But having established this, let us leave it behind, because the song holds much more. When listening to it, we grasp it in part, but it also leaves us bewildered. We know its delirium, loneliness, and anger, can hear its conversations, can step into the darkness with it, can almost dare to look in that strange mirror where our own reflection might be a lamb, or possibly a ship. As the night goes on, words dissemble and disassemble; something so terrifying happens that we wish hail would come pounding in sideways and blast it to bits.

Now we can leave even this behind and take in the language of the music: the stormy beat with its syncopations, the contrast between the quieter first two lines and more explosive second two lines of each verse. It was this explosive but tuneful, foot-tapping quality that first drew me into the song: the rapturous rhythm and texture, the somber-playful mood. I have played the song (on cello, accompanying Sándor Sárkány) and felt the possibilities within the lines, the contrasts within and across the verses.

There is another essential difference between "A vidéki rokon" and "Keresztben jégeső": both songs were written by Cseh, Másik, and

Bereményi (Cseh and Másik wrote the music, and Bereményi the lyrics), but at the time when "A vidéki rokon" was released, Cseh and Másik were not speaking to each other. They had had a falling out and had no contact for about fifteen years. Then Bereményi suggested to Cseh that they write a continuation of their first album, *Levél nővéremnek*, and Cseh replied that this could only be done together with Másik. Bereményi spoke with Másik, who agreed to take part; the three of them sat down and began working on *Levél nővéremnek 2*, which was released in 1994 and consists entirely of previously unreleased songs.[4] From then on, the friendship between Cseh and Másik had no more interruptions.

With this in mind, one can understand "Keresztben jégeső" partly in terms of the relationship between the three of them: without tracing it directly to events in their lives, one gleans that it has something to do with a world where friends disappear and identity falls apart. The three of them had seen ruptures, not only among them, but in the lives of others: deaths, emigration, broken relationships, betrayals.

When I first heard the song, in the song-play *Füst a szemében* ("Smoke in His Eyes"), created and directed by Miklós H. Vecsei and performed by Vecsei, Balázs Szabó, and Huba Ratkóczi, what drew me in, besides the rhythm and mood, were the dialogue and final verse; despite the bitterness of the lyrics, which I only gleaned later, the actual performance of the song was full of friendship and repartee. In other words, the song has a layer even beyond its meanings, mysteries and music: the performance, the people performing it, the rapport between them (or, if it is performed solo, the rapport with the audience). There is also something special about the way each performer articulates the phrases; in this case, I loved "*Számban az íz, valami íz és nem múlik el*" ("the taste's in my mouth, some kind of taste, it won't go away").

People came to Cseh's concerts, or the concerts of Cseh and Másik, not only for the songs, albums, and shows themselves, but for the people who inhabited them, as we always do to some degree. Cseh's concerts were intimate, and the after-concerts even more so; those who attended imagined that they knew him, and a few actually did. His relationships with Bereményi, Másik, and others could be felt in the performances. People came in part for these relationships, even when Cseh performed entirely on his own.

In "Keresztben jégeső," as in Cseh and Bereményi's songs overall, the friendships are between men. Women enter the songs in many ways, but not as friends. The male friends sometimes approach the status of spouses: in the case of Antoine and Désiré, or Vizi and Ecsédi, they go on countless escapades and talk about all kinds of things except the friendship itself (except when it comes to a crisis). Somewhat like Cseh and Bereményi themselves, these pairs are both more and less than friends to each other. Within their game, the friendship is infinite and intimate: but the game can come to an end at any moment. "Keresztben jégeső" suggests a world where one can not even recognize oneself, let alone another; only terror and transaction remain. Yet the very performance of the song—itself an act of camaraderie—suggests that friendship has survived. In other words, the act of performance adds a layer to the song; this can be felt in the musical rapport between Cseh and Másik.

In this song I hear an allusion (perhaps unintended) to the folk song "Lesz még kedvem" ("I will be cheerful again"), which the nineteenth-century poet János Arany included in his personal folk song collection, and which laments a world that has lost its light and fragrance and has become *kétszínűvé* ("two colored").[5] Take, for instance, the third verse:

> *A szegénység ütött nálam tanyát,*
> *Kivel elmúlattam sok éjszakát,*
> *De a remény mindig jó barátom,*
> *Kifizeti minden adósságom.*

This can be translated roughly as follows:

> Poverty, my partner of many nights,
> Has set up a homestead in me,
> But hope is always my good friend,
> And will pay off all my debts.

"Keresztben jégeső," too, is filled with suffering and a kind of poverty—but while "Lesz még kedvem" resolves this suffering through hope, "Keresztben jégeső" can manage a grimace at best. In "Lesz még kedvem," payment is a kind of redemption; in "Keresztben jégeső," there is no redemption at all, except in the existence and performance of the song itself.

Perhaps that is part of its essence: that it conveys seemingly opposite realities, which come together in the ear. There is no grace, redemption, or meaning, except right there, in the act of performing for others, with others. We come together again and again to live out depictions of worlds that have come apart. This on its own does not make "Keresztben jégeső" unusual. What sets it apart from other songs is every element of it, taken together with the rest: the haunting words, the dark and thrilling music, the mirror held to us all. The abyss of "Keresztben jégeső" is one I tap my feet to and know all too well. This ragged-souled song takes me home.

Chapter 10

Opening the Jar:
Grácia Kerényi and the Cseh-Bereményi Opus

To some extent we can know musicians and songwriters by their ardent supporters. Fanhood has dignity; it is fans who share the artists' dedication and carry their legacy forward. Granted, fanhood can go wrong by tipping toward adulation, obsession, and greed—but it also blazes with life. Fans of the arts contribute more than they receive credit for; some are artists themselves, some write about the arts, some offer financial and logistical support, some create collections and archives, and many simply show up.

The writer and translator Grácia Kerényi (1925–1985) was not only a groundbreaker in her own right but an exceptional supporter and critic of Cseh and Bereményi's work, attending performance after performance, collecting recordings and memorabilia, writing lively and probing reviews, and even translating some of their songs for a Polish tour that she organized for Cseh and his fellow composer-musician István Márta. Through examining her life approximately a century since her birth, we can glean what drew her to these songs and what she gave them in turn.[1] In several ways, her work opened a jar.

Gifted, energetic, and dedicated, Kerényi had a prolific though somewhat obscure career: she translated numerous Polish writers, including Maria Dąbrowska, Wiktor Woroszylski, Adam Mickiewicz, Miron Białoszewski, Zbigniew Herbert, Tadeusz Różewicz, and Sławomir Mrożek, as well as ancient Greek writers; released volumes of her own poetry and prose; assisted Polish poets in translating Hungarian verse; supported protest movements, particularly Solidarność in Poland; and formed lasting collegial friendships. Her life trajectory—her studies of classical languages; her anti-Nazi protest at the age of eighteen, which landed her as a political prisoner in a Gestapo prison, then Auschwitz, then Ravensbrück; her dedication to literary and cultural translation; and her ardent Catholicism combined with unmentioned Jewish roots—suggests rich combinations that may have found something kindred in the cryptic, enchanting opus of Cseh and Bereményi.

Kerényi not only loved their work and Cseh's performances but contributed to them in remarkable ways. In her article on the 1979 premiere of *Frontátvonulás* ("Frontal Passage"), held on October 18 at the Castle Theatre in Budapest, she recalls that in the olden days, in the 1960s, well before meeting Bereményi, Cseh had already begun seeking lyrics other than his own; at one point, in 1966, he came upon Kerényi's translation of Konstanty Ildefons Gałczyński's 1946 poem "Dlaczego ogórek nie śpiewa?" ("Why Doesn't the Pickle Sing?"); according to Kerényi, this was the first time Cseh composed a song with lyrics that were not his own.[2] If the story is accurate, this must have marked a turning point for Cseh, opening him to the possibility of future collaboration. For Kerényi, this may have been more than a source of pride; it may have answered a yearning to bring people together through art.

Kerényi was born on September 9, 1925, in Budapest.[3] Her father, Károly Kerényi, was a renowned professor of classical philology; her mother, Erzsébet Stamberger, taught Latin and Greek at the Veres Pálné Secondary School, as well as three other secondary schools, over the course of her career. Stamberger's parents—Kerényi's maternal grandparents— were buried in the Rákoskeresztúr Jewish Cemetery of Budapest in 1914 and 1931; thus, by Jewish law as well as the Hungarian racial laws passed between 1938 and 1941, Kerényi would have been considered Jewish. However, Kerényi had a Catholic upbringing; neither her own writings nor others' biographical accounts mention her Jewish ancestry. In the late nineteenth and early twentieth centuries, it was common for bourgeois, non-Orthodox Jews in Budapest to assimilate, assuming an emphatically Hungarian identity; in the early twentieth century, many families and individuals concealed their Jewish origins for sheer survival. It appears that Kerényi's mother had taken this route, or some version of it; whether Kerényi even knew of her Jewish origins is unclear.[4]

Taking an early interest in classical languages and literatures, in 1943 Kerényi began her university studies in Hungarian, Latin, and Greek at the Pázmány Péter Catholic University. Outspoken and uncompromising, she was arrested in 1944 by the Gestapo for her anti-Nazi activities (among other things, she had written "Down with the Germans" with her finger on the fogged university windows) and sent to prison, then Auschwitz, and then Ravensbrück, before her release about a year later. Throughout her imprisonment, she was classified as a political prisoner; her own writings, which describe her experience and the camps themselves in revealing detail, refer compassionately to the Jews but do not hint that she could have been considered one of them.[5]

On November 7, 1943, possibly as a result of her father's multiple appeals on her behalf—from Switzerland, where he had emigrated several years earlier—Kerényi was released from Auschwitz, then, after a month of quarantine, transferred to Ravensbrück, where she stayed until April 1945. At the time of her transfer, one of the Gestapo police recognized her; he was one of the officers who had originally taken her to prison. He explained to the others that she was "the plump girl with short pigtails and pink bows who was always walking around in the prison courtyard with her golden-furred teddy bear."[6] (Her teddy bear was confiscated at the time of her transfer to Auschwitz.) Four months after her release from Ravensbrück, in August 1945, she finally returned home, emaciated and feverish. For months she had been dreaming of entering her home secretly, sneaking up behind her mother, covering her eyes, and saying, "Who am I?" But her sister—who met her on the street and accompanied her home—was so joyous that she shouted her name all along the way.[7]

While in the concentration camps, Kerényi began to learn Polish from her fellow prisoners. Despite illness, physical pain, and terrifying conditions, she made friends, shared information, and absorbed as much knowledge as possible. Upon returning home, she finished her studies in Hungarian, Latin, and Greek; her father wanted to make her an adjunct professor, but she chose instead to teach at a high school. Because Polish philology interested her more and more, she soon left her teaching position to work at the Library of the Hungarian Parliament, then as an intern at the Eötvös Loránd University. Her initial application for a passport to travel to Poland was unsuccessful, as the internal affairs officers deemed her a "class enemy" on account of her "petty-bourgeois-intellectual" status. Kerényi managed to continue her studies of Polish language and literature with the help of Polish associates in Hungary. Treated with increasing hostility by Hungarian officials, she focused on Polish literature, which she began translating into Hungarian; she translated from Latin and Greek as well, and from Hungarian into Polish. Unlike other young translators who took what assignments they were given, she selected her own projects.[8]

With the political situation improving slightly after the 1956 Revolution, she began visiting Poland frequently. In the 1960s she divided her time between Budapest and Warsaw. She translated and wrote prolifically in both Hungarian and Polish; her translations, poems, stories, essays, and scholarly articles appeared in both languages. Her activities in Poland were closely monitored by the Hungarian government; on several occasions she was summoned to the Ministry of the Interior for interrogation. Unable to secure employment, she began living off of her translations and an inheritance from her father, who had died in Switzerland. She began to associate with other Hungarian writers who had likewise been deemed enemies of the regime. While her own writings were rarely published by official presses, she released them through unofficial channels and in Poland. She became close to the poets Miron Bialoszewski and Wiktor Woroszylski, who often wrote about her; her friendship with Woroszylski was particularly intimate and lasted the rest of her life. She obtained her doctorate in Warsaw in 1968. In 1970 she received Poland's most prestigious cultural designation: "Worthy Creator of Polish Culture." Other international awards followed.[9]

During the 1970s, Kerényi, well acquainted with Cseh and Bereményi's music, organized a Polish tour for Cseh, for which she translated some of the songs into Polish. A poster advertises a concert held on March 16, 1975, featuring Cseh, István Márta, the actress Ewa Benesz (who read aloud Kerényi's translations of the songs) and Kerényi (the event organizer). Márta reminisced about this concert in a 2023 interview:

She organized a tour for the two of us, which seemed quite risky, since [Cseh] could not imagine that the Poles would understand his lyrical songs, which are typically aimed at Hungarian intellectuals. We were joined by a Polish actress who read the lyrics in Polish, in Grácia's translation, before each song. Tamás dazzled the Poles with his personal magic. It was an amazing success, the Poles experienced the performance profoundly, despite the fact that they could not grasp the meanings and metaphors between the lines of the songs. It may have been precisely apropos of this trip that the song "Krakkói vonat" ("Kraków Train") was born, which I even made into a short film.[10]

From the late 1970s to the end of her life she taught in the Polish department at the Eötvös Loránd University. Gizella Csisztay recalls: "Grácia's classes were very popular; as a graduate I too attended her literary translation seminars. We sat there in the midst of the Piarista, on the fourth floor, next to the unmissable Moscow cakes, and we could learn everything from her about Polish literature and culture—but not only about these. We also learned from her that it is worthwhile to be generous, because it is always a good investment."[11]

In the early 1980s Kerényi was active in Hungarian and Polish opposition movements, particularly Solidarność. She moved to Warsaw but made frequent trip to Szeged to receive money and documents to hand over to the organization. To avoid being stopped by border guards, she often traveled with go-cart racer and pilot Lajos Kizmann. She herself did not like to drive; in fact, she was afraid of technology in general. She had a Trabant car, which she never drove herself; her students usually drove her. In the autumn of 1984, on the way to the town of Máriapócs, the car in which she was riding swerved into a ditch; the others were unharmed, but she broke her spine.[12] She spent the rest of her life in a hospital, where she died in April 1985, at the age of fifty-nine. She had no children.

According to the poet György Gömöri, who knew her well, she had difficulties in her intimate life. She was briefly married, but men generally found her "too intellectual, bluestocking-ish." It was through her literary and political work that she found the richest connections with others. Gömöri writes that "Grácia was always in solidarity with the persecuted, the disowned, the oppressed; even at the end of her life, bedridden with a broken spine, she still signed the Hungarian letter protesting the cruel murder of Father Popiełuszko." (Jerzy Popiełuszko, a Polish catholic priest associated with Solidarność, was murdered in 1984 by three members of the Polish secret police, who kidnapped him, beat him to death, and tossed him in the Vistula Water Reservoir.) In addition, according to Gömöri, Kerényi did more to contribute to Hungarian and Polish culture than she took credit for; she assisted Polish poets in translating Hungarian poetry, often providing them with literal translations.[13]

Even from the above biographical sketch, one can glean some of Kerényi's apparent contradictions or combinations: political outspokenness and subtle aesthetic sense, unflappable courage and marked phobias (of driving, for instance); a highly public life combined with solitude and obscurity; a devotion to international (particularly Polish) culture and a sympathy for the oppressed, along with an emphatically Hungarian and Christian identity. Given her background, interests, and passions, it is no surprise that she was drawn to Cseh and Bereményi's songs and shows, which also have contradictions and paradoxes at their core, albeit different ones. A close look at a few of her articles can help us understand some of what she found in their work.

Her article on one of the premiere performances, by Cseh and János Másik, of *Levél nővéremnek* ("Letter to My Sister")—which she must have seen between February 1 and March 6, 1976—begins with a reflection on the beginning of Plato's *Phaedrus*, where Socrates, walking through a grove with Phaedrus, observes the tall plane-tree, the plants, and the stream, and judges that this must be a sacred spot to Aphelous and the Nymphs. Phaedrus marvels that Socrates does not know the place; to which Socrates replies that he is a lover of knowledge, and it is the men in the city, not the trees, who have something to teach him. They then proceed to converse about the kind of friendship that is free of lust.[14]

Kerényi frames her concert review with this story; according to her description, the main character of this *Levél nővéremnek* stage show (which differs somewhat from the album version), broken into two personae, lives by his compulsions; "with his egocentrism, his street fragments, where the people are his people and the rain his rain," he enters an espresso bar, sits down, and writes a letter to his sister (whom Kerényi does not name). According to Kerényi, this man, "no longer an attractive swindler, not yet a repulsive villain, not quite tragic and not quite grotesque ... drifts between ready-made thought patterns and rests on emotional anchors." Yet there is something sympathetic about him; at the end, she says, "and for this we love him after all, and we wish him the kind of lust-free friendship that Socrates spoke with Phaedrus about on the banks of the Ilisus river.[15]

In beginning and ending with the *Phaedrus*, Kerényi situates this music in a larger canon and points out a hidden theme within it: loneliness, fragmentation, selfishness, pursuit of momentary desires. She begins her description with a quotation from a song that seems to be lost altogether (and which influenced her interpretation of the whole): "Az emberek, akik voltak nekem" ("The people I used to have"), which begins, "This street is closed, rain falls upon it, people stand on the closed street and gaze, who are they? And who closed that street? I, I myself. Enclosed people who I used to have." She specifies that Másik sings these words of Bereményi, by way of prologue, at the beginning of the show. (This song was already absent from the March 26, 1976, show at the R Klub.)[16]

Kerényi's observations and perceptions—besides mentioning a song that has since vanished—bring something out of the show that must have been present and that few others would have been able to express so keenly: in her view, the show depicts a city where people live for quick satisfaction and where love, or life purpose, can only be distantly apprehended. With her reference to *Phaedrus* (which she simplifies and sweetens somewhat, sidestepping the discussion of love between a man and a boy), she brings out a secret ache that she senses in this work of Cseh, Bereményi, and Másik, perhaps similar to her own.

As mentioned earlier, in her review of the *Frontátvonulás* premiere, Kerényi mentions that, thirteen years earlier, presumably in 1966, Cseh came upon her translation of Gałczyński's poem "Dlaczego ogórek nie śpiewa" ("Why Doesn't the Pickle Sing?"); this serves as the starting point of her description of Cseh's trajectory. In those days, according to Kerényi, he still sang only for his friends; he had not yet performed on stage. She apparently was present at some of these gatherings, for she described them: "In those days he sang in the company of friends, and only when the mood hit him; one couldn't quite say good spirits, as a good-humored or cheerful temperament was still remote from him."[17] In the article, she presents this as a point of origin in order to trace the path to *Frontátvonulás*, describing all of the earlier shows along the way.

Kerényi's personal knowledge of Cseh and Bereményi sometimes affected her interpretations of the music (for better or worse). When describing the *Frontátvonulás* premiere, she quotes the character Vizi's words, "My God, if only I could sing to people." She interprets this as an expression of Bereményi's own unrealized musical longing, which he self-ironically put into words for Cseh to perform, because Bereményi, she explains, was tone-deaf, could not keep a tune; yet, on the other hand, as a literary master, capable of surrealistic floating, he was perfectly suited to the task of enabling Cseh to sing.[18] While Kerényi may have read too much biography into Vizi's words, she perceived that Cseh and Bereményi's work was born not only of their individual artistic gifts, but of their relationship, and that it contains many hidden references and somber jokes.

Her attendance at numerous performances allowed her to perceive the overall development of their work: in this same article, she describes the arc. Where Cseh's debut performance (in 1973—but she gives 1974 as the date) consisted of a collection of songs, *Levél nővéremnek* frames the songs within a (sung) letter, whose fragments ultimately make a whole. *Désiré és Antoine* takes a step further by introducing spoken text; yet the stories are episodic, not tied together into a larger movement or plot. It is *Fehér babák takarodója* ("White Dolls' Curfew") that takes the next (in her view, imperfect) experimental step that would then lead to *Frontátvonulás*.[19] Although highly critical of aspects of *Fehér babák takarodója*, she ultimately forgives it because of where it leads.

Besides describing the progression of Cseh and Bereményi's work, Kerényi was able to highlight some of its most important and poignant moments. She ends her article on *Frontátvonulás* by quoting the song "Születtem Magyarországon" ("I was born in Hungary") in its entirety. This song—which had also been part of their *Désiré és Antoine* show—is sung here by the character of the eighty-seven-year-old man, who has some hidden wisdom to impart (that Vizi, impatient to leave, has no room for). By ending her article on this note (the song ends, "How will these survivors fare? / Something is taking a bad turn. / I'd like to ask, in a hundred years, / who here will speak Hungarian?") she brings out the subtle urgencies of Cseh and Bereményi's work: its grappling, at some level, with survival, not to be taken for granted, and its ultimate Hungarian identity, which nonetheless makes ample room for allusions to U.S. American, French, Russian, and other literatures and cultures.

Thus Kerényi's reviews of Cseh and Bereményi's performances draw on her knowledge of ancient and modern literature and offer uncommon insight. They reveal her avid devotion to Cseh and Bereményi's work; at one point in the *Frontátvonulás* review, she writes, "Let us set aside the knowledge that we bring with us, and let us sit in the audience as if our drawers at home were not filled with Cseh tapes, cassettes, and albums, as if we had come in off the street just to watch a performance, a solo stage performance. What is going on here?"[20] We can assume that her drawers, and those of many other audience members, were filled with "Cseh tapes, cassettes, and albums"; that she not only attended and wrote about these performances, but adored them, even at their weaker moments.

While I have known nothing like what Kerényi lived through, and am not inclined toward overt political protest, I find a kindred spirit in her: in our love of languages, both ancient and modern; our devotion to translation; our joy in bringing cultures together through events; our unabashed enthusiasm for favorite songwriters and musicians (Cseh and Beremènyi included); our combination of playful and serious language; and our solitude—never mind our mixed ancestry, Jewish and non-Jewish, which may have affected us in similar ways. For this reason I can imagine what it might have been like to be Kerényi in the audience, to take in those songs again and again, and to try to convey their brilliance to others.

I also sense a loneliness: Kerényi, who was married only briefly, seems to have pursued her work with emotional as well as intellectual intensity. While many appreciated her, especially in Poland, she probably had times when she could speak to no one or when her work went unrecognized. She probably had difficult sides as well. (Who doesn't?) According to Márta, she eagerly mothered Cseh, writing to his wife about how thin he looked or about how he should wear a scarf in the cold.[21] Yet instead of giving in to sorrow or self-pity, she led a lively, empathetic, and thoughtful life.

When considering whether to bring up her Jewish background here, I considered the following questions: Would she have wanted this to be revealed? Is it important in general? Is it important to this discussion? To the first question I have no answers, but if asked whether I would want something to be revealed after my death that could clarify something about my own and others' lives, I would say yes, if it were presented in the spirit of enlargement rather than reduction. In any case, her family origins were at one point public: her maternal grandmother's obituary, published on April 30, 1931, in the *Pesti Hírlap* ("Pest Newspaper"), mentions Kerényi, her sister, and her mother among the survivors.[22] Indeed, this is important: one's background accounts for a dimension of who one is: not the whole, but a depth of it. Her Jewish roots take nothing away from her; they only contribute. As to the third question, I believe that Kerényi's story relates in some way to Cseh and Beremènyi's music: set in Hungary, expressed in Hungarian, and filled with Hungarian soul, but also tinged with Rimbaud, Shakespeare, the Wild West, ancient folk song, and more, and thrillingly expansive within their brevity. Moreover, Cseh and Beremènyi both sought their origins in a way: Cseh through his spiritual identification with Native Americans, Beremènyi through his connection with his Italian ancestry (the

Vetró surname crops up here and there in the songs and texts). Beyond all of this, the *titok* ("secret") plays an essential role in their work.

Perhaps each of us yearns for translation into the secret language of who we actually are; perhaps a kind of music speaks to this yearning. If Kerényi ever read John Donne's "Meditation XVII," famous for its declaration that "no man is an island," she may well have been drawn to this passage: "when one man dies, one chapter is not torn out of the book, but translated into a better language; and every chapter must be so translated; God employs several translators; some pieces are translated by age, some by sickness, some by war, some by justice; but God's hand is in every translation, and his hand shall bind up all our scattered leaves again, for that library where every book shall lie open to one another...."[23]

In music and song, we find ourselves translated, not statically, but in time; as a concert plays itself out, we unconsciously live out our own passing, which turns us into something we were not before. To take part in a concert that one loves—whether as performer or audience member—is to have our "scattered leaves" gathered up. Those shut off from this—who have no audience and nothing to listen to—live without knowing who they might be and become. From what I understand, Kerényi sought to break through such isolation—her own and that of others—and to both seek and resist completion.

It seems fitting to end here with my English translation of Kerényi's Hungarian translation of Gałczyński's poem. When translating the translation, I also consulted the original text, lest I drift too far astray—yet it was Kerényi's translation that illuminated the poem for me.[24] Gałczyński was a complex, contradictory figure and gifted versemaker; this particular poem, while supremely silly, hints at something far more serious than its apparent theme. It seems a telling prelude to the songs of Cseh and Bereményi. With her translation, Kerényi opened a jar.

Why Doesn't the Pickle Sing?

This question, which the title
shoves boldly beneath our eyes,
calls out for a solution,
whatever pain might arise.

For if the pickle has never
made a musical attempt,
perhaps it's the will of heaven:
the poor thing obviously can't.

But if he wished! Oh swell!
More sparkling than a star!
If late at night he'd spill
green tears inside his jar!

Winters and summers pass,
here sunshine, there grey sky,
and we indifferently
pass many a pickle by.

Chapter 11

Cseh and Bereményi's Influence Today
(What Is "Influence"?)

When musicians, actors, and other artists name Cseh and Bereményi among their most important influences, they take part not in a trend, but the opposite; anyone who listens closely to Cseh and Bereményi's work will respond to it uniquely. Some artists are drawn to its emotional depth, some to its lyrical ingenuity, some to its musical idiosyncrasy, some to its play with musical genres, some to its encoded political and social commentary, some to its candor, some to its understatedness, some to aspects difficult to name. Sometimes people are attracted to the work for opposite reasons; "their" Cseh and Bereményi might look nothing like another's. Yet all these listeners are brought together by a sense that there is more to the songs than may appear at a given time—and that, to this day, no one writes songs like these.[*]

Influence is elusive; we don't always know what influences us (or what this means in the first place). Sometimes our strongest influences are not the ones that we recognize. Let us define artistic influence as a lasting effect: something that changes our conception of what art can be, or that grows in importance for us over time. Or more simply: something that moves us, excites our imagination, and becomes part of us.

Those who knew Cseh personally associate him with specific experiences and concerts. Cseh had a remarkable gift for performance and a charismatic personality; these qualities, along with late-night songs and conversations,

---

[*] This chapter draws on written sources (newspaper articles, interviews, etc.), recorded talks (particularly those held at *Helyzetjelentések*, the Tamás Cseh exhibition at the Petőfi Literary Museum) in 2023 and 2024, and direct correspondence and conversation. I attended several of the Petőfi Literary Museum talks cited in this chapter and listened to their recordings later (on April 23, 2025) at the Cseh Tamás Archívum.

might play in the memory of those who met him even once. Those who never met him are more likely to focus on the songs themselves, particularly the album versions.

Today many Hungarian artists occupy a space between underground and officialdom; they perform in some of the most coveted and popular venues and may receive state funding, yet they take care to preserve their artistic freedom and resist encroachments on it. What they share is not a political view but a commitment to serious art as they know it.

In addition, many of these artists break taboos and conventions of some kind, whether gently or roughly. They avoid clichés; they steep themselves in literature, music, and film. They bring up difficult subjects; they require the audience's attention. They break barriers between "high" and "low" culture, bringing elements of both into their work. Most do not lead celebrity lifestyles, or anything close; they live and walk in the same world as their audiences. In all of this, the artists may find something kindred in the songs of Cseh and Bereményi.

I will begin by mentioning a few artists who knew Cseh during his lifetime; while this chapter focuses mainly on younger generations, one cannot approach the subject without first mentioning Bereményi himself, Gábor Hanák, László Bérczes, János Másik, János Novák, and István Márta. These mentions will be far briefer than the individuals deserve—and there are other important musicians and groups that I do not bring up here. This is just a glimpse into Cseh and Bereményi's legacy.

Bereményi, who largely avoided the spotlight during his collaboration with Cseh, not only takes the stage at events commemorating his and Cseh's work, but also supports younger artists who bring Cseh and Bereményi's work to new audiences. He has taken part in various performances of Miklós H. Vecsei's *Füst a szemében* ("Smoke in His Eyes"), SICC Production's *Frontátvonulás*, and other renditions of their opus—and has recently begun writing songs with Cseh's son, András. Behind the scenes, he encourages and speaks highly of these artists. In my own correspondence with Bereményi (over this book and associated articles), I have found him appreciative of my efforts and generous with his time.

When asked in interviews about his favorite songs that he and Cseh wrote, Bereményi often brings up "Csönded vagyok" ("I Am Your Silence"), a song that says much about both of them. One day, long ago, Bereményi received a letter from a couple whose seventeen-year-old son had died after a long illness. Their son had asked them to pass on to Bereményi a few lines he had written to him; now, half a year after his death, they decided they had an obligation to do so. Bereményi read the lines the boy had written: "*Most elmondom, mid vagyok, mid nem neked: vártál ha magadról szép éneket, dicsérő éneked én nem leszek, mi más is lehetnék, csak csönd neked.*" ("Now I will tell you what I am of yours, what I am not: if you were expecting a nice song about you, I will not be your song of praise; what else could I be, only silence to you.") He knew neither whether they were meant personally for him, nor what to do with them, so he sat down and continued them, turning them into a song. It took the form of a dialogue with the boy, where the boy begins, and at the end Bereményi says the boy's own words back to him.[1]

The song, which first appeared on Cseh and Bereményi's 1990 album *Új dalok* ("New Songs"), says much about what a younger person might find in their music. The song invites the person to sit in the lack of praise, where there is "no sign, no flame, just silence, which reaches the skies." The boy anticipating his own death might have found something kindred in Bereményi's reticence, his dislike of obsequious fans. He might have heard a silence throughout the songs, in the sense that Cseh and Bereményi kept their songs sparse and essential, without decoration, and not only did not pursue mainstream popularity, but rejected it. Beyond that, the song has to do with legacy: what is it that I can hand down to you before I die? What can I be to you after I am gone? The humble reply to this question conceals a greatness: to be someone's silence is to meet the part of them that the world does not know.

The historian and documentary director Gábor Hanák met Cseh in 1971, when the film director Miklós Jancsó was working on *Még kér a nép* (English title: *Red Psalm*), for which Cseh was the singer. Hanák and Ferenc Grunwalsky managed to make an illegal recording of Cseh's songs at the Magyar Radio studio. Hanák was making a television series at the time; he included a Cseh-Bereményi song in each episode. Their friendship persisted over the years; when Cseh was dying, he asked Hanák to take care of his legacy. This led Hanák to found the Cseh Tamás Archívum, which opened in 2014 and continues to this day; and later, in 2023, to release the *Cseh-Víg Album*, a triple album of Cseh and Bereményi's songs as performed by Cseh and Mihály Víg (separately). Hanák has also taken care to protect Cseh's legacy from kitsch and distortion, to the extent that he can. He has spoken of Cseh's way of conveying intense emotion without spilling into excess.[2]

The writer, actor, and director László Bérczes (1951–), first met Cseh when still a teacher at the Varga Katalin Gimnázium in Szolnok; after giving a concert in Szolnok, Cseh had nowhere to sleep, so Bérczes offered his place. The next day, Bérczes introduced Cseh to his students on a class excursion; Cseh played a few songs for them.[3] They became close friends; over the years, Bérczes, who had turned to theatre directing, arranged many concerts and theatrical performances for him over the years, directed the documentary of Cseh's final concert, and interviewed him for a "conversation book." In 2008, while Cseh was still alive, Bérczes and Mónika Kiss founded the Ördögkatlan Festival and named Cseh and the legendary actress Mari Töröcsik as the festival's patrons. In naming these patrons, they affirmed that they would never sacrifice quality for money and would never let the festival be influenced by politics.[4]

It would be difficult to pinpoint or summarize what Cseh's work means to Bérczes, but he would likely point to Cseh's songs, musicianship, and presence; his artistic integrity; his lack of concern for financial gain; his simple and generous lifestyle (he had a habit of giving away his guitars); and their years of working together and coming to know each other. He also knew Cseh as fully human and fallible: an inveterate smoker, even when ill; a man who loved his wife and family but traveled continually to perform.[5] When speaking of his conversation book, Bérczes has emphasized that he intended it not as an accurate account but rather as a genre of its own: moving freely through time and themes, conveying impressions and memories and two friends speaking with each other.

As for János Másik (1952–), a book could be written about his own musicianship and his work with Cseh: their early collaboration, their falling out, their later reunion, and everything that Másik has done to continue Cseh's legacy. A composer and multi-instrumentalist (bandoneon, piano, guitar, percussion), he has given a number of concerts in Cseh's memory, some of these with Bereményi (who reads excerpts from his autobiography, *Magyar Copperfield*). Másik is essential to Cseh and Bereményi's work in that he took part in the making of it: particularly *Levél nővéremnek* ("Letter to My Sister") and its later incarnations. He has also collaborated and toured with bands strongly influenced by Cseh and Bereményi, such as Balaton and Európa Kiadó.

Part of what makes Másik's role so interesting is that he, classically trained and proficient in a wide range of styles, perceived the ingenuity in Cseh and Bereményi's simple-seeming songs. This in turn speaks to the absence, in their music, of rigid divisions between formal and informal, classical and popular. Cseh and Bereményi's music takes part in a larger art where opposites converge and genres intertwine.

At the final event of *Helyzetjelentések – Cseh Tamás 80*, the exhibition at the Petőfi Literary Museum commemorating Cseh and Bereményi's songs, Másik spoke of how his jazz background allowed him to approach songs like "Lee van Cleef." He told of how, when he, Cseh, Bereményi, and others began working together, they would meet and play frequently, turning song fragments into songs. In this way, the songs of the first album, *Levél nővéremnek* ("Letter to My Sister"), were composed within approximately two weeks. (Twenty years later, it took them much longer to compose the sequel, *Levél nővéremnek 2*; Másik quipped that by then they had "grown up.") Commenting on what stands out in Cseh and Bereményi's music, Másik noted that, on the one hand, the phrases in the songs are sharply evocative, bringing up memories, emotions, and associations; on the other, they constitute a kind of musical theatre in themselves.[6]

János Novák (1952–), the cellist, composer, director, who contributed to several of the Cseh-Bereményi albums, has likewise helped to continue Cseh's legacy, participating in events and speaking of his memories of Cseh. In addition to working with Cseh and Bereményi on several of their albums, he also invited Cseh to perform and record his (Novák's) musical renditions of poems by the nineteenth-century poet Endre Ady. Released in 2004 on the Gryllus label, the album, in its exuberant variety of styles, hints at what Novák finds special in Cseh's musicianship. According to the Cseh Tamás Archívum, Cseh had told Novák that he had tried to play true rock, true tango, but that it didn't work and that instead he discovered pseudo-rock, pseudo-tango, which allude to the actual genres but are not identical to them. Novák believed that he and his fellow musicians were able to help Cseh develop these musical allusions and reworkings.[7]

Another important musical collaborator is the composer István Márta (1952–), founder of the festival Művészetek Völgye ("Valley of the Arts"), who, like Másik and Novák, worked intensively with Cseh and Bereményi in the early period and toured with Cseh several times. He finds it difficult to talk about Cseh, first of all, because many of the stories are not public, and second, because the key points are difficult to pinpoint. Even before working with Cseh and Bereményi, he admired Bereményi's talent as a writer. When László Gyurkó suggested that he and Novák accompany Cseh at his debut public concert at the 25th Theatre (Gábor Kecskeméti also joined on flute), Márta was apprehensive, since they came from such different musical worlds. But then he found that they were able to accompany him in a way that reflected the songs instead of interfering with them. To Márta, Cseh and Bereményi's songs broke the expectations of conservative audiences that did not regard this as music, while also differing from the politically explicit Beat artists. The songs had so many sides that, for instance, when Cseh performed in Romania on tour, the audiences' responses differed from those of Hungarian audiences. Márta also points to Cseh's ability to move audiences who did not understand a word of the songs.[8]

Let us now consider some of the musicians and writers whose lives intersected with Cseh's, who may have met and worked with him briefly, but who did not know him intimately. They have less to say about Cseh's stage charisma and offstage presence (although they, too, may be affected by them); their focus is primarily on the songs and albums. Again, I leave out many important figures and only briefly discuss the following three: Mihály Víg, János Háy, and Zoltán Beck.

The composer, musician, and actor Mihály Víg (1957–), one of the most dedicated bearers of Cseh and Bereményi's legacy, belongs to a somewhat younger generation and did not work directly with Cseh except on an album in memory of "Dixi" (János Gémes). Known for his musicianship in the bands Trabant and Balaton, and for his composition of sound tracks for numerous films, including Béla Tarr's eight-hour *Sátántangó*, in which he also plays the lead role of Irimiás, Víg plays Cseh's songs in venues large and small, departing markedly from Cseh's own renditions, but cutting to their essence with his melodic drawl and guitar or piano. As mentioned earlier, in 2023 he released a triple album of Cseh and Bereményi's songs, half of them performed by him in his renditions, and half by Cseh in previously unreleased recordings.

When I first heard Víg perform Cseh and Bereményi's songs, I was startled that his version of "Az ócska cipő" ("Shabby Shoes") lacked the song's signature *tárá-ráálá-rálárám* refrain; then I understood that it was there in the absence. I do not know whether this was Víg's intent, but the omission seemed to acknowledge that Cseh was gone and that no one could replace him. Now I understand it still more simply; even if Cseh were still alive, Víg might play the song this way; perhaps he plays it as he hears it internally.[9]

The writer, playwright, poet, and illustrator János Háy (1960–) began attending Cseh's concerts as a teenager. At the time, he had dreams of becoming a rock guitarist, but since disco music predominated during this era, he began looking for music that interested him. Someone recommended Cseh to him; he was drawn to the songs' unique and familiar world. He also enjoyed the musical eclecticism, where you could find everything. He describes this encounter with Cseh and Bereményi's songs as liberating.

In the 1960s, according to Háy, it was not yet clear what language Hungarian popular music would be in; it was Metró and other bands that decided it would be in Hungarian. Bereményi brought something to the song lyrics that no other lyricist at the time could: good, simple (but clever) rhymes, good rhythm, poetry in song. To Háy, the songs have a reflective and ironic quality; they make indirect statements while playing with nostalgia and memory. In addition, as others mention, Cseh brought something special to the stage: both his own presence and the theatrical quality of the songs.

Háy was moved by Cseh as a person; he even called him at his parents' home once when feeling depressed. When Cseh's father said, "Tamás isn't here," Háy immediately felt comfort and cheer over having come so close.

Háy speaks of how audience responses to the songs differed by generation. He and his peers found the songs very funny, whereas the older members of the audience took them seriously and reverently. This sometimes led to a kind of friendly competition at the shows: which group was closer to Cseh's music? The atmosphere at these concerts was congenial and intimate; according to Háy, a pressing question during socialism had to do with public appearances. What kind of public appearance did an artist want: performance, publication, or both? Certain kinds of publicity and public appearance carried the threat of compromise: once you packaged your work in some way, you would be expected to replicate it, and replication was deadly.

Háy began distancing himself from Cseh and Bereményi's work when it became extremely popular. In the latter half of the 1990s, he returned to it with new appreciation; he could now hear the songs afresh, without tension or apprehension. In 2008, at the inaugural program of the Ördögkatlan Festival, Háy held a conversation with Cseh before an audience.[10]

The composer, writer, and scholar Zoltán Beck (1971–), founder and songwriter of the band 30Y, defies expectations and stereotypes of rock musicians. Active in literary and multidisciplinary events, a docent at the University of Pécs in the Department of Romology and Sociology of Education, as well as the founder and professional director of the same university's Music University, he brings together performance, composition and writing, scholarship, and leadership. For Beck, it is not a contradiction to perform before exuberant crowds and then, the next day, sit down in a seminar room to discuss poetry. These aspects of his life not only coexist but intertwine; perhaps he finds a kindred versatility and openness in the music of Cseh and Bereményi. He likewise finds no contradiction between understanding the songs as art and understanding the people who made them; to him, Cseh the person is essential to the songs.[11]

When speaking of Cseh and Bereményi, Beck has emphasized that we do not always encounter music in a linear or chronological way. The first of their albums to become important to him was *Új dalok* ("New Songs"), released in 1990; he worked backwards from there. One of the songs on the album, "A képzelet szálfái közt" ("In the Sapwoods of the Imagination") he did not understand at first; when he returned to it later, he was astonished both that he had not understood it before and that he understood it now. For Beck, a song brings to life a reality that you can enter and believe, like the floating glass of *Frontátvonulás* (see Chapter 5). When Cseh, as Vizi, releases the glass, we see and hear it fall on the ground and break, but it nonetheless floats in the air for us; a song likewise makes magic in the midst of broken things.

Beck has been instrumental in supporting Cseh and Bereményi's legacy; not only has he taken part in numerous Cseh events, but in 2018 he directed a documentary film about a concert in memory of Cseh and Leonard Cohen (who came close to having a joint concert during their lifetime). In 2021 he and Krisztián Szűcs reworked and completed Cseh and Dénes Csengey's unreleased performance *Másnap* ("The Next Day"), which until now had existed only in draft form. This became a concert, then an album. In 2024 he was involved in the creation of the special album *Western dalok* ("Western Songs"), featuring Cseh's performances (likewise previously unreleased) of his and Bereményi's songs on Western themes, some of them unfamiliar to listeners, others well known.[12]

Continuing onward to younger artists, one can see increasing attention to the internal workings of the songs. László Sallai, the frontman and songwriter of Felső Tízezer, The Somersault Boy, and Captain Average, and the bassist of Galaxisok and Platon Karataev, says that when he first listened to *Levél nővéremnek* as a high school student, he was stunned, primarily by the lyrics, which were "an entirely different dimension" from typical Hungarian lyrics of the album's era. Most lyrics at that time, according to Sallai, were simple, focused on love, and easily singable, following the models of American and English bands. Cseh and Bereményi, in contrast, drew their influence mainly from French and Russian *chanson*; their songs captured the world of Sallai's parents' youth, and the creative collaboration of Cseh and Bereményi was perhaps unique even internationally. Sallai considers the pair an important influence on the Hungarian new wave of the 1980s (such as Kontroll Csoport, Európa Kiadó) and the alternative rock music emerging from the 1990s (such as 30Y and Kispál és a Borz). "There is no Tamás Cseh template," says Sallai; while many of the songs have common characteristics, they also differ widely, as Cseh was able to "renew himself musically and lyrically" many times and "bring in influences that further colored his universe." In his own songs, Sallai strives for the quality of live speech, as Cseh and Bereményi did with quoted sentences, slang, and allusions; in addition, he considers their songs' storytelling an important standard for his work.[13]

Márton Hó (1981–2025), one of Hungary's most revered and beloved songwriters, spoke in January 2018, on the seventy-fifth anniversary of Cseh's birth, of how Cseh inhabited Bereményi's lyrics, thus bringing music, words, and performance together: "the stories, the four chords, the songs, whose lyrics he did not write, but still could perform as if he had written them." He went on to say that Cseh "felt at home in this, in Bereményi's world, which then became his own, easily accessible universe. The first Hungarian singer-songwriter? I don't know, but he was certainly the first Hungarian storyteller to give soul to Bereményi's lyrics." In Hó's own songs, one can hear possibilities in simplicity and human limitation. He is quoted as saying, "I am not a great singer. On the guitar I can play about four chords. Solos, for example, I can't do." Yet like Cseh and Bereményi, though differently, he not only brings brilliance out of the limitations, but makes meaning and meaninglessness of them, creating a place in the world for others like him who cannot and will not strive for fake success. Commenting on Hó's first full-length album, *Dalok a fürdőszobából* ("Songs from the Bathroom"), which he created in 2011 with his band Hó Márton és a Jégkorszak, or "Márton Hó and the Ice Age," Sallai said that "the songs lacked philosophical verbiage, they had simple, relatable and clever lyrics. Musically, [his work] was nourished mainly by international indie; it was very different from the Hungarian alternative music that pervaded Petőfi Radio at the time. It was more personal, more lovable, and it bravely dared to be different in the era of imitator bands."[14]

Dalok a fürdőszobából has musical traces of Cseh and Bereményi (the opening song, "Hello Purgatórium!" has a hint of "Jóslat" in my ears, and "Négy évszak: tél, tél, tél, tél" ("Four Seasons: Winter, Winter, Winter, Winter") sounds almost as if Cseh and Bereményi could have written it. Still, the songs resemble Cseh and Bereményi's primarily in their freshness, independence, and daring. They ask something similar of the listener: that we come to it without pretense or defenses. Hó's ten albums are foundational in many musicians' collections and minds; the musician Erik Sumo said about Hó after his death, "I think my Tamás Cseh is not Tamás Cseh, but Marci Hó."[15]

The last lineup of Hó's band A Jégkorszak ("The Ice Age") included the musician and composer Dávid Konsiczky, the co-founder, with the lyricist and singer Olivér Csepella, of the band Csaknekedkislány ("Just for You, Girl"). Csepella and Konsiczky have spoken of how, when they began playing music together, they had few musical favorites in common, but Cseh was one. They too are a songwriting pair, but their roles differ from those of Cseh and Bereményi: Csepella describes Konsiczky, the music writer and guitarist, as more introverted, and himself, the lyricist and singer, as more extraverted. Csepella met Cseh only through his recordings; Konsiczky met him in person once, in rather embarrassing circumstances for him. He and his mother were heading to a Cseh senecert, and on the way he spotted a poster. "Look, Mom!" he cried. "Tomi Cseh!" At that moment, Cseh appeared right behind him.

In Csepella's view, the music of Cseh and Bereményi differs from other music of the era, because while the latter evokes specific time periods, Cseh and Bereményi's work seems to exist outside of time. As a teenager he related strongly to the songs: to the conflicts, the breathlessness, the struggle within confines, the sense of not being the ruler of one's own life. The songs arise from Cseh or Bereményi's experiences, or both; it is less important to him where they come from than what kind of world they create. The songs have to do with actions and witnessing: what was seen, who went where, what was said. To both Csepella and Konsiczky, they have a film-like quality; Csepella describes "Váróterem" ("Waiting Room"—see Chapter 8) as a film script.

The duo also finds something kindred in the songs' intentional contrasts and contradictions: the way Bereményi might write humorous lyrics to Cseh's somber melody, for instance. They, too, work with such pairings and juxtapositions. In my own understanding, the band combines intellect with party instinct; keen, sophisticated, and thoughtful, they know how to have a good time and to bring the audience into their fun.[16]

According to Csepella, he and Konsiczky wrote their song "Cseh Tamás" in the early period of their "friendship verging on love," when they listened to his and Bereményi's album *Levél nővéremnek* some two hundred times; it is among their earliest songs that they still play today. Written in a mellow tango-like style reminiscent of Cseh and Bereményi's "Demonstráció" and other songs, it imagines Cseh as barred from heaven because he is too difficult a person, yet also barred from hell because it is already filled to the brim with musicians. Cseh himself then speaks up, saying that he is entirely unsuited to the matter of death and belongs only on earth; he offers to sacrifice himself, "shoes, coat, body, dream, song, and cancer," so that those on earth will carry it all forward from there. The guardians of heaven and hell give their assent, and Cseh is scattered over the earth, with "as much cancer as there is mold on bread, as much treasure as there are street musicians." He cries out, "Géza, if you come over, we'll can write songs, / The pipes will buzz them, and the birds will sing them." The songs comments, "A hoarse announcer is speaking like this somewhere." It ends: "Take out the guitar, the fight / Is the same, just the act differs! / [Fight] with our lives against death, / As Tamás Cseh did back then." The song has the refrain, "Take out the guitar, / [Defeat] death with life!" This wry and profoundly respectful tribute suggests that not only Csepella and Konsiczky, but all the musicians who carry on something of Cseh's fighting spark are indebted to him, that the music of Cseh and Bereményi has something to do with the fight itself.[17]

Some artists respond to Cseh and Bereményi's influence by resisting it somewhat—that is, acknowledging it but marking out their distinct path. Benedek Szabó, the songwriter, musician, and frontman of Galaxisok, said in a 2015 interview that Cseh's influence on him was undeniable, that he considers Bereményi's lyrics the best of all time and a great influence on his work, but that he hates being called the new Cseh. Still, to him, it is impossible to write the kind of songs he writes without the influence of both. He remarked that few musicians today are actually working from that influence, as they avoid touching the topics that Bereményi was so "brutally honest" about. They don't discuss drugs or sex, or anything that would make them look bad; instead, they refine their words, not only in interviews, but probably in their songs as well.[18] Szabó's songs, while filled with musical and lyrical delight, spare no punches; they might talk of drunkenness, depression, death, and political repression and stupidity, just as they might tell of surreal dreams or speak of teenage love, a happy afternoon, a walk over a soccer field at night. The music, according to the band's self-description, has elements of punk, "twee pop, bossa nova, tropicalia, soukous, Peruvian folk, shoegaze and psychedelic rock," among others. The band members listen to music from around the world and across the eras. Szabó is an avid and discerning reader; he spends hours with his favorite books and continually adds to his knowledge. While this in itself speaks of no Cseh-Bereményi influence or relation, it suggests a somewhat kindred relation to the world. In 2025, when the news outlet Telex.hu asked him which Hungarian album he considered the most important, he named Cseh and Bereményi's *Levél nővéremnek,* not only because it is essentially a story collection in song, and not only because it captures an era in Hungary, but because of its exceptional songwriting.[19]

The list of writers, musicians, actors, and others influenced by Cseh and Bereményi (to different degrees, in different ways) could go on indefinitely; yet the point is not to include everyone (or exclude anyone, for that matter), but rather to consider why Cseh and Bereményi's work has such vitality for artists today. The reasons considered so far are many, but they all have to do with imagination and integrity. Even those words fail to capture what attracts these artists: maybe a phrase, a melodic turn, a song, then an album that they end up playing hundreds of times. Something playful and bold; some truth shining through the mischief. Influence is impossible to pinpoint exactly; it often happens without our awareness. Nonetheless, from all of these examples we can see that Cseh and Bereményi's legacy not only lives on, but gives rise to new versions, new works, and everyday surprises.

In January 2024, on Cseh's birthday, I introduced my students to Cseh and Bereményi's "Csönded vagyok." When the lesson ended, they said goodbye as usual and headed down the stairs. I was gathering up my things when I heard a student whistling the melody in the stairwell; the sound filled the space. Maybe influence happens this way too: a humming, a whistling, something carried on without conscious intent. We will never know how far Cseh and Bereményi's music has spread, what lives it has entered, what music, plays, poems it has affected. Still, even when not attending Cseh events or listening to Cseh-reworkings, we may catch something in the air. But what? As soon as we try to grasp it, it slips away, so that the only thing left to do is chase it around the corner.

Chapter 12

"What Roads I Have Had":
My Entry Into Cseh and Beremény's Work

I wrote this book not as a Cseh and Beremény expert, nor as a musicologist, but as a listener with literary and musical background who yearned to bring this music to those who had never heard of it. In the midst of the writing, I ended up performing four of their songs in a small concert with Sándor Sárkány, whom I had already mentioned in the first chapter. The world of Cseh and Beremény is so densely knit that, once part of it, you could eventually meet anyone in it who is still alive. It seems at times that Cseh is in the room.

People often ask me what brought me to Hungary (where, at the time of this writing, I have been living for seven and a half years); each time I tell a slightly different story, not because I'm making it up, but because there is no single or complete answer. In brief: I was just finishing my second book when a colleague in Istanbul, Dr. Nimet Küçük, who I had met through my school's philosophy journal, *Contrariwise*, invited me to be a guest teacher at her school for two weeks. I would teach philosophy classes and take part in a school ceremony. They would board me at the school, a centrally located Catholic lycée; I could come and go freely (security guards worked around the clock). I gratefully accepted the invitation.

When planning my trip, I decided to spend a few days in Hungary after Istanbul. I had a dream of bicycling in the Zemplén area and then going up to Košice, Slovakia (formerly Kassa, Hungary) and from there to the village where my great-grandfather was born. Although I spoke no Hungarian, I was able to make all the arrangements: purchasing train tickets, reserving a room at a rural guesthouse, renting a bicycle.

The Istanbul visit was much more than a tourist's foray. At the school I met with bright, bold students (they had no fear of challenging my assumptions, and this led into thoughtful discussions) and dedicated and accomoplished teachers. I had many conversations with my host, the philosophy teacher Dr. Nimet Kucuk, who oversaw my stay, introduced me to faculty and students, and showed me a few special places in the city, including several synagogues. The school had a teachers' room—a fixture of Hungarian schools as well, I would learn later—where each teacher had a desk and espresso was routinely served. In addition, there was a quiet room, serene and elegant, where no chatting whatsoever took place. Anyone wishing to work, relax, or think without distraction could go there.

In my free time I explored the city; when not with my host, I romped around alone. My favorite pastime was to walk along İstiklal Avenue and listen to the Turkish, Kurdish, Iranian, Syrian, and other musicians. The music took on many moods: lively, melancholic, dreamy, angry. Several times I heard a blind ashik (troubadour) who sang and played the oud. He became my favorite; I loved his sparse, haunting songs. A young man held the microphone for him and kept an eye on the surroundings. I also became fond of an Iranian duo, a Kurdish duo, and a Syrian ensemble. While always alert, I felt safe, even late at night. Sometimes I would stop at a hole-in-the-wall restaurant for a doner kebab or at a fruit stand for a pomegranate (they were broken open so that you could see the juicy red seeds). Like many others, I admired and fed the street cats.

After that, it seemed that anything would be a letdown, but Hungary proved a quiet counterpart to those lively days. In Zemplén, I picked up a bike from a rental place in Sátoraljaújhely and stayed at a bed-and-breakfast place in Vajdácska. I found myself bicycling through fields and meadows, listening to the sounds of farm animals early in the morning, and gazing at the glow of the two churches on the hill at sundown. My trip to my grandfather's village was likewise low-key: I took the train to Košice (where I walked around and went on a tour of the synagogues), then took the bus to Györke through hills and dark green forests. There was not much to see there, at least for me at that time—I walked around for half an hour and then took the bus back—but I saw Hungarian-Slovak and Roma children walking together, passed by a wooden church, saw men lounging outside a pub, and looked at the surrounding hills.

I also visited Budapest (where I attended a concert and went on a tour of the Dohány Street Synagogue), but it was the Zemplén trip that stirred my imagination. Being able to bicycle around alone, in quiet and without fanfare, to take part in life there even as a visitor, left me thinking that something along these lines could continue.

The fresh memories of the two visits—to Istanbul and to Hungary—stirred up an idea: what if I were to teach in Hungary? I had left my previous teaching a year earlier (with ample advance notice and planning) to write my book; nothing held me back from taking a new direction. One day I searched online for teaching opportunities in Hungary and came upon the Central European Teaching Program, which enables teachers from the U.S. to teach in Hungarian schools. I wrote to the director immediately; she replied promptly and asked whether I would be interested in an opportunity in Szolnok, at the Varga Katalin Gimnázium (Katalin Varga Secondary School). I looked up the school and found that they had, among other things, a legendary drama club. I replied immediately to say that I was interested. I would not be able to start until November, since the person I was replacing, also an American, was going on long-term maternity leave and would be teaching until then. So I had to hold tight for a few weeks. Once she disclosed her plans and mentioned me as a possible replacement, the principal responded enthusiastically, and I was set.

I managed to go to Hungary again in September—primarily to visit the school and take care of some of the paperwork, but also to visit Budapest, Szeged, Baja, and Albertirsa. In the latter two, I attended synagogue concerts by members of the Budapest Festival Orchestra. The orchestra has an ongoing synagogue concert series; their goal is to play in every synagogue and former synagogue in Hungary. In Budapest, I attended two Shabbat services held by the congregation Szim Salom and leyned (chanted Torah) at the morning service. I had been in touch with Rabbi Katalin Kelemen beforehand, and she had welcomed me warmly. (She was Hungary's first and at the time only female rabbi.) The Torah chanting at Szim Salom led to much more than I could have foreseen. Shortly after I moved to Hungary, they invited me to be their lay cantor; I served in that role for six years and continue to leyn there on occasion.

When I came to Hungary to teach, at the end of October 2017, I already knew that this was not a short stay and that I wanted to get on my feet with Hungarian as soon as possible. Within the first week, I felt at home at the school with its tranquil atmosphere and bright, funny, attentive students. I considerable freedom to bring literature, music, and drama into my English classes and to initiate projects. Colleagues told me that I didn't need to attend faculty meetings, since I wouldn't understand anything, but it was precisely for that reason that I wanted to attend. I knew (just as with Hebrew and other languages I have learned to different degrees) that the best way for me to learn a language is to plunge into what I don't understand. The mind starts to figure it out. At first, two colleagues tried translating the meetings for me on the spot, in the back of the room, but I found it more helpful to sit near the front and focus on every word, without translation.

In my second year at the school, two events changed the course of everything that would follow. First, I discovered that one of my colleagues, Gyula Jenei, was a poet and that his wife, Marianna Fekete, wrote literary criticism. I had never spoken with Gyula before, but one day I walked up to him and recited one of his poems. He was taken aback and pleased. Not long afterward, I read Marianna's essay—published in the literary journal *Eső*, of which Gyula is the founder and editor-in-chief—about the haiku poems of Béla Markó. I had an idea: what if I translated a few of Gyula's poems (from his 2018 collection) and this essay? I talked with them, mainly through Marianna (my Hungarian was halting at this point), and they were delighted with the idea. "A few poems" turned into the entire collection; the book was eventually published by Deep Vellum in 2022, and my translation of Marianna's essay appeared in *Literary Matters*. The Cowan Center for Education at the Dallas Institute of Humanities and Culture (where I had been teaching in the summers since 2011) invited the three of us to hold several literary events; we went in the fall of 2019 and had a memorable five days there.

I was not at all a novice translator; I had previously translated (from Lithuanian) many poems by Tomas Venclova, and I had been translating poetry from various languages for decades. My undergraduate thesis consisted of translations of Russian poetry, along with commentary on the poems themselves and the challenges of translating them. My approach to translation, which has grown subtler and more flexible over time, was to immerse myself in the sound of the original until comparable sounds and forms in English arose in my mind.

Another important (recurring) event that year was being the teacher of Marcell Bajnai, one of the most outspoken and thoughtful young people I have ever met. I taught his group just once a week and saw him paying keen attention whenever we focused on literature (for instance, Percy Bysshe Shelley's "Ozymandias"). A colleague told me that Marcell had just released an album with his band; he procured a copy for me, and I was struck by the song "Maradok ember" ("I will stay human" or "I will remain a person"). I created a cello version of the song and sent him the recording; I feared that he would not like it, but he approached me in the hallway to tell me how moved he was by it. (I later played this cello cover at the Dallas Institute and taught the chorus to everyone.) At the end of the year, when Marcell graduated, I met his family; in stumbling Hungarian, I tried to express to them what an extraordinary student and person he was. Over time, I came to know the family better, and my Hungarian improved to the point where I could converse freely with them. (Marcell has since earned a master's degree as a philologist of literary and cultural studies and writes for *Magyar Narancs*.)

I stared noticing Marcell's online musical recommendations. One group that came up repeatedly was Platon Karataev (named after a character in Tolstoy's *War and Peace*). I listened to the band's recordings and fell in love with their music. I first heard them play as a duo, in August 2020 (the founding members, Gergely Balla and Sebestyén Czakó-Kuraly, often give concerts together). Like many audience members, I found myself listening to their songs and albums over and over, attending as many of their concerts (duo and full-band) as possible, and entering deeper and deeper into the songs. I rarely stayed after the concerts for conversation (since I had to get back to Szolnok and am not good at after-concert conversation anyway), but conversations started up nonetheless.

Two years later, a group including them, the poet Csenger Kertai, and two graphics students came to the 2022 conference of the Association of Literary Scholars, Critics, and Writers (ALSCW) to present in my seminar on "Setting Poetry to Music." Another two years later, the duo performed in DC, at the 2024 ALSCW conference. In the meantime, I had been steeped in the music of Platon Karataev, had attended scores of their concerts, and had been introduced to the music of related bands and individuals: Cz.K. Sebő (Czakó-Kuraly's solo and band project, which also has an electronic project, capsule boy), Galaxisok, Felső Tízezer, Cappuccino Projekt (Dávid Korándi), Noémi Barkóczi, Norbert Kristóf, and many others. Just as with cantillation previously, and with the Hungarian language, I loved (and love) going to these concerts alone and concentrating on the sounds and forms. I started translating some of the lyrics. In addition, I translated a memoir by Sándor Czakó, the father of Sebestyén Czakó-Kuraly and one of the founding members of the band Vágtázó Halottkémek (Galloping Coroners). The book was published by Serving House Books in March 2026.

Both the music and I went through changes during these years; my Hungarian expanded, I grew older (like everyone), and Platon Karataev went deeper down their musical, sonic, and lyrical path, which is so introspective that it goes beyond the self. Although I am different from them (and they from each other—individually, they take quite different musical directions), it seems to me that we have been through something together and meet at unexpected times. I listen to them with new and old awe.

The worlds of music, literature, and theatre in Hungary intertwine. Musicians take part in literary events and create musical renditions of literary works; actors and directors set literary works (including authors' letters and diaries) to music. One of the most important examples of this for me is Miklós H. Vecsei's solo play based on the poems and letters of Attila József, with guitar accompaniment by Gergely Balla. I attended this performance in several locations, including a music festival in the mountains of Transylvania and the famed Fiumei Road Graveyard in Budapest, where they performed near József's gravestone. The latter was so overwhelming—not only for me but apparently for Vecsei himself—that Vecsei stumbled over and mixed up some of his lines, an essential and beautiful blunder that belonged to us all, as we were encountering something much larger than ourselves.

I began hearing Tamás Cseh mentioned here and there. One day Gyula wrote to me to say that he thought I would like his songs (he mentioned that Cseh and Bereményi wrote them together). He sent a few to me, and not only did I like them, but I knew I would be listening to more. The songs seemed closely related to what I was listening to now, but older, perhaps one of its origins. I was drawn in by the simplicity, melancholy, and utter lack of cliché, among unnamable things.

Gyula also told me about the director and writer László Bérczes, who had taught at the Varga Katalin Gimnázium in the 1980s and was a close friend of Cseh (he wrote a book based on conversations with him, which I have cited extensively here). Bérczes is the co-founder, along with the dramaturge Mónika Kiss, of the Ördögkatlan Festival, first held in 2008 (and attended by Cseh). Cseh and the film actress Mari Törőcsik were named the festival's patrons at the time of founding. The founders envisioned a festival that would bring the arts and people together in small villages—and would respect not only the performers and guests, but the caterers, technicians, artisans, and residents, as well as the history of the location. A portion of the festival is devoted to events in honor of Tamás Cseh (and Géza Bereményi and others associated with Cseh). It is an immense festival of music, theatre, literature, and more: tiny and large events, discussions, exhibitions, and a seven-kilometer run.

Now that I was aware of Cseh, I began hearing his name repeatedly. Musicians referred to him as an important influence and played covers of his work. I became aware that one cannot bring up Cseh without also mentioning Bereményi, since they wrote the songs together. By the time my Cseh and Bereményi listening had taken off, the events honoring eighty years since Cseh's birth were underway: events hosted by the Tamás Cseh Archive, the Petőfi Literary Museum, the Ördögkatlan Festival, and all sorts of other institutions, large and small, official and unofficial.

I had been mulling over ideas for my next book. One of the early ideas was for a book called *Speaking "Emberül"* (which may still come into being). The title refers to the Platon Karataev song "Elmerül" ("Sinking"), which has the lyrics, "Nem beszélem nyelved, de beszélek emberül" ("I don't speak your language, but I speak the human tongue"). The book was to be about my encounters with music and songwriting in Hungary. But as I thought about it, I grew wary of writing about people I knew personally, even if the acquaintance was slight. It seemed too soon for this, and I wasn't sure I could do anything but praise them. I wanted some distance from the topic but also wanted it to be close to me. It then occurred to me that the book should be about Cseh and Bereményi's songwriting partnership.

But do I understand it? I wondered. Do I have anything to say about it?

After seeing Vecsei's song-play *Füst a szemében* ("Smoke in His Eyes"), based on *Cseh Tamás: Bérczes László beszélgetőkönyve* ("Tamás Cseh: László Bérczes's Conversation Book") and performed with Balázs Szabó and Huba Ratkóczi, I walked out of the theatre exuberant, my mind brimming with an understanding that had no words yet. I knew that I "got it"—not just the play, but the songs themselves—but didn't know exactly what that meant. I was moved that Vecsei didn't imitate Cseh at all; instead, he understood him from the inside. Vecsei's Cseh brings to mind the words of the eleventh- and twelfth-century rabbi Rashi (as quoted at the beginning of the Coen brothers' movie *A Serious Man*): "Receive with simplicity everything that happens to you."

If *Füst a szemében* convinced me that I had a book to write, it was the performance of *Frontátvonulás* ("Frontal Passage") by graduates of the University of Theatre and Film Arts that hurled my thoughts into a new dimension. They have since formed their own company, SICC Production; I describe their *Frontátvonulás* in detail the fifth chapter, in some ways the heart of this book. By that time, I had already written two articles on Cseh and Bereményi and was close to finishing the third (on *Frontátvonulás* itself); I had visited the Tamás Cseh Archive several times, and the book was in progress. It was a staff member at the Cseh Tamás Archívum who told me about the performance; I went, saw it, and walked out floating like Vizi's glass (and have seen it many more times since then).

Every time I see the performance, it strikes me in a different way, or I pick up on different details. It has personal meaning for me too; my life plays out in it. I am both Vizi and Ecsédi; there was even a bit of both Vizi and Ecsédi in my impulse to come to Hungary. I wanted to start a new life and was grappling with a friendship I had lost. Starting a new life, and looking for a friend, are among the clearest, most essential impulses I have known; they contrast with all the muddy things that we are supposed to want in life (success, status, influence, etc.). This personal connection to the play combines with admiration of its details: the stage set, instruments, direction, choreography, music, acting, text, enunciation, structure, ritual, humor, and wonder.

Around the time of my first *Frontátvonulás*, I made the acquaintance of Cseh's son, András, the founder of Offline Rezervátum, a place and a group that emphasizes being offline. I was present when he first performed Cseh's songs in public (at a small private club in Szolnok), on March 28, 2024. Until then, he had resisted doing so because the songs were so close to him that they seemed untouchable. He enjoyed the evening so much that he started holding more Cseh sing-alongs: in various clubs in Budapest, at the Ördögkatlan Festival, and elsewhere. At Ördögkatlan, these sing-alongs took place almost every night, in Beremend, at the Offline Rezervátum, which had a campfire and many teepees. We sat around the fire and sang into the night, sometimes with special guests such as Mihály Víg. One night the sing-along took place in Nagyharsány, in front of (and with) a large audience. Many people attended, maybe two hundred. András was apprehensive about having so many "online" people present (that is, people using their phones), but most of them seemed eager to sing Cseh's songs without distraction. We sang with love and glee. Then came the rain.

The audience stuck it out when the drops started coming down, splashing the lyrics books—but when big streaks of lightning ripped the sky, most of the crowd rushed out, leaving just fifteen to twenty of us, who kept singing and singing. The rain got thicker, so we went under a tree for just a few more songs—and I remember the sight of András spreading his arms in the downpour and singing with full heart and joy, singing as himself but honoring his father, honoring the songs.

All of this leads up to the question: what was it that I "got" (and get) about the music? This book contains the answer, or part of it, but I will add a few more possibilities.

As an undergraduate and graduate student, I was intrigued and enchanted by the work of Nikolai Gogol, ultimately the topic of my doctoral dissertation. Looking back, I see that I was drawn not only to his idiosyncratic wit, not only to his cadences, not only to the strangeness (and poignancy) of his characters and situations, but to a vision of the world in which the tragic and comic merge (and which is far more than "tragicomic"). This vision can be conveyed in a turn of phrase, a strange story about a nose, or an epic novel.

I sense a kindred vision in the songs of Cseh and Bereményi. As the earlier chapters explore, the songs can be at once supremely silly and trenchant; different listeners tended to hear one or the other side of them, but really these opposites connect. I have yearned for this union, or something like it.

In an era of polarization (caused by cheapened online discourse, political rhetoric, self-help fads, and more), each of us gets defined, willy-nilly, as one thing or another: serious or silly, weak or strong, beautiful or plain, masculine or feminine, introverted or extraverted, religious or atheistic, political or apolitical—and these divisions chop up the soul. We are made not only of multitudes, but of seeming opposites, which turn out not to be opposites at all. There is music, theatre, and literature that gathers up the pieces and shows the paradox. This needs to be done well. Cseh and Bereményi do it well.

Much suffering comes from the belief that we can occupy only one side of these poles: this belief makes us lie to ourselves, contort ourselves, tell partial tales. Nothing in the world is more complex than identity; in a sense we come to know ourselves when we stop trying to identify ourselves at all.

Or rather: identity markers mean something, but not everything; the danger lies not in having them, but in mistaking them for the whole.

In my sporadic correspondence with Bereményi over the course of this project, I asked him now and then about the source of inspiration for certain songs, or the presence of a particular allusion. He would answer that the songs came to him as they are; for the most part, he didn't want to explain them, except to clarify certain meanings here and there. The songwriter's task, he said once, is to create the song; it is on others to interpret it.

This outlook allows the songs to resist allocation to crude categories. If critics choose to categorize them, that is their business, but the songwriter does not have to participate. Songs come largely from intuition; to pin them down is to flatten them. That does not mean we should not write about songs, interpret them, raise questions about them. But we must leave an opening.

There is much about Cseh and Bereményi that will always remain unknown to me. As a performer, Cseh had a devoted following; I cannot know what they saw and heard. Videos and recordings cannot convey what it was like to be there in the room. I do sense that Cseh had the ability to live each moment of the song. Bereményi described this quality: in László Bérczes's words to Cseh, "Géza often says that you sing as though the words were born right then and there."[1]

As for Bereményi, he wisely protects his creative privacy, letting his work speak for itself. The *titok* ("secret") is essential to his creations: not only a hidden meaning or reference, but even something that goes beyond what we know as meaning. There are meanings to the songs that I may never grasp; inside jokes, passing thoughts, hunches; and beyond that, the way and language of song, which cannot be translated into other forms of speech.

The songs change for me even as I write, even up to the final edits. My Hungarian has deepened, and with it my understanding of the songs. In addition, much has happened since this book began: besides Cseh events and releases of previously unpublished songs, Bereményi has begun writing songs with Cseh's son, András. At an event honoring Bereményi's eightieth birthday, I heard some of these songs alongside songs Bereményi had written for other musicians, as well as a few of the old Cseh-Bereményi favorites. Even these favorites—such as "Budapest," "Az ócska cipő," and "Keresztben jégeső"—came to me in a new way. My fingers on the keyboard will never catch up with these changes; they continue in my mind.

Over time, I have become more alert and open to the political aspects of the songs: that is, those details and phrases that illuminate the structures and systems in which we live. The songs' own characters, situations, language, wordplay, and music prevail but also respond to the features of the room. Vizi and Ecsédi differ from the other characters of *Frontátvonulás* because they dare to break through the edifice, even temporarily, even in something like a hallucination or dream. This breakthrough is infinitely meaningful and meaningless, because the structures we live in are countless. Some of these structures house and protect us, some hold us back; some we don't see or feel, others we knock against again and again, and still others we knock down. Within all of this, there is a chance at dignity, a risk of absurdity, a way to have both at once.

The point of this book was never to pinpoint the songs or explain them through and through, but simply to introduce them. At some point the words fall away. I end this book with "Désiré megnémul" ("Désiré Falls Silent), the last song on the *Antoine és Désiré* album. I mentioned it in the first chapter but translate it differently here, with more liberties. It has been quoted many times in Hungarian, maybe even to excess, but not in English; and there is something to be said for having this book end (more or less) where it began.

What roads I have had,
said Désiré, now that I recall,
what a mess, how many mistakes,
maybe I lied too, and there was a small,
and there was a small, I don't know what to call it,
maybe one or two evenings,
which passed without naming,
and nameless is the way
they are likely to stay.

Tárárárárám, tárárárárám, tárárárárárárárá rárárám,
tárárárárám, tárárárárárám, tárárárárárárárárám.

If I don't name it, and no one else
names it, that little something,
that little something, I don't know what it is,

in which I played a part...
but now, it seems, my speech has gone numb,
and it will be lost for all time to come,
that little, I don't know what to call it,
maybe just this: there were one or two evenings...

Táráráráram, táráráráram, tárárárárárárá ráráram,
táráráráram, táráráráram, táráráráráráráram.

Biographies of Cseh and Bereményi

These brief biographies give a basic overview of the lives of Cseh and Bereményi. More biographical information comes up over the course of the book.

Tamás Cseh was born in Budapest on January 22, 1943, and lived in the village of Tordas (in Fejér County) until his thirteenth year. In 1956, just after the revolution, the family moved to Budapest. He received a guitar from his grandparents as a high school graduation present; he then formed a band with two neighbors, boys with some musical knowledge. In high school, he had already begun exploring the "Indian" (i.e., Native American) lifestyle with some friends; later, he started an "Indian" camp in the Vértes mountains that shortly moved to the village of Bakonybél, where it remained. The activities included rugged outdoor survival, roleplay, dances and other rituals. For Cseh and his companions, as well as many others in Hungary and Eastern Europe, the Native American lifestyle represented freedom and simplicity, as well as implicit resistance to the political and social system.

In 1961 Cseh applied to the Képzőművészeti Főiskola ("Hungarian University of Fine Arts") but was rejected. After working for a year as a mason's assistant and then as an apprentice painter and being rejected once more by the Hungarian University of Fine Arts, he decided to become an art teacher. During his training period, he began teaching in the small village of Perkáta, where he played guitar in the evenings, setting his melodies to English lyrics. In 1965, after a sudden illness, he left the village and moved back to Budapest, where he worked first in Kelenföld at a vocational training school and then, after receiving his teaching diploma, as an art teacher in Kőbánya. In 1970 he met Bereményi and began collaborating with him. One of their songs reached the film director Miklós Jancsó; Cseh played it in Jancsó's 1972 film *Még kér a nép* (official English-language title: *Red Psalm*). From then on, Cseh acted and played in numerous films by Jancsó and others, as well as on stage.

Over the decades of their collaboration, Cseh and Bereményi created twenty full-length albums (some of them concert recordings or compilations) in addition to numerous bootlegs and unrecorded work.

During Bereményi's hiatus from songwriting, Cseh and Dénes Csengey created and released the album *Mélyrepülés* ("Flying Low" or "Deep Dive"). Besides Bereményi and Csengey, Cseh's significant collaborators included, among others, János Másik, who with Cseh composed the music for the first album, *Levél nővéremnek* ("Letter to My Sister"), and its two later sequels; the cellist János Novák, who played on a number of the albums and also contributed to the composition of *Levél nővéremnek*; the composer István Mártha; and the composer, poet, and guitarist Mihály Víg. In 1993, Cseh received the Ferenc Liszt Prize and, in 2001, along with Bereményi, the Kossuth Prize (among many other awards over the years).

Cseh married Éva Császár Bíró in 1980. Their son, András, was born in 1981; their daughter, Borbála, in 1989.

On August 26, 2006, Cseh, by now ill with lung cancer, performed his last full concert on Bakáts Square in Budapest. On August 7, 2009, he died at his home on Béla Bartók Street in Budapest. Several thousand people attended his funeral. In 2013, a statue was erected in his memory.

Géza Bereményi (whose early life story is depicted in his film *Eldorádó* and his autobiographical novel *Magyar Copperfield*), was born in Budapest in 1946; his mother was seventeen at the time of his birth. His name at birth was Géza Vetró; his Italian ancestor Giovanni Vetro had moved to Hungary in the eighteenth century. His grandparents, who ran a vegetable business on Teleki Square, raised him until the age of six, when his mother and her husband adopted him. From age six to twenty-four, he carried the surname Rózner, after his stepfather. When his first collection of stories, *A svéd király* ("The Swedish King"), was about to be published, he was informed that he needed to choose a Hungarian surname. The possibility arose of reverting to Vetró, but instead he chose his grandparents' surname, Bereményi.

In 1964, Bereményi graduated from the Türr István Gimnázium és Kollégium ("István Türr High School and Dormitory") in Pápa, after attending two other high schools. After a year of military service, he attended Eötvös Loránd Tudományegyetem Bölcsészettudományi Kar ("Eötvös Loránd University Faculty of Humanities"), from which he graduated in 1970 with a degree in Hungarian and Italian.

Bereményi and Cseh worked together from 1970 until Bereményi's songwriting hiatus in 1982, and then again from 1989 almost until Cseh's death in 2009. Together they not only wrote hundreds of songs and released twenty albums, but created a particular genre, akin to a musical, in which songs combined with narration tell a story for the stage. While Cseh performed these song-stories alone (and occasionally with fellow musicians), Bereményi was always the author of the text and lyrics, except during his hiatus, when Cseh and Dénes Csengey created the show and album *Mélyrepülés* ("Deep Dive," "Plummeting," or "Low-altitude Flying").

Bereményi worked first in book advertising, then as a dubbing dramaturg. Since 1978, he has worked independently as an independent writer and director; he also taught for years at Budapest's Színház- és Filmművészeti Főiskola ("Academy of Theatre and Film Arts"), which later became the Színház- és Filmművészeti Egyetem ("University of Theatre and Film Arts"). The author of songs, stories, novels, plays, screenplays, and two autobiographies, and the winner of numerous awards (including the Attila József Prize in 1984, the Kossuth Prize—with Cseh—in 2001, the Prima Primissima Prize in 2011, the Petőfi Music Prize in 2016, and the Libri Literary Prize in 2021).

In addition to his song lyrics and his memoir, *Magyar Copperfield*, he has published numerous stories, novels, poems, plays, and screenplays. The portrait film *Bereményi kalapja* ("Bereményi's Hat"), directed by Gábor Zsigmond Papp, was released in 2022. Today Bereményi appears on stage in joint performances, readings, and interviews. He has begun writing songs with Tamás Cseh's son, András; this project premiered at the Szkéné Theatre on March 6, 2026, with András Cseh, Endre Kertész (cello), and György Bartók (piano).

Bereményi married Tünde Hámos in 1999, after three prior marriages. He has four children: Anna Pásztor (1972), Sára Bereményi (1978), Márk Bereményi (1999), and Bálint Bereményi (2003).

NOTES

Preface

[1] Géza Bereményi, "Egy dologba vagyok szerelmes: az A4-es papírba" ("I Am In Love with One Thing: A-4 Paper"), interview by Gergely Bödők, *Új Szó* ("New Word"), November 14, 2022, https://ujszo.com/szalon/egy-dologba-vagyok-szerelmes-az-a4-es-papirba.

Chapter 1

[2] Cseh told László Bérczes, "A nevek, a helyszínek, a szavak Géza birodalma, abba nehéz beledumálni" ("The names, places, and words are Géza's realm; it's hard to speculate about them"). László Bérczes, *Cseh Tamás: Bérczes László beszélgetőkönyve* ("Tamás Cseh: László Bérczes's Conversation Book") (Budapest: Európa Könyvkiadó, 2019), 317.

[1] This is a description of a pub concert I attended at the Sárga söröző ("Yellow Brewery") in Szolnok, Hungary, on January 19, 2024. The song "Antoine, Désiré és a szél" ("Antoine, Désiré, and the Wind") appears as the first track on Cseh and Bereményi's album *Antoine és Désiré* (Budapest: Pepita SLPX 17548, 1978, 33⅓ rpm). I will discuss it further in the fourth chapter.

[2] László Bérczes, Sándor Sárkány Sr. and others frequently tell stories of Cseh's late-night concerts and escapades.

[3] An outstanding example of this can be found in the translator, poet, and critic Grácia Kerényi (1925–1985), the subject of this book's tenth chapter.

[4] Anna Szemere, *Up from the Underground: The Culture of Rock Music in Postsocialist Hungary* (University Park: The Pennsylvania State University Press, 2001), 122n. For an English-language explanation of the "Three Ts," see Hungarian National Gallery, "Within Frames: The Art of the Sixties in Hungary (1958–1968)," https://en.mng.hu/exhibitions/within-frames-the-art-of-the-sixties-in-hungary-1958-1968/; for Bereményi's comments on self-censorship, see Bereményi, "Bereményi Géza: Én gyáva voltam, ő meg tudatlan" ("Géza Bereményi: I was a coward, and he was ignorant"), interview by Fruzsina Lázár, *Magyar Nemzet* ("Hungarian Nation"), March 5, 2017, https://magyarnemzet.hu/nagyinterju-a-magazinban/2017/03/beremenyi-geza-en-gyava-voltam-o-meg-tudatlan#google_vignette.

[5] The official name of the *sanzonbizottság* was the *Táncdal- és Sanzonbizottság* ("Dance Song and Chanson Committee"). For an analysis of the changes in arts policy during the last three decades of Hungary's socialist era, see Gábor Bolvári-Takács, "Arts Policy in Kádár Era in Hungary, 1957–1989," *Hungarian Studies*, vol. 37, no. 2, https://akjournals.com/view/journals/044/37/2/article-p318.xml; for insights into the censorship that Cseh and Bereményi faced, see Bence Csatári, "Csatári Bence a rendszerkritikus Cseh Tamásról és a mai napig ható életművéről" ("Bence Csatári on the system critic Tamás Cseh and his life work, which still affects us today"), interview with Attila Ditzendy, *Magyar Nemzet* ("Hungarian Nation"), January 22, 2023, https://magyarnemzet.hu/lugas-rovat/2023/01/csatari-bence-a-rendszerkritikus-cseh-tamasrol-es-maig-hato-eletmuverol.

6 Bereményi and Cseh, *Titkos dalok* (DVD), Mirax, 2009. Cseh often spoke of the "secret" aspect of the songs; see, for instance, his 1994 interview with Stefánia Horváth, "A titok a dalokban van" ("The Secret Is in the Songs"), *Bel-Ami*, August 29, 1994, https://csehtamasarchivum.hu/tortenet/titok-dalokban-van.

7 László Bérczes, *Cseh Tamás: Bérczes László beszélgetőkönyve* ("Tamás Cseh: László Bérczes's Conversation Book"), 161; Géza Bereményi, "Bereményi Géza: Én gyáva voltam, ő meg tudatlan" ("Géza Bereményi: I was a coward, and he was ignorant"), interview by Fruzsina Lázár, *Magyar Nemzet* ("Hungarian Nation"), March 5, 2017.

8 This story is adapted from Tamás Cseh's own telling of it to László Bérczes in Bérczes, 104–108. It has been told many times, with slight variations. Bereményi describes the terms of their working relationship in Bereményi, "Egy dologba vagyok szerelmes: az A4-es papírba" ("I Am in Love with One Thing: A-4 Paper"), interview by Gergely Bödők, *Új Szó* ("New Word"), November 14, 2022, https://ujszo.com/szalon/egy-dologba-vagyok-szerelmes-az-a4-es-papirba.

9 Bereményi and Cseh, *Összekacsintó* (Hungarian television program), no. 3: "Még lesznek dalok."

10 The song "Az ócska cipő" ("Shabby Shoes") appears as the eighth track on Cseh and Bereményi's 1978 album *Antoine és Désiré*.

11 "I Love You So" is the second song on Cseh and Bereményi's 1979 album *Fehér babák takarodója* ("White Dolls' Curfew").

12 For a close analysis of the differences between *Levél nővéremnek* ("Letter to My Sister") and *Levél nővéremnek 2*, see Cecília Horsch, "Társadalomkép és társadalomkritika Cseh Tamás dalaiban: Az 1976-os és az 1994-es Levél nővéremnek és a Levél nővéremnek 2. albumok összehasonlítása" ("Social Image and social Criticism in the Songs of Tamás Cseh: A Comparison of the 1976 and 1994 albums *Letter to My Sister* and *Letter to My Sister 2*"), *Tanulmányok a társadalomról: a Szegedi Tudományegyetem JGYPK Alkalmazott Társadalomismereti Tanszék tudományos diákköri munkái* ("Studies on society: scientific student works of the JGYPK Department of Applied Social Sciences of the University of Szeged"), vol. 1, 2013: 102–128, http://acta.bibl.u-szeged.hu/72912/.

13 For a personal perspective (from a member of the Cheyenne people) on the history of "Indians" in Hungary, see Lance Henson, "Indians," *The Continental Literary Magazine*, November 10, 2021, https://continentalmagazine.com/2021/11/10/indians/. For an examination of the roots of Indian lore in Germany, see H. Glenn Penny, "The German Love Affair with American Indians: Rudolf Cronau's Epiphany," *Commonplace*, vol. 11, no. 4 (July 2011), https://commonplace.online/article/the-german-love-affair-with-american-indians/.

14 Bérczes, 312–316.

15 "Pridem" (to be discussed in the sixth chapter) was part of the stage performance of *Jóslat* ("Prophecy") but first appeared on the 1987 double album *Utóirat* ("Postscript").

16 Bérczes, 200–203, 209–210.

17 András Szeredás, "Parafrázisok a Dalra. A Dal nélkül: Cseh Tamás estje a 25. Színházban" ("Paraphrases for a Song. Without Song: The Tamás Cseh Evening at the 25th Theatre"), *Színház* ("Theatre"), vol. 6, no. 9 (September 1973), 28–29.

18 Sándor Fodor, Cseh Tamás – interjúregény ("Tamás Cseh: Interview Novel") (Budapest: Graffiti, n.d.), 197.

19 Cseh, János Másik, János Novák, and Bereményi. *Levél nővéremnek* ("Letter to My Sister"), Budapest: Pepita SLPX 17524, 1977, 33⅓ rpm; *Spotify,*

https://open.spotify.com/album/4qh8OwdAisw2pj6ZaL7dMM; *Cseh Tamás Archívum,* https://csehtamasarchivum.hu/lemezgyujtemeny/level-noveremnek.
20 Bérczes, 238.
21 Ibid., 11; László Bérczes and Jenő Hartyándi, directors, *Cseh Tamás – Az utolsó koncert* ("Tamás Cseh: The Last Concert") (film), MEDIAWAVE Alapítvány - BÁRKA Színház, 2006–2009,
https://www.mediawavearchivum.hu/index.php?modul=filmek&kod=3333&nf=
1&nyelv=hun.
22 See Bereményi's comments in Fodor, 103.

Chapter 2

1 Dénes Csengey, ... *és mi most itt vagyunk* ("And We Are Here Now") (Budapest: Magvető, 1983). The work is available digitally in *A kétségbeesés méltósága* ("The Dignity of Despair") (Budapest: Digitális Irodalmi Akadémia, 2021), https://reader.dia.hu/document/Csengey_Denes-A_ketsegbeeses_meltosaga-34425.
2 Gábor Bolvári-Takács, "Arts Policy in Kádár Era in Hungary, 1957–1989," *Hungarian Studies*, vol. 37, no. 2,
https://akjournals.com/view/journals/044/37/2/article-p318.xml.
3 Gábor Hanák, "A dal átváltozásai—Interjú Hanák Gáborral" ("Transformations of the Song: Interview with Gábor Hanák"), interview with Gábor Mórocz, *Irodalmi Magazin* ("Literary Magazine"), 2018, no. 1, 5–13, available at Cseh Tamás Archívum website, https://csehtamasarchivum.hu/tortenet/dal-atvaltozasai-interju-hanak-gaborral.
4 László Bérczes, *Cseh Tamás: Bérczes László beszélgetőkönyve* ("Tamás Cseh: László Bérczes's Conversation Book") (Budapest: Európa Könyvkiadó, 2019), 120; Cseh Tamás Archívum, "Életesemények" ("Life Events") (1943 and 1944), https://csehtamasarchivum.hu/lifeevents.
5 Géza Bereményi, "Egy dologba vagyok szerelmes: az A4-es papírba" ("I Am In Love with One Thing: A-4 Paper"), interview by Gergely Bödők, *Új Szó* ("New Word"), November 14, 2022, https://ujszo.com/szalon/egy-dologba-vagyok-szerelmes-az-a4-es-papirba.
6 Géza Bereményi, *Magyar Copperfield* ("Hungarian Copperfield") (Budapest: Magvető, 2021), 249–255.
7 Bérczes, 30–31.
8 Attila Horváth, "The Educational Policy of the Soviet Dictatorship in Hungary," *Civic Review*, vol. 13, Special Issue (2017) 335–356, https://eng.polgariszemle.hu/archive/141-vol-13-special-issue-2017/hungarian-history/897-the-educational-policy-of-the-soviet-dictatorship-in-hungary.
9 Csengey, 14.
10 Bérczes, 29–30.
11 Ibid., 70–71.
12 Sándor Fodor, *Cseh Tamás: Interjúregény* ("Tamás Cseh: Interview Novel") (Budapest: Graffiti, n.d.), 43, 68–69.
13 Director of National Intelligence, Central Intelligence Agency, "Hungary: The Waning of the Kádár Era: National Intelligence Estimate," Central Intelligence Agency, approved May 15, 1986, https://www.cia.gov/readingroom/docs/CIA-RDP90T00155R000900120002-0.pdf.
14 "Indián," Cseh Tamás Archívum, n.d., https://csehtamasarchivum.hu/indian.
15 Sándor Horváth, "A 'nagy generáció' emlékezete - alternatív Kádár-korszak" ("A Remembrance of the 'Great Generation': An Alternative Kádár Era"), *Műút :*

irodalmi, művészeti és kritikai folyóirat ("Art's Way: A Literary, Artistic, and Critical Journal), 2010, http://epa.oszk.hu/02300/02381/00020/pdf/EPA02381_Muut_2010_020_05 0-053.pdf, 50.

16 Csengey, 29–31.

17 Zoltan Rihmer, Xenia Gonda, Balazs Kapitany, and Peter Dome, "Suicide in Hungary—Epidemiological and Clinical Perspectives," *Annals of General Psychiatry*, vol. 12, no. 21 (2013), https://pmc.ncbi.nlm.nih.gov/articles/PMC3698008/.

18 "Örök lázadó—Baksa-Soós János 75 éve született" ("Eternal Rebel: János Baksa-Soós Was Born 75 Years Ago"), *Kultura*, September 20, 2023, https://kultura.hu/orok-lazado-baksa-soos-janos-75-eve-szuletett/; László Sallai, "Egy szent grál a beatkorszakban—Baksa-Soós János és a Kex" ("A Holy Grail in the Beat Era: János Baksa-Soós and Kex," *Recorder*, October 1, 2021, https://recorder.blog.hu/2021/10/01/_egy_szent_gral_a_beatkorszakban_baks a-soos_janos_es_a_kex.

19 Ibid; Attila Arisztid Ditzendy, "Baksa-Soós Kexe megakadt a hatalom torkán" ("Baksa-Soós' Kex Got Stuck in the Throat of the Authorities"), *Index*, September 20, 2023, https://index.hu/kultur/popkult/2023/09/20/baksa-soos-janos-syrius-kex-meszaros-marta-illes-zenekar-taurus-kisfaludy-andras-/.

20 Tamás Szőnyei, "'Sötétben káprázó jelenés': Dixi–Gémes János (1943–2002)" ("'A Dazzling Apparition in the Dark': Dixi–jános Gémes [1943–2002]"), *Magyar Narancs* ("Hungarian Orange"), June 27, 2002, https://magyarnarancs.hu/lelek/sotetben_kaprazo_jelenes_dixi_-_gemes_janos_1943-2002-59793; Dixiblogg, "Dixi könyv & videó" ("Dixi Book and Video"), June 18, 2013, http://dixiblogg.blogspot.com/2013/06/dixi-konyv-video.html.

21 Dixi, "?," Dixiworld.hu, February 21, 2021, https://poems.dixiworld.com/107-2/.

22 Mihály Víg, "Dixi" (eulogy), September 12, 2002, https://artpool.hu/ketseg/dixi/vig.html.

23 András Fiath, "Dixi Gemes Janos 1999" [sic], YouTube, https://www.youtube.com/watch?v=JFLtt_18LFc; Lehel Oláh, *Dixi* (documentary film), Inforg, 2004, https://inforgfilm.org/filmek/dixi/.

24 László Majnik, "'Talán egy szép napon, a végtelent lezárhatom'—ötven éve jelent meg Koncz Zsuzsa *Gyerekjátékok* című lemeze" ("'Maybe One Fine Day I Can Close the Infinite': Zsuzsa Koncz's Album *Children's Games* Was Released 50 Years Ago"), *Beatkorszak* ("Beat Era"), April 2, 2024, https://beatkorszak.blog.hu/2024/04/02/koncz_zsuzsa_gyerekjatekok_774.

25 Zsuzsa Koncz, "Koncz Zsuzsa: Ha én rózsa volnék! 1986" ("Zsuzsa Koncz: If I Were a Rose! 1986"), YouTube, posted on by kaszkadoor, August 5, 2010, https://www.youtube.com/watch?v=ESyDyHsDhY4.

26 Zsuzsa Koncz, "Koncz Zsuzsa a *Narancs*nak: 'Most is aktuális a Majomország'" ("Zsuzsa Koncz to the *Orange*: 'Even Now, Monkey-Country Is Current'"), interview with Tibor Legát, *Magyar Narancs* ("Hungarian Orange"), November 26, 2019, https://magyarnarancs.hu/sorkoz/koncz-zsuzsa-most-is-aktualis-a-majomorszag-124792. For the poem itself and an excellent English translation by Edwin Morgan, see Sándor Weöres, "Majomország" ("Monkey-Country"), Babel Web Anthology, https://www.babelmatrix.org/works/hu/We%C3%B6res_S%C3%A1ndor-1913/Majomorsz%C3%A1g; the song itself appears on Koncz's 2019 album *Így volt*

szép ("It Was Nice This Way"), double CD, Hungaroton, https://open.spotify.com/album/2koiLuW6Ffl9HVYXuI9n3y.

27 See, for instance, Origo, "Ezek a rockzenészek voltak a kommunista rezsim áldozatai" ("These Rock Musicians Were the Victims of the Communist Regime"), *Origo*, August 2, 2020, https://www.origo.hu/itthon/2020/08/koncz-zsuzsa-cenzurat-kialt.

28 Attila Ághassi, "Nyolcvan éve született Szécsi Pál, az egyik legnagyobb hatású magyar énekes" ("Szécsi Pál, One of the Most Influential Hungarian Singers, Was Born Eighty Years Ago"), *Telex*, March 19, 2024, https://telex.hu/eszkombajn/2024/03/19/szecsi-pal-rejtelyes-elete-80-eves-lenne.

29 Márk Herczeg, "Segédmunkásból lett a nők bálványa – 70 éve született Szécsi Pál" ("He turned from a Laborer into a Womens' Idol: Pál Szécsi Was Born 70 Years Ago"), 444.hu, March 19, 2014, https://444.hu/2014/03/19/szecsipal70.

30 This plot description combines elements of the standard summary (found on Port and elsewhere) with my own observations. See "A nagy generáció," Port, https://port.hu/adatlap/film/tv/a-nagy-generacio-a-nagy-generacio/movie-1753.

31 Ferenc András, "'Ronda generáció, szép nemzedék'—András Ferenc filmrendező" ("'Ugly Cohort, Lovely Generation': Film Director Ferenc András"), interview with Brigitta Hegyi Ombódi, *HVG*, November 26, 2012, https://hvg.hu/kultura/20121126_Ronda_generacio_szep_nemzedek__Andras_Fer.

32 Csengey, 49–53, 64.

33 Ibid., 92, 96.

34 Ibid., 188–189.

35 Ibid., 189.

36 Sándor Fodor, Cseh Tamás – interjúregény ("Tamás Cseh: Interview Novel") (Budapest: Graffiti, n.d.), 142.

37 On January 22, 2024—the eighty-first anniversary of Cseh's birth—I attended a Cseh concert at the Alternatív Közgazdasági Gimnázium ("Alternative High School of Economics") in Budapest. Several hundred people crowded into an auditorium to hear students, teachers, and guests—including János Novák—perform Cseh and Bereményi's songs. See Diana Senechal, "Tamás Cseh's Birthday," *Take Away the Takeaway* (blog), January 22, 2024, https://dianasenechal.wordpress.com/2024/01/22/tamas-csehs-birthday/.

Chapter 3

38 Cseh is quoted in the April 1980 issue of *Látóhatár* ("Horizon"), an anthology of news articles, as saying, "A mi időnk most gyors, a dalokat gyorsabban meg lehet hallgatni, mint egy regényt, s ha jók, akkor viszonylag pontos információkat is közölnek. Nem azt mondom, hogy teljeseket, mert ezek helyzetjelentések. Az emberek ebben a felgyorsult időben a saját kétséges helyzeteik között borzasztó kíváncsiak egy pontos helyzetre." ("Our time is fast, you can listen to songs faster than a novel, and if they are good, they convey relatively precise information. I'm not saying they are complete, because these are situation reports. In this accelerated time, in the midst of their own dubious situations, people are terribly eager for a precise situation.") *Látóhatár*, April 1980, 280. The quote appears also on the Petőfi Literary Museum website, "Helyzetjelentések – Cseh Tamás 80," https://pim.hu/kiallitas/helyzetjelentesek-cseh-tamas-80. Bereményi used the term in an interview with Dénes Csengey, "Tíz év után: Csengey Dénes interjúja

Cseh Tamással és Bereményi Gézával" ("After Ten Years: Dénes Csengey's Interview with Tamás Cseh and Géza Bereményi"), *Alföld*, 1981(3), 70–78.

[1] *Levél nővéremnek* ("Letter to My Sister"), recording of concert at the R. Klub on March 25, 1976, featuring Tamás Cseh and János Másik in a performance of songs by Cseh, Másik, János Novák, and Géza Bereményi (lyricist), Cseh Tamás Archívum, https://csehtamasarchivum.hu/level-noveremnek.

[2] Cseh, Másik, Novák, and Bereményi. *Levél nővéremnek* ("Letter to My Sister"), Budapest: Pepita SLPX 17524, 1977, 33⅓ rpm; *Spotify*, https://open.spotify.com/album/4qh8OwdAisw2pj6ZaL7dMM; *Cseh Tamás Archívum*, https://csehtamasarchivum.hu/lemezgyujtemeny/level-noveremnek.

[3] Anna Szemere, "Let's Turn Hegel from His Head onto His Feet: Hopes, Myths, and Memories of the 1960s in Tamás Cseh's Musical Album 'A Letter to My Sister,'" *Slavic Review* 77, no. 4 (Winter 2018), 881–889; 888.

[4] In an email dated November 16, 2023, Géza Bereményi explained the role of the *házmester* under socialism—and also explained that the line regarding the envelope suggests that the speaker himself is the letter being sent. As for the "black hole," in his autobiography Magyar Copperfield, Bereményi refers to the 1956 Revolution as a "black hole" in that he and his classmate did not mention it when discussing history; see Bereményi, Magyar Copperfield (Budapest: Magvető, 2021), 356.

[5] Sándor Fodor, *Cseh Tamás – interjúregény* ("Tamás Cseh: Interview Novel") (Budapest: Graffiti, n.d.), 60.

[6] For a political analysis of "Presszó," see Szemere, 887: "The 'presszó' stands as a metaphor of entrapment in a country bereft of public spaces for creative and critical thought."

[7] Szemere (op. cit., 883), translates the line as "The years succeed each other in an uncanny way," which I especially like but did not want to steal.

[8] Szemere, 884.

[9] Ibid., 887.

[10] Mariann Makádi, "A hazai földrajztanítás története" ("The History of Geography Instruction in Hungary") (Budapest: Eötvös Loránd University, 1973), https://geogo.elte.hu/images/Hazai_foldrajztanitas_toretenete.pdf.

Chapter 4

[1] László Bérczes, *Cseh Tamás: Bérczes László beszélgetőkönyve* ("Tamás Cseh: László Bérczes's Conversation Book") (Budapest: Európa Könyvkiadó, 2019), 106–108.

[2] Grácia Kerényi, "A daloló uborkától az egyszemélyes színházig" ("From the Singing Pickle to the One-Person Theatre"), *Színház*, January 1980: 27–30, 28.

[3] Tamás Cseh and Géza Bereményi, *Antoine és Desiré* (album), with Gábor Kecskeméti, Győző Lukácsházi, István Mártha, János Novák, Péter Román, and Ágnes Szakály (Budapest: Pepita SLPX 17548, 1978, 33⅓ rpm); Bereményi and János Vető, *Antoine és Désiré: Fényképregény az 1970-es évekből* ("Antoine and Désiré: Photograph Novel from the 1970s") (Budapest: Corvina, 2017).

[4] Bérczes, 221–222, 238.

[5] Dénes Csengey. *... és mi most itt vagyunk* (Budapest: Magvető, 1983), 134, 138, in *A kétségbeesés méltósága* ("The Dignity of Despair"), (Budapest: Digitális Irodalmi Akadémia, 2021), https://reader.dia.hu/document/Csengey_Denes-A_ketsegbeeses_meltosaga-34425; Bereményi and Cseh, *Összekacsintó*

(Hungarian television program), no. 3: "Még lesznek dalok," interview by Pál Sándor, 1980, courtesy of the Cseh Tamás Archívum.
[6] The two fictional biographies can be found in the insert in Bereményi and Cseh, *Antoine és Désiré*, 1978, as well as in the Cseh Tamás Archívum, https://csehtamasarchivum.hu/lemezgyujtemeny/antoine-es-desire.
[7] Sándor Fodor, *Cseh Tamás – interjúregény* ("Tamás Cseh: Interview Novel") (Budapest: Graffiti, n.d.), 73; Cseh comments that "Tangó" is one of his favorites.
[8] Fodor, 73.
[9] Dénes Csengey. *... és mi most itt vagyunk*, 134.

Chapter 5

[1] The text of the stage performance of *Frontátvonulás* appears in Bereményi, *Kelet-nyugati pályaudvar* ("Keleti-Nyugati Station") (Budapest: T-Twins Kiadó, 1993); the text quoted here appears on page 26.
[2] An earlier and substantially different version of this chapter appeared as an article: "*Frontátvonulás* ("Frontal Passage"): Tamás Cseh and Géza Bereményi's Album of No Return," *Hungarian Cultural Studies*, September 2024, https://ahea.pitt.edu/ojs/ahea/article/view/561.
[3] Grácia Kerényi, "A daloló uborkától az egyszemélyes színházig" ("From the Singing Pickle to the One-Person Theatre"), *Színház*, January 1980: 27–30, 30.
[4] See, for instance, Albert Gazda, "Félig vagyok" ("I'm Half of Myself"). *Magyar Hang* ("Hungarian Voice"), June 2, 2024, https://hang.hu/kritika/felig-vagyok-frontatvonulas-cseh-tamas-164434. After its March 2024 debut in Budapest, the SZFE production of *Frontátvonulás* traveled to the Holnaput31 Fesztival in Nagyvárad (Romania), Ördögkatlan Fesztivál (Hungary), the Őriszentpéter Fesztivál (Hungary), and and numerous venues in Hungary and Romania. In December 2024, the cast and director announced the founding of their own theatre company, SICC Production; the *Frontátvonulás* performances continue, along with their newer productions.
[5] First opened in 1884, and significantly damaged during World War II, the Keleti train station underwent repair in the 1950s and 60s; the ticket windows and restaurant, added during that time, figure prominently in *Frontátvonulás*. The 1970s can be considered the station's second golden age after that of the early 1900s. With its express international as well as domestic lines, the station represented a connection to the outside world. In *Frontátvonulás*, however, all travel ceases; the trains are not running at all until the breakthrough at the end. For more about the station's history, see Indóház Online ("Station Online"), "Isten éltessen, Keleti pályaudvar! – 1. rész" ("Long Live Keleti Station! – Part 1"), *IHO.hu*, August16, 2014, https://iho.hu/hirek/isten-eltessen-keleti-palyaudvar-1-resz-140816;"Isten éltessen, Keleti pályaudvar! – 2. rész" („Long Live Keleti Station! – Part 2"), *IHO.hu*, August 17, 2014, https://iho.hu/hirek/isten-eltessen-keleti-palyaudvar-2-resz-140817.
[6] See Dénes Csengey, *... és mi most itt vagyunk* ("And We Are Here Now") (Budapest: Magvető, 1983), 188–189, in *A kétségbeesés méltósága* ("The Dignity of Despair") (Budapest: Digitális Irodalmi Akadémia, 2021), https://reader.dia.hu/document/Csengey_Denes-A_ketsegbeeses_meltosaga-34425..
[7] At the Cseh Tamás Archívum, on January 4, 2024, I listened to two complete unreleased recordings of *Frontátvonulás* concerts: a performance at the Ifjúsági Ház ("Youth House") in Szeged on October 30, 1979, and one at the Szkéné Theatre in Budapest in 1980. In addition, I watched an eight-minute video of a

performance of *Frontátvonulás,* which includes the part where Cseh, in the character of Vizi, releases the glass.

8 The reader can find the lyrics and sound recording at https://csehtamasarchivum.hu/lemezgyujtemeny/frontatvonulas and https://open.spotify.com/album/3x9OV7SvFjyaarmFJnWYFl?si=_inkq9NwRD KWU03zc13pLg, respectively.

9 Tamás Cseh and Géza Bereményi, *Frontátvonulás* ("Frontal Passage"), Budapest: Krém SLPX 17756, 1983, 33⅓ rpm. *Spotify,* https://open.spotify.com/album/3x9OV7SvFjyaarmFJnWYFl. *Cseh Tamás Archívum* https://csehtamasarchivum.hu/lemezgyujtemeny/frontatvonulas. The quoted definition of *frontátvonulás* can be found in Mariann Makádi, *Foldrajzi fogalomtár: A közoktatásban használt legfontosabb foldrajzi fogalmak* ("Geographical glossary: The most important geographical concepts used in public education"), Budapest: Eötvös Loránd Tudományegyetem, Természettudományi Kar, Földrajz- és Földtudományi Intézet ("Eötvös Loránd University, Faculty of Natural Sciences, Institute of Geography and Earth Sciences"), 2015, updated 2018, http://geogo.elte.hu/images/Foldrajzi_fogalomtar.pdf, 29. I would like to thank the editors of *Hungarian Cultural Studies* for pointing out the additional connotation.

10 Kerényi, 29; Cseh, "Nehéz könnyűzene" ("Heavy Popular Music"), interview by Judit Magyar, *Magyar Ifjúság* ("Hungarian Youth"), April 1980, 36.

11 The song is sung by Cseh in the character of *Sas elvtárs* ("Comrade Sas," or "Comrade Eagle"), but its official title is "Sors elvtárs dala" ("Song of Comrade Fate").

12 I had the opportunity to speak with Kristóf Fülöp about Frontátvonulás over Zoom on October 15, 2025 and with Vilmos Krasznai over Messenger on October 21, 2025. Fülöp also spoke about *Frontátvonulás* at a discussion hosted by the critic portal Revizor at the DANTE Közösségi Alkotótér ("DANTE Community Creator Space") on Tuesday, September 30, 2025. As for the stage set, I saw them assemble it at the Ördögkatlan Fesztivál on August 3, 2024. (See Diana Senechal, "Ördögkatlan (the last two days)," *Take Away The Takeaway* (blog), August 4, 2024, https://dianasenechal.wordpress.com/2024/08/04/ordogkatlan-the-last-two-days/.

13 Kristóf Fülöp, Zoom interview with Diana Senechal, October 15, 2025, 7 p.m. CET; Vilmos Krasznai, Messenger interview with Diana Senechal, Messenger, October 21, 2025, 5:20 p.m. CET.

14 Ibid.

15 Kristóf Fülöp, Zoom interview with Diana Senechal, October 15, 2025, 7 p.m. CET.

16 Ibid.

17 Kristóf Fülöp, Zoom interview with Diana Senechal, October 15, 2025, 7 p.m. CET; Vilmos Krasznai, Messenger interview with Diana Senechal, Messenger, October 21, 2025, 5:20 p.m. CET.

18 Ibid.

19 Ibid.

20 Ibid.

Chapter 6

1 Kerényi, "Jóslat: Cseh Tamás–est a Katona József Színházban," 31. The Petőfi poem quoted here is "Falu végén kurta kocsma" ("A squat pub at the end of the

village"), written in Szatmár in 1847 (for the text, see https://mek.oszk.hu/01000/01006/html/vs184705.htm#91).

2 Attila Michnai, "Michnai Attila emlékezése, Cseh Tamás Archívum: Jóslat" ("Attila Michnai's Recollections, Tamás Cseh Archive: Jóslat"), n.d., https://csehtamasarchivum.hu/tortenet/michnai-attila-emlekezese. The text of the stage performance of *Jóslat* can be found in Bereményi, *Kelet-nyugati pályaudvar* ("Keleti-Nyugati Station"). Budapest: T-Twins, 1993. Cseh's last stage performance of *Jóslat*, on May 2, 1986 at the Csurgó, can be viewed on the Cseh Tamás Archívum website, https://csehtamasarchivum.hu/az-utolso-joslat-koncert. The album, which differs markedly from the stage performance, is Cseh and Bereményi, *Jóslat* ("Prophecy") (Budapest: Krém SLPM 17857, 1984), 33⅓ rpm, *Spotify*, https://open.spotify.com/album/2OGUSGDhfr6E41NjGBCvz0, *Cseh Tamás Archívum*, https://csehtamasarchivum.hu/lemezgyujtemeny/joslat.

3 Kerényi, 30–31; Péter Fábri, "Jóslat elmúlt időkről," *Magyar Ifjúság*, June 22, 1984, 26–27.

4 An image of the poster for the opening night of *Jóslat* is available at the Cseh Tamás Archívum.

5 When writing "Az égboltsapkájú" in 1972 or 1973, Bereményi did not realize that he was quoting Weöres; he later asked Weöres for permission to publish the song and did not receive it at the time. Weöres eventually granted permission; the song appeared, with permission and credit, on *Jóslat*. See Gábor Hanák, "A dalírás gesztusai" ("The Gestures of Songwriting"), *Országút*, February 1, 2023, https://orszagut.com/eloadomuveszet/cseh-tamas-beremenyi-geza-a-daliras-gesztusai-3817.

6 On the Cseh Tamás Archívum website, the description of the March 26, 1976, concert at the R Klub explains: "Certain songs can be heard in the *Levél nővéremnek* show that were left off of the album that appeared one year later, in March 1977. One such song, for instance, is "70 or 60" ("Prophecy"), which became the opening and title song on the 1984 *Prophecy* album; or "A Beetle," which was recorded for the *Antoine és Désiré* album." See https://csehtamasarchivum.hu/level-noveremnek.

7 Kerényi, 31.

8 The song "Megholt feleségem" appears in a folk song collection handwritten from memory by the poet János Arany for István Bartalus: Bartalus, ed., *Régi Népdalok, melyeket Népdalgyűjteményem számára Arany János gyermekkori emlékeiből sajátkezüleg írt le hangjegyekkel* ("Old Folk Songs, which János Arany wrote out with music notes in his own hand for my Folk Song collection"), 1874, http://arany.btk.mta.hu/verseskotetek/regi-nepdalok.

9 Sándor Fodor, *Cseh Tamás: Interjúregény* ("Tamás Cseh: Interview Novel") (Budapest: Graffiti, n.d.), 122.

10 Ibid., 123.

11 Ibid., 124.

12 Ibid.

Chapter 7

1 For a detailed examination of the release of Hollywood films in the Kádár era, see Róbert Takács, "Hollywood Ascendant: American Films in Hungary in the 1970s," *Hungarian Journal of English and American Studies*, vol. 24, no. 1 (Spring 2018), 191–218.

2 "Hungarian Eastern—Stories of the Outlaw," Hungarian National Digital Archive, n.d., https://en.mandadb.hu/cikk/924070/Hungarian_eastern__Stories_of_the_out law.

3 Tamás Cseh and Géza Bereményi, "Mindig csak végig" ("Always to the End"), Cseh Tamás Archívum, https://csehtamasarchivum.hu/dal/classic/mindig-csak-vegig-filmdal.

4 Tamás Cseh, *Western dalok* ("Western Songs") (Budapest: PIM – Cseh Tamás Archívum, 2024).

5 Howard Hughes, *Once Upon a Time in the Italian West: A Filmgoer's Guide to Spaghetti Westerns* (London: I.B. Tauris, 2005), 45.

6 Thanks to my colleague Gyula Jenei for an explication of this line.

7 Bence Aradi, "Lee van Cleef,...avagy olykor egy kissé Csehül állunk" ("Lee van Cleef...or, Sometimes We Are a Bit Cseh-like"), *Irodalmi dimenziók* ("Literary Dimensions"), August 6, 2016, https://aradib.blog.hu/2016/08/06/lee_van_cleef_902.

8 The correct spelling is Kearny, but I am deliberately leaving it as Carney, for reasons to be explained later.

9 Robert Burns, "John Barleycorn: A Ballad" (1782), Burns Country (website), https://www.robertburns.org/works/27.shtml.

10 Ákos Somos, "Benne van az egész világ: A tíz legszebb Cseh Tamás-ballada" ('The Whole World Is In It: The Ten Most Beautiful Tamás Cseh Ballads"), *WMN*, January 22, 2016, https://wmn.hu/kult/21774-benne-van-az-egesz-vilag-a-tiz-legszebb-cseh-tamas-ballada.

Chapter 8

1 Tamás Cseh, "Az *Utóirat* után: Beszélgetés Cseh Tamással" ("After the *Postscript*: Conversation with Tamás Cseh"), interview with Zoltán Szentgáli, *EF-lapok* ("EF-Pages"), 1987, issue 12, 102–103.

2 Jánosz Szász, Utóirat (short film), 1988, viewable on YouTube in two parts, https://www.youtube.com/watch?v=4RGHGf-BTXs and
 https://www.youtube.com/watch?v=ooaa3leVMD8.

3 Attila Kovács, "Cseh Tamás: Utóirat" ("Tamás Cseh: Postscript"), *Népújság* ("People's News"), August 26, 1987, 5.

4 F. László Földényi, *A melankólia dicsérete* ("In Praise of Melancholy") (Budapest: Jelenkor, 2017), 23, 39–40, 51.

5 Cseh, interview on *Stúdió '87* (Magyar Televízió).

6 "Szász János," Nemzeti Színház ("National Theatre"), https://nemzetiszinhaz.hu/muvesz/szasz-janos; Peter Marks, "With 'Angels in America,' a Hungarian Director Puts Down Roots in U.S.," Washington Post, March 24, 2023, https://www.washingtonpost.com/theater-dance/2023/03/24/janos-szasz-arena-angels-kushner/; "János Szász: Biography," American Repertory Theater, https://americanrepertorytheater.org/bio/janos-szasz/; "János Szász: Awards," IMDB, https://www.imdb.com/name/nm0844444/awards/; Szász, "Jövőre elmúlik, ami most Magyarországon van, egy év múlva otthon leszek" ("Next Year What is Now in Hungary Will Pass; In a Year I Will Be at Home"), interview with Júlia Váradi, *Klubrádió*, May 18, 2025, https://www.klubradio.hu/adasok/szasz-janos-jovore-elmulik-ami-most-magyarorszagon-van-egy-ev-mulva-otthon-leszek-152533.

7   Mihály   Babits,   "Kosztolányi,"   *Nyugat*,   1936,   issue   12, https://www.arcanum.com/hu/online-kiadvanyok/Nyugat-nyugat-1908-1941-FFFF0002/1936-458B99/1936-12-szam-48C399/babits-mihaly-kosztolanyi-4BC399/; the quote appears in English in Hanna Zelma Horányi, "Dezső Kosztolányi: Anna Édes," *Hungarian Literature Online*, December 27, 2024, https://hlo.hu/zoom/dezso-kosztolanyi-anna-edes.html.
8 Péter Pál Tóth, "Cseh Tamás énekel" ("Tamás Cseh Sings"), *Kapu* ("Gate"), 1990:6, 70–71.

Chapter 9

1 Tamás Cseh, János Másik, Géza Bereményi, "Keresztben jégeső" ("Sideways Hail"), *Az igazi levél nővéremnek* ("The True Letter to My Sister") (Budapest: Intuison IR007-D, 2004), CD; lyrics available on the Cseh Tamás Archívum website,   https://csehtamasarchivum.hu/lemezgyujtemeny-track/keresztben-jegeso-0;   Spotify, https://open.spotify.com/track/62CGG89JOm7HcdbkAbc6Gc?si=24b1a23b2bd 9424a.
2 Bereményi, *Magyar Copperfield* (Budapest: Magvető, 2020), 485–516; Bérczes, 75.
3 Gábor Losonci-Kovács, "Keresztben jégeső," *kovaboR.hu* (blog), October 29, 2008, https://blog.kovabor.hu/2008/10/keresztben-jegeso/.
4 For Cseh's account of the falling out, see Bérczes, 221–222; for his account of the reconciliation, see Sándor Fodor, *Cseh Tamás – interjúregény* ("Tamás Cseh: Interview Novel") (Budapest: Graffiti, n.d.), 198.
5 János Arany, Ágost Gyulai, and Zoltán Kodály, eds., *Arany János népdalgyűjteménye - Az 1952-ben megjelent, Kodály Zoltán széljegyzeteivel ellátott gyűjtemény hasonmás kiadása* ("János Arany's Folk Song Collection: A Facsimile Edition of the Collection Published in 1952 with Marginal Notes by Zoltán Kodály") (Budapest: Argumentum, 2011). I became aware of this song through the performance by Ágoston Liber and Martos Domonkos, featured in the 2024 film *Bolond Istók* ("Istók the Fool") and in a related music video directed by Gábor Attila Kovács (https://www.youtube.com/watch?v=GgGjjMGR3Dg).

Chapter 10

1 The basic biographical facts in this essay—except for the details about Kerényi's Jewish background and her specific experiences as a political prisoner—are drawn from "Kerényi Grácia," *Magyar életrajzi lexikon* ("Hungarian Biographical Lexicon"), ed. Ágnes Kenyeres, *Arcanum*, n.d., https://www.arcanum.com/hu/online-kiadvanyok/Lexikonok-magyar-eletrajzi-lexikon-7428D/k-760F2/kerenyi-gracia-76340/); some of the lesser-known details come from Gizella Csisztay, "Kerényi Grácia, a lehetetlen ostromlója" ("Grácia Kerényi, Besieger of the Impossible"), *Óbudai Anziksz*, Winter 2017–2018,   https://obudaianziksz.hu/csisztay-gizella-kerenyi-gracia-a-lehetetlen-ostromloja-3/; and György Gömöri, "Kerényi Grácia 'halacskái'" ("Grácia Kerényi's 'Fish'"), *Egy szigetlakó feljegyzéseiből: Esszék* ("From the Notes of an Islander: Essays") (Budapest: Cserépfalvi, 1996), published online at Magyar Elektronikus Könyvtár ("Hungarian Electronic Library"), https://www.mek.oszk.hu/02500/02562/02562.htm. Further sources, including Kerényi's own writing, are cited as appropriate.

² Kerényi, "A daloló uborkától az egyszemélyes színházig" ("From the Singing Pickle to the One-Person Theatre"), *Színház*, January 1980: 27–30. Konstanty Ildefons Gałczyński's 1946 poem "Dlaczego ogórek nie śpiewa" ("Why Doesn't the Pickle Sing?") was published by Świat Książki in his 2003 collection by the same title; according to his website, it is from the unfinished work entitled *Miłosierdzie* ("Mercy"). The text can be found at http://www.kigalczynski.pl/wiersze/dlaczego_ogorek_nie_spiewa.html. Kerényi's translation was published in *Világirodalmi antológia* ("World Literature Anthology") VI, vol. 2 (Budapest: Tankönyvkiadó, 1962), p. 293; the text can be found at https://versnaptar.blog.hu/2019/08/28/augusztus_28_konstanty_ildefons_gal czynsky_miert_nem_dalol_az_uborka. According to the staff at the Cseh Tamás Archívum, there is no known recording of Cseh singing the poem and no evidence, beyond Kerényi's word, that these were the first lyrics that he sang that were not his own.

³ Some sources give April 9 as her birthdate, but this is an error.

⁴ Information on Erzsébet Stamberger's parents' burial can be found in Péter Kozák, "Kerényi Károly," *Névpont*, https://www.nevpont.hu/palyakep/kerenyi-karoly-228e3; this information, based on published obituaries, is carefully documented in the accompanying notes. For insight into Jewish assimilation in Hungary, see Gábor Gyáni, "Image versus Identity: Assimilation and Discrimination of Hungary's Jewry," *Hungarian Studies*, vol. 18, no. 2 (2004), 153–162, http://efolyoirat.niif.hu/01400/01462/00032/pdf/153-162.pdf.

⁵ The first 128 pages of Kerényi's *Utazások könyve* ("Book of Travels") (Budapest: Szépirodalmi Könyvkiadó, 1979) describe and document her stay at the concentration camps. Her 1974 essay "Nem Mindegy" ("It Isn't All the Same"), about the Warsaw Ghetto Uprising and about moral choice in the face of death, was published in 1984 in her volume of that title (Budapest: Szépirodalmi Könyvkiadó). Some accounts claim that she wrote "Le a németekkel" ("Down with the Germans") on a wall at the university; however, in her essay "Amikor én ellenáltam" ("When I Protested"), *Topográfia* (Budapest: self-published, n.d.), 16, she specifies that she drew the words in the fogged up windows of the university's third floor (called the second floor in Hungary). In addition, she made and distributed cockades (knots of ribbons) in Hungary's national colors.

⁶ Ibid., 29. For a detailed account of Károly Kerényi's attempts to have his daughter released, see "Egyéb dokumentumok" ("Other Documents"), ibid., 117–128, as well as László Karsai, "Kislány rövid copfokkal, aranyszínű mackóval: Kerényi Grácia Auschwitzban" ("Little Girl with Short Pigtails, Golden Teddy Bear: Grácia Kerényi in Auschwitz," *Kritika*, vol. 90, no. 9 (1990), 410–414. This article documents how Kerényi's mother wrote to a colleague of the father (as did Kerényi's father separately), emphasizing Kerényi's innocence and Christian identity, and signing the letter with both her husband's name and her own (the latter as "dr. Kerényi Károlyné," with no "Stamberger"). Karsai—entirely unaware of the mother's Jewish origins—could not grasp why she signed the letter with both her married name and her ex-husband's, but it appears to me that she wanted to intervene for her daughter without raising questions or causing further harm.

⁷ Kerényi, "Amikor én ellenáltam" ("When I Protested"), *Topográfia* (Budapest: self-published, n.d.), 18–19; Kerényi, "Bandi búcsújója" ("Farewell to Bandi"), *Dalok könyve* ("Book of Songs") (self-published, 1982), 53–55.

⁸ Regarding Kerényi's translation activities and how they differed from those of her fellow translators, see Csisztay, op. cit.

---

[9] Csisztay (op. cit.) also describes Kerényi's friendships and associations with Polish writers.

[10] The poster can be viewed on the website of the Cseh Tamás Archívum, https://csehtamasarchivum.hu/dokumentum/piosenki-i-wiersze-wegierskie-magyar-dalok-es-versek-koncertplakat; for Márta's interview, see István Márta, "Cseh Tamás az irónia és az önirónia művésze volt" ("Tamás Cseh Was an Artist of Irony and Self-Irony"), interview with Zsolt Sütő-Nagy, *Magyar Hírlap* ("Hungarian Newspaper"), January 22, 2023 (updated January 27, 2023), https://www.magyarhirlap.hu/kultura/20230122-cseh-tamas-az-ironia-es-az-onironia-muvesze-volt.

[11] Csisztay, op. cit.

[12] Ibid.

[13] Gömöri, "Kerényi Grácia 'halacskái'" ("Grácia Kerényi's 'Fish'"); John Moody and Roger Boyes, *The Priest and the Policeman: The Courageous Life and Cruel Murder of Father Jerzy Popieluszko* (New York: Summit Books, 1987).

[14] Kerényi, "Levél nővéremnek" ("Letter to My Sister"), *Film Színház Muzsika* ("Film, Theatre, Music"), March 6, 1976, https://csehtamasarchivum.hu/tortenet/kerenyi-gracia-level-noveremnek; Kerényi gives the dates of the premiere of *Levél nővéremnek* in her article "A daloló uborkától az egyszemélyes színházig" ('From the Singing Pickle to the One-Person Theatre'), *Színház*, January 1980: 27–30, 27.

[15] Kerényi, "Levél nővéremnek" ("Letter to My Sister").

[16] Ibid; a recording, available on the Cseh Tamás Archívum website, of the March 26, 1976, show at the R Klub, suggests the song's absence from that show (https://csehtamasarchivum.hu/level-noveremnek).

[17] Kerényi, "A daloló uborkától az egyszemélyes színházig" ('From the Singing Pickle to the One-Person Theatre'), 27.

[18] Ibid.

[19] Ibid., 28–30.

[20] Ibid., 28–29.

[21] Márta, "Cseh Tamás az irónia és az önirónia művésze volt" ("Tamás Cseh Was an Artist of Irony and Self-Irony").

[22] The obituary of Dr. Stamberger Salamonné (i.e., the wife of Dr. Salamon Stamberger), née Franciska Strausz, was published in *Pesti Hírlap* ("Pest Newspaper"), April 30, 1931. It mentions her burial in the Rákoskeresztúr "Israelite" cemetery and lists Kerényi, her mother, and her sister among her survivors. Kerényi's maternal grandfather, Dr. Salamon Stamberger, died in 1914 (eleven years before Kerényi's birth) and was buried in the same cemetery.

[23] John Donne, "Meditation XVII," in *Devotions upon Emergent Occasions* (1623), in *The Works of John Donne*, ed. Henry Alford (London: John W. Parker), 1839, 574–575.

[24] I am aware of two other English translations of Gałczyński's poem: one by S. Barańczak and C. Cavanagh, and another by Aniela Korzeniowska. Both can be found at http://www.bokorlang.com/journal/18soundapp.htm.

Chapter 11

[1] "Hátborzongatóan szép történet áll Bereményi Géza legnépszerűbb dalszövete mögött" ("An Eerily Beautiful Story Behind Géza Bereményi's Most Popular Song Lyrics"), *Fidelio*, December 5, 2022, https://fidelio.hu/jazz-world/hatborzongatoan-szep-tortenet-all-beremenyi-geza-legnepszerubb-

dalszovege-mogott-176020.html. (I have heard Bereményi tell slightly different versions of this story, but the essence is the same.)

2 Gábor Hanák, "'Kegyetlen keményen tudta énekelni'—Hanák Gábor Cseh Tamásról, Víg Mihályról és az új tripla lemezükről" ("'He could sing it brutally hard': Gábor Hanák on Tamás Cseh, Mihály Víg and Their New Triple Album"), interview with Tamás Soós, *Recorder*, December 5, 2023, https://recorder.blog.hu/2023/12/05/kegyetlen_kemenyen_tudta_enekelni_ha nak_gabor_cseh_tamasrol_vig_mihalyrol_tripla_lemezukrol_interju.

3 Bérczes, *Cseh Tamás: Bérczes László beszélgetőkönyve* ("Tamás Cseh: László Bérczes' Conversation Book") (Budapest: Európa Könyvkiadó, 2019), 6; Bérczes, with Balázs Csengey, "Tárlatvezetés" ("Guided Tour"), *Helyzetjelentések – Cseh Tamás 80* ("Situation Reports—Tamás Cseh 80"), exhibition event, Petőfi Literary Museum, Budapest, January 21, 2024. Recording accessed at the Tamás Cseh Archívum on April 23, 2025.

4 Ördögkatlan Fesztivál (website), "A Katlan," 2025, https://ordogkatlan.hu/2020/05/12/a-katlan; ; about his smoking, see 19–21, about the strain that his performance schedule placed on his family life, see 291–294.

5 About Cseh's habit of giving away his guitars (including one given to him by Másik), see Bérczes, 68.

6 János Másik, with Balázs Csengey, "Finisszázs a *Helyzetjelentések – Cseh Tamás 80* kiállításban" ("Finissage at the *Situation Reports—Tamás Cseh 80* Exhibition"), Petőfi Literary Museum, Budapest, April 24, 2024. Recording accessed at the Tamás Cseh Archívum on April 23, 2025.

7 "Novák János emlékezése" ("János Novák's Reminiscence"), Cseh Tamás Archívum, 2025, https://csehtamasarchivum.hu/tortenet/novak-janos-emlekezese.

8 István Márta, with Balázs Csengey, "Tárlatvezetés" ("Guided Tour"), *Helyzetjelentések – Cseh Tamás 80* ("Situation Reports—Tamás Cseh 80"), exhibition event, Petőfi Literary Museum, Budapest, September 27, 2023. Recording accessed at the Tamás Cseh Archívum on April 23, 2025.

9 A recording of Víg performing Cseh and Bereményi's "Az ócska cipő" in a 2017 concert at the Lumen can be found on YouTube at https://www.youtube.com/watch?v=E2kEoaIoohI.

10 János Háy, with Balázs Csengey, "Tárlatvezetés" ("Guided Tour"), *Helyzetjelentések – Cseh Tamás 80* ("Situation Reports—Tamás Cseh 80"), exhibition event, Petőfi Literary Museum, Budapest, December 5, 2023. Recording accessed at the Tamás Cseh Archívum on April 23, 2025.

11 Zoltán Beck, "'Egy kitalált személy neve' – a színpadon álló személyről" ("'The Name of an Invented Person': About the Person on the Stage"), plenary lecture, *Helyzetjelentések: A Cseh Tamás–életmű megközelítési lehetőségei és hatásai* ("Situation Reports: Approaches and impacts of the Oeuvre of Tamás Cseh"), conference held by the PTE BTK, Irodalom és Kultúratudományi Doktori Iskola and the MNMKK Petőfi Irodalmi Múzeum – Cseh Tamás Archívum at the University of Pécs, November 6–7, 2025.

12 Zoltán Beck and Krisztián Szűcs, with Balázs Csengey, "Tárlatvezetés" ("Guided Tour"), *Helyzetjelentések – Cseh Tamás 80* ("Situation Reports—Tamás Cseh 80"), exhibition event, Petőfi Literary Museum, Budapest, June 24, 2023. Recording accessed at the Tamás Cseh Archívum on April 23, 2025. "Hvg.hu premier: Itt a teljes film a Cseh Tamás – Leonard Cohen emlékkoncertről" ("Hvg.hu Premiere: Here Is the Complete Film of the Tamás Cseh – Leonard Cohen Memorial Concert"), *Hvg.hu*, July 14, 2018,

https://hvg.hu/kultura/20180714_Hvghupremier_Itt_a_teljes_film_a_Cseh_T
amasLeonard_Cohen_emlekkoncertrol ; "Megjelent Beck Zoli, Cseh Tamás,
Csengey Dénes és Szűcs Krisztián lemeze" ("An Album by Zoli Beck, Tamás Cseh,
Dénes Csengey, and Krisztián Szűcs Has Been Released"), *Kultura*, May 31, 2023,
https://kultura.hu/megjelent-a-masnap-beck-zoli-cseh-tamas-csengey-denes-es-
szucs-krisztian-lemeze/; Cseh and Bereményi, with János Novák, *Western dalok*
("Western Songs") (Budapest: PIM – Cseh Tamás Archívum, 2024).

[13] László Sallai, email to Diana Senechal on October 5, 2025.

[14] Márton Hó et al., "'Volt egy hős, akinek sikerült' – zenészek Cseh Tamásról"
("'There Was a Hero Who Succeeded': Musicians on Tamás Cseh"), *Recorder*,
January 22, 2018,
https://recorder.blog.hu/2018/01/22/_volt_egy_hos_akinek_sikerult_zeneszek
_cseh_tamasrol; Ádám Bicsérdi-Fülöp, "Egyedülálló férfi megosztaná életét,
álmát, tudását" ("A Solitary Man Would Share His Life, Dream, Knowledge"),
Telex, January 16, 2025, https://telex.hu/after/2025/01/16/ho-marton-horvath-
marton-jegkorszak-enekes-dalszerzo-eletmu.

[15] Hó Márton és a Jégkorszak, "Dalok a fürdőszobából" ("Songs from the
Bathroom"), 2011, https://jegkorszak.bandcamp.com/album/dalok-a-f-rd-szob-
b-l; Erik Sumo, Facebook post, January 19, 2025,
https://www.facebook.com/eriksumo/posts/pfbidopSmyNuWk6rayU64M64RK
mAY9DGNnjgcUqZkC6Qo57RDykuDJdUL4CXGV9jfqmJWvl.

[16] Olivér Csepella and Dávid Konsiczky, with Balázs Csengey, "Tárlatvezetés"
("Guided Tour"), *Helyzetjelentések – Cseh Tamás 80* ("Situation Reports—Tamás
Cseh 80"), exhibition event, Petőfi Literary Museum, Budapest, March 27, 2024.
Recording accessed at the Tamás Cseh Archívum on April 23, 2025.

[17] Olivér Csepella, "Nem ilyen fejet képzelsz el egy rocksztárnak" ("You don't
imagine such a head for a rockstar"), interview with Dávid Sajó, *Index*, November
25, 2015,
https://index.hu/kultur/zene/2015/11/25/csaknekedkislany_csepella_oliver_int
erju_klip_lemez/; Csaknekedkislány ("Justforyougirl"), "Cseh Tamás," *Na ná ba
bám* (album), 2015, https://www.youtube.com/watch?v=rDRotSMToTs.

[18] Benedek Szabó, "Amikor különben egyáltalán nem volt jó" ("When it was
otherwise not good at all"), interview with Endre Dömötör, *Recorder*, June 3, 2015,
https://recorder.blog.hu/2015/06/03/_amikor_kulonben_egyaltalan_nem_volt
_jo_szabo_benedek-interju.

[19] Szabó on the Hungarian album he considers most important, *Telexafter*
(Telex.hu), September 14, 2025,
https://www.instagram.com/p/DOl5HBRDBgM/?e=3771259e-908a-4099-ad37-
62a07587d44a&g=5.

Chapter 12

[1] László Bérczes, *Cseh Tamás: Bérczes László beszélgetőkönyve* ("Tamás Cseh:
László Bérczes's Conversation Book") (Budapest: Európa Könyvkiadó, 2019), 39.

Select Bibliography

András, Ferenc. "'Ronda generáció, szép nemzedék'—András Ferenc filmrendező" ("'Ugly Cohort, Lovely Generation': Film Director Ferenc András"). Interview with Brigitta Hegyi Ombódi. *HVG*, November 26, 2012, https://hvg.hu/kultura/20121126_Ronda_generacio_szep_nemzedek__An dras_Fer. Accessed October 28, 2025.

Barna, Emília, and Ágnes Patakfalvi-Csirják. *"The 'System of National Cooperation' hit factory: the aesthetic of Hungarian government-commissioned songs between 2010 and 2020." Popular Music 41, no. 3 (2022): 333–353.*

Bérczes, László. *Cseh Tamás: Bérczes László beszélgetőkönyve* ("Tamás Cseh: László Bérczes's Conversation Book"). Budapest: Európa Könyvkiadó, 2019.

Bérczes, László, and Jenő Hartyándi, directors. *Cseh Tamás – Az utolsó koncert* ("Tamás Cseh: The Last Concert") (film). MEDIAWAVE Alapítvány - BÁRKA Színház, 2006–2009, https://www.mediawavearchivum.hu/index.php?modul=filmek&kod=3333 &nf=1&nyelv=hun. Accessed October 28, 2025.

Bereményi, Géza. "Bereményi Géza: Én gyáva voltam, ő meg tudatlan" ("Géza Bereményi: I was a coward, and he was ignorant"). Interview by Fruzsina Lázár. *Magyar Nemzet* ("Hungarian Nation"), March 5, 2017, https://magyarnemzet.hu/nagyinterju-a-magazinban/2017/03/beremenyi-geza-en-gyava-voltam-o-meg-tudatlan. Accessed October 28, 2025.

——. *Magyar Copperfield* ("Hungarian Copperfield"). Budapest: Magvető, 2021.

——. "Bereményi Géza: Ezek angyali pillanatok voltak" ("Géza Bereményi: These Were Angelic Moments"). Interview by Éva Tarnócai. *Pepita Magazin*, September 14. 2022, https://pepitamagazin.com/beremenyi-geza-ezek-angyali-pillanatok-voltak/. Accessed October 28, 2025.

——. "Egy dologba vagyok szerelmes: az A4-es papírba" ("I Am in Love with One Thing: A4 Paper"). Interview by Gergely Bödők. *Új Szó* ("New Word"), November 14, 2022, https://ujszo.com/szalon/egy-dologba-vagyok-szerelmes-az-a4-es-papirba. Accessed October 28, 2025.

——. *Kelet-nyugati pályaudvar* ("Keleti-Nyugati Station"). Budapest: T-Twins, 1993.

——. *Magyar Copperfield* ("Hungarian Copperfield"). Budapest: Magvető, 2021.

——. *Versek* ("Poems"). Budapest: Magvető, 2020.

Bereményi, Géza, and János Vető. *Antoine és Désiré: Fényképregény az 1970-es évekből* ("Antoine and Désiré: Photograph Novel from the 1970s"). Budapest: Corvina, 2017.

Bolvári-Takács, Gábor. "Arts Policy in Kádár Era in Hungary, 1957–1989." *Hungarian Studies*, vol. 37, no. 2, https://akjournals.com/view/journals/044/37/2/article-p318.xml. Accessed October 28, 2025.

Cseh, Tamás. "Nehéz könnyűzene" ("Heavy Popular Music"). Interview by Judit Magyar. *Magyar Ifjúság* ("Hungarian Youth"), April 1980, 36.

——. "A titok a dalokban van" ("The Secret Is in the Songs"). Interview by Stefánia Horváth. *Bel-Ami*, August 29, 1994, https://csehtamasarchivum.hu/tortenet/titok-dalokban-van. Accessed October 28, 2025.

——. Western dalok ("Western Songs"). Budapest: PIM – Cseh Tamás Archívum, 2024, 33⅓ rpm.

Cseh, Tamás, and Géza Bereményi. Television interview by Pál Sándor. *Összekacsintó* ("Wink") 3: "Még lesznek dalok" ("There Will Be More Songs"), 1980.

——. *Antoine és Désiré* ("Antoine and Désiré"). Budapest: Pepita SLPX 17548, 1978, 33⅓ rpm. *Spotify*, https://open.spotify.com/album/316XLlIN1xyyT8sxQkXRTI. *Cseh Tamás Archívum*, https://csehtamasarchivum.hu/lemezgyujtemeny/antoine-es-desire. Accessed October 28, 2025.

——. *Fehér babák takarodója* ("White Dolls' Curfew"). Budapest: Pepita, SLPX 17595, 1979, 33⅓ rpm. *Spotify*, https://open.spotify.com/album/3M6gziJ4dgImv5815vOp5o. *Cseh Tamás Archívum*, https://csehtamasarchivum.hu/lemezgyujtemeny/feher-babak-takarodoja. Accessed October 28, 2025.

——. *Frontátvonulás* ("Frontal Passage"). Budapest: Krém SLPX 17756, 1983, 33⅓ rpm. *Spotify*, https://open.spotify.com/album/3x9OV7SvFjyaarmFJnWYFl. *Cseh Tamás Archívum*, https://csehtamasarchivum.hu/lemezgyujtemeny/frontatvonulas. Accessed October 28, 2025.

——. *Jóslat* ("Prophecy"). Budapest: Krém SLPM 17857, 1984, 33⅓ rpm. *Spotify*, https://open.spotify.com/album/2OGUSGDhfr6E41NjGBCvzo. *Cseh Tamás Archívum*, https://csehtamasarchivum.hu/lemezgyujtemeny/joslat. Accessed October 28, 2025.

——. *Műcsarnok* ("Art Gallery"). Budapest: Krém SLPX 17656, 1981, 33⅓ rpm. *Spotify,* https://open.spotify.com/album/4moGupbtnFoWqQJIeqMeMy. *Cseh Tamás Archívum,* https://csehtamasarchivum.hu/lemezgyujtemeny/mucsarnok. Accessed October 28, 2025.

——. *Titkos dalok* (DVD). Mirax, 2009.

——. *Utóirat* ("Postscript"). Budapest: Hungaroton SLPX 14061–62, 1987. *Spotify,* https://open.spotify.com/album/5llyI6dkTXKowJKkBVcRGy. *Cseh Tamás Archívum,* https://csehtamasarchivum.hu/lemezgyujtemeny/utoirat. Accessed October 28, 2025.

Cseh, Tamás, and Dénes Csengey. *Mélyrepülés* ("Flying Low" or "Deep Dive"). Budapest: Hungaroton SLPX 14114, 1988, 33⅓ rpm. *Spotify,* https://open.spotify.com/album/31NFJuIO7UcaebxT4qQBdc. *Cseh Tamás Archívum,* https://csehtamasarchivum.hu/lemezgyujtemeny/melyrepules. Accessed October 28, 2025.

Cseh, Tamás, János Másik, and Géza Bereményi. *Levél nővéremnek* ("Letter to My Sister"). Budapest: Pepita SLPX 17524, 1977, 33⅓ rpm. *Spotify,* https://open.spotify.com/album/4qh8OwdAisw2pj6ZaL7dMM. *Cseh Tamás Archívum,* https://csehtamasarchivum.hu/lemezgyujtemeny/level-noveremnek. Accessed October 28, 2025.

Cseh Tamás Archívum ("Tamás Cseh Archive"). Budapest: Cseh Tamás Archívum, 2024,http2://csehtamasarchivum.hu Accessed October 28, 2025.

Csengey, Dénes. … *és mi most itt vagyunk* ("And We Are Here Now"). Budapest: Magvető, 1983. In *A kétségbeesés méltósága* ("The Dignity of Despair"). E-book, Budapest: Digitális Irodalmi Akadémia ("Digital Literary Academy"), 2021, https://reader.dia.hu/document/Csengey_Denes-A_ketsegbeeses_meltosaga-34425. Accessed October 28, 2025.

Csisztay, Gizella. "Kerényi Grácia, a lehetetlen ostromlója" ("Grácia Kerényi, Besieger of the Impossible"). *Óbudai Anziksz,* Winter 2017–2018, https://obudaianziksz.hu/csisztay-gizella-kerenyi-gracia-a-lehetetlen-ostromloja-3/. Accessed October 28, 2025.

Csorba, Loránt, et al. "Volt egy hős, akinek sikerült—zenészek Cseh Tamásról" ("There Was a Hero Who Succeeded: Musicians on Tamás Cseh"). *Recorder.hu,* January 22, 2018, https://recorder.blog.hu/2018/01/22/_volt_egy_hos_akinek_sikerult_zeneszek_cseh_tamasrol. Accessed October 28, 2025.

Danczi, Csaba László. "*Fehér babák takarodója*—rekviem egy utolsó lélekért: Utolsó búcsúm Cseh Tamástól" ("*White Dolls' Curfew*: Requiem for a Last Soul; My Last Farewell to Tamás Cseh"). *Prae.hu*, August 27, 2009, https://www.prae.hu/article/2232-feher-babak-takarodoja-rekviem-egy-utolso-lelekert/. Accessed October 28, 2025.

Director of National Intelligence, Central Intelligence Agency. "Hungary: The Waning of the Kádár Era: National Intelligence Estimate." Central Intelligence Agency, approved May 15, 1986, https://www.cia.gov/readingroom/docs/CIA-RDP90T00155R000900120002-0.pdf. Accessed October 28, 2025.

Fábri, Péter. "Jóslat elmúlt időkről" ("Prophecy About the Past"). *Magyar Ifjúság* ("Hungarian Youth"), June 22, 1984, 26–27.

Fodor, Sándor. *Cseh Tamás: Interjúregény* ("Tamás Cseh: Interview Novel"). Budapest: Graffiti, n.d.

Földényi, F. László. *A melankólia dicsérete* ("In Praise of Melancholy"). Budapest: Jelenkor, 2017.

Gazda, Albert. "Félig vagyok" ("I'm Half of Myself"). *Magyar Hang* ("Hungarian Voice"), June 2, 2024, https://hang.hu/kritika/felig-vagyok-frontatvonulas-cseh-tamas-164434. Accessed October 28, 2025.

Gömöri, György. "Kerényi Grácia 'halacskái'" ("Grácia Kerényi's 'Fish'"). In *Egy szigetlakó feljegyzéseiből: Esszék* ("From the Notes of an Islander: Essays"). Budapest: Cserépfalvi, 1996. Published online at Magyar Elektronikus Könyvtár ("Hungarian Electronic Library"), https://www.mek.oszk.hu/02500/02562/02562.htm. Accessed October 28, 2025.

Hanák, Gábor. "A dal átváltozásai—Interjú Hanák Gáborral" ("Transformations of the Song: Interview with Gábor Hanák"). Interview with Gábor Mórocz. *Irodalmi Magazin* ("Literary Magazine"), 2018, no. 1, 5–13. Cseh Tamás Archívum, https://csehtamasarchivum.hu/tortenet/dal-atvaltozasai-interju-hanak-gaborral. Accessed October 28, 2025.

Henson, Lance. "Indians." *The Continental Literary Magazine*, November 10, 2021, https://continentalmagazine.com/2021/11/10/indians/. Accessed October 28, 2025.

Horsch, Cecília. "Társadalomkép és társadalomkritika Cseh Tamás dalaiban: Az 1976-os és az 1994-es Levél nővéremnek és a Levél nővéremnek 2. albumok összehasonlítása" ("Social Image and social Criticism in the Songs of Tamás Cseh: A Comparison of the 1976 and 1994 albums *Letter to My Sister* and *Letter to My Sister 2*"). *Tanulmányok a társadalomról: a Szegedi Tudományegyetem JGYPK Alkalmazott Társadalomismereti Tanszék tudományos diákköri munkái* ("Studies on society: scientific student works of the JGYPK Department of Applied Social Sciences of the University of Szeged") 1, 2013: 102–128, http://acta.bibl.u-szeged.hu/72912/. Accessed October 28, 2025.

Hughes, Howard. *Once Upon a Time in the Italian West: A Filmgoer's Guide to Spaghetti Westerns*. London: I.B. Tauris, 2005.

Hungarian National Gallery. "Within Frames: The Art of the Sixties in Hungary (1958–1968)," https://en.mng.hu/exhibitions/within-frames-the-art-of-the-sixties-in-hungary-1958-1968/. Accessed October 28, 2025.

Indóház Online ("Station Online"). "Isten éltessen, Keleti pályaudvar! — 1. rész" ("Long Live Keleti Station! — Part 1"). *IHO.hu*, August 16, 2014, https://iho.hu/hirek/isten-eltessen-keleti-palyaudvar-1-resz-140816. Accessed October 28, 2025.

——. "Isten éltessen, Keleti pályaudvar! — 2. rész" ("Long Live Keleti Station! — Part 2"). *IHO.hu*, August 17, 2014, https://iho.hu/hirek/isten-eltessen-keleti-palyaudvar-2-resz-140817. Accessed October 28, 2025.

Juhász, Tibor. "Helyzetjelentés: Nemzedékiség és térpoétika Cseh Tamás és Bereményi Géza *Frontátvonulás* című monodrámájában" ("Situation Report: Generationality and Spatial Poetics in Tamás Cseh and Géza Bereményi's Monodrama *Frontal Passage*"). *Literatura* 45, no. 2 (2019): 196–208, https://ojs.mtak.hu/index.php/literatura/article/view/2042/1361. Accessed October 28, 2025.

Kerényi, Grácia. *Dalok könyve* ("Book of Songs"). Budapest: n.p., 1982.

——. "A daloló uborkától az egyszemélyes színházig" ("From the Singing Pickle to the One-Person Theatre"). *Színház*, January 1980: 27–30.

——. "*Jóslat*: Cseh Tamás–est a Katona József Színházban" ("*Prophecy*: A Tamás Cseh Evening at the József Katona Theatre"). *Színház*, July 1, 1984, 30–31.

——. "Levél nővéremnek" ("Letter to My Sister"). *Film Színház Muzsika* ("Film, Theatre, Music"), March 6, 1976, https://csehtamasarchivum.hu/tortenet/kerenyi-gracia-level-noveremnek. Accessed October 28, 2025.

——. *Utazások könyve* ("Book of Travels"). Budapest: Szépirodalmi Könyvkiadó, 1979.

Márta, István. "Cseh Tamás az irónia és az önirónia művésze volt" ("Tamás Cseh Was an Artist of Irony and Self-Irony"), interview with Zsolt Sütő-Nagy, *Magyar Hírlap* ("Hungarian Newspaper"), January 22, 2023 (updated

January 27, 2023), https://www.magyarhirlap.hu/kultura/20230122-cseh-tamas-az-ironia-es-az-onironia-muvesze-volt. Accessed October 28, 2025.

Moody, John, and Roger Boyes. *The Priest and the Policeman: The Courageous Life and Cruel Murder of Father Jerzy Popieluszko.* New York: Summit Books, 1987.

Penny, H. Glenn. "The German Love Affair with American Indians: Rudolf Cronau's Epiphany." *Commonplace*, vol. 11, no. 4 (July 2011), https://commonplace.online/article/the-german-love-affair-with-american-indians/. Accessed October 28, 2025.

Petőfi Irodalmi Múzeum ("Petőfi Literary Museum"). "Helyzetjelentések—Cseh Tamás 80" ("Situation Reports: Tamás Cseh 80"). Budapest: Petőfi Irodalmi Múzeum, (2023), https://pim.hu/kiallitas/helyzetjelentesek-cseh-tamas-80. Accessed October 28, 2025.

Senechal, Diana. *Frontátvonulás* ("Frontal Passage"): Tamás Cseh and Géza Bereményi's Album of No Return," *Hungarian Cultural Studies*, September 2024, https://ahea.pitt.edu/ojs/ahea/article/view/561. Accessed October 28, 2025.

——. "*Frontátvonulás* at the Akvárium." *Take Away the Takeaway* (blog), June 5 2024, https://dianasenechal.wordpress.com/2024/06/05/frontatvonulas-at-the-akvarium/. Accessed October 28, 2025.

——. "A Syllable That Turns Into the World: On Translating 'Lee van Cleef' by Géza Bereményi and Tamás Cseh." *Asymptote*, April 2024, https://www.asymptotejournal.com/special-feature/a-syllable-that-turns-into-the-world-diana-senechal/. Accessed October 28, 2025.

——. "'Tárá-ráálá-rálárám': The First Two Albums of Tamás Cseh and Géza Bereményi." *Literary Matters* 16, no. 2, 2024, https://www.literarymatters.org/16-2-senechal-tara/. Accessed October 28, 2025.

Somos, Ákos. "Benne van az egész világ: A tíz legszebb Cseh Tamás-ballada" ("The Whole World Is in It: The Ten Most Beautiful Tamás Cseh Ballads"). *WMN*, January 22, 2016, https://wmn.hu/kult/21774-benne-van-az-egesz-vilag-a-tiz-legszebb-cseh-tamas-ballada. Accessed October 28, 2025.

Szabó, István. "Daltörténetek I.—Jóslat" ("Song Stories I.—Prophecy"). Cseh Tamás Archívum, https://csehtamasarchivum.hu/tortenet/szabo-istvan-daltortenetek-i-joslat. Accessed October 28, 2025.

Szabolcsi, Bence. *A Concise History of Hungarian Music*, translated by Sára Karig and Fred Macnicol, translation revised by Florence Knepler. 2nd ed. Budapest: Corvina Press, 1974. Available online at mek.osk.hu Accessed October 28, 2025.

Szemere, Anna. "Let's Turn Hegel from His Head onto His Feet: Hopes, Myths, and Memories of the 1960s in Tamás Cseh's Musical Album 'A Letter to My Sister.'" *Slavic Review* 77, no. 4 (Winter 2018), 881–889.

——. *Up from the Underground: The Culture of Rock Music in Postsocialist Hungary.* University Park: The Pennsylvania State University Press, 2001.

Szeredás, András. "Parafrázisok a Dalra. A Dal nélkül: Cseh Tamás estje a 25. Színházban" ("Paraphrases for a Song. Without Song: The Tamás Cseh Evening at the 25th Theatre"). *Színház* ("Theatre"), vol. 6, no. 9 (September 1973), 28–29.

Takács, Róbert. "Hollywood Ascendant: American Films in Hungary in the 1970s." *Hungarian Journal of English and American Studies*, vol. 24, no. 1 (Spring 2018), 191–218.

Torkos, Matilt. "Itt éltek, itt élnek közöttünk a magyar indiánok" ("Here Lived, Here Live the Hungarian Indians Among Us"). *Index*, August 4. 2021, https://index.hu/kultur/multkep/2021/08/04/nemzeti-fototar-indian-indiantabor-cseh-tamas-bakonybel-baktay-ervin/. Accessed October 28, 2025.

About the Author

Diana Senechal is the author of *Solo Concert* (poems), *Republic of Noise: The Loss of Solitude in Schools and Culture* (nonfiction), and *Mind over Memes: Passive Listening, Toxic Talk, and Other Modern Language Follies* (nonfiction), as well as numerous essays, stories, songs, and translations. Born in Tucson, Arizona, she grew up in western and eastern Massachusetts (with a year apiece in the Netherlands and the Soviet Union), earned her B.A., M.A., and Ph.D. at Yale University, and taught for nine years in New York City public schools. Since 2017 she has been living and teaching in Szolnok, Hungary.

About the Cover Art

The front cover features an adaptation (with slight color changes) of Juan Gris' oil-on-canvas painting *Still Life with a Guitar* (1913). Diana Senechal chose it for its loose association with some of the themes of the book (a guitar, a glass, a fragment of French), its multiple perspectives, its disconnected shadows, and its overall texture and mood. The glass's shadow seems almost as if Vizi of *Frontátvonulás* had released it and it had stayed floating in the air. If Gris (1887–1927) had lived during Cseh and Bereményi's time, traveled to Hungary, and met them, perhaps he would have painted their songs.

www.ingramcontent.com/pod-product-compliance
Lightning Source LLC
Chambersburg PA
CBHW061422160726

47995CB00003B/722